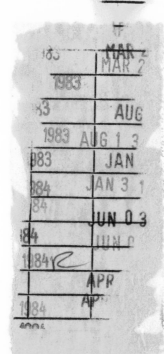

The Story of Jazz

The Story of Jazz

From New Orleans to Rock Jazz

Edited by
Joachim-Ernst Berendt

With contributions from

Werner Burkhardt, Reimer von Essen,
Leonard Feather, Ekkehard Jost,
Karl Lippegaus, Manfred Miller
and Dan Morgenstern

PRENTICE–HALL INC

Englewood Cliffs New Jersey 07647

Library of Congress Cataloging in Publication Data

Berendt Joachim
The Story of Jazz

A Spectrum Book
Includes bibliography
Jazz forms and careers of artist

The Story of Jazz
77–18428
ISBN 0–13–850248–X
ISBN 0–13–850230–7 Pbk.

ⓒ 1978 in the United States by Prentice-Hall Inc. Englewood Cliffs New
Jersey 07647
ⓒ Translation copyright ELS Consultant Linguists Ltd.
Produced by Computer-controlled phototypesetting
using OCR input techniques and printed offset in Great Britain
by UNWIN BROTHERS LIMITED
The Gresham Press Old Woking Surrey

PRENTICE-HALL INTERNATIONAL INC *London*
PRENTICE-HALL OF AUSTRALIA PTY LIMITED *Sydney*
PRENTICE-HALL OF CANADA LTD *Toronto*
PRENTICE-HALL OF INDIA PRIVATE LTD *New Delhi*
PRENTICE-HALL OF JAPAN INC *Tokyo*
PRENTICE-HALL OF SOUTHEAST ASIA PTE LTD *Singapore*
WHITEHALL BOOKS LIMITED *Wellington New Zealand*

Contents

Joachim-Ernst Berendt

Introduction

So what is jazz? We find definitions in dictionaries and specialized literature but they are often amateurish—"Jazz is a dance music of the American Negro, crude, decadent, syncopated, of African origin". Some years ago the editor of this book offered the following, based on a number of earlier definitions by American experts:

"Jazz is a form of art music which orginated in the United States through the confrontation of the Negro with European music. The instrumentation, melody, and harmony of jazz are in the main derived from Western musical tradition. Rhythm, phrasing and production of sound, and the elements of blues harmony are derived from African music and from the musical conception of the American Negro. Jazz differs from European music in three basic elements:

1. A special relationship to time, defined as 'swing'.
2. A spontaneity and vitality of musical production in which improvisation plays a rôle.
3. A sonority and manner of phrasing which mirror the individuality of the performing jazz musician.

These three basic characteristics create a novel climate of tension, in which the emphasis no longer is on great arcs of tension, as in European music, but on a wealth of tension-creating elements, which continuously rise and fall. The various styles and stages of development through which jazz has passed since its origin around the turn of the century are largely characterised by the fact that the three basic elements of jazz temporarily achieve varying degrees of importance, and that the relationship between them is constantly changing".

But definitions of this kind, like any others, are bound to be incomplete. The question with which this book opens means—What is jazz for those who experience it and live it?

Jazz "ain't what you do, it's the way that you do it", said Fats Waller, Harlem's great jazz pianist of the twenties and thirties. "If you don't have the whole spiritual thing, I don't think jazz is complete", states Jimmy Heath, the tenor saxophonist from Philadelphia. "Jazz is the cosmos, the all. *You* are jazz, it's all inside you", writes Sun Ra, Free Jazz orchestrator and leader of the "Galactic Orchestra". One man who unlike most others quoted here is not a jazz musician but a poet, Jean Cocteau, wrote: "I'm astonished that there hasn't always been jazz. Nothing is intensive enough—except maybe jazz". "Jazz is shit" (Johnny Griffin) and "Jazz is love—what happens between you and me" (Teddy Wilson). "If you haven't lived it, it doesn't come out of your horn" (Charlie Parker). "Jazz is Black music" (Archie Shepp). "Jazz is a white man's word" (Miles Davis). "There's nothing specially African about jazz. Rabbis in the synagogue and gypsies sound more like jazz than anything in Africa" (Lennie Tristano). "Jazz is why this century sounds different from any other" (Dizzy Gillespie). "Jazz is the sound of the universe" (Sun Ra). "Jazz is freedom" (Archie Shepp). "Jazz is the freedom which takes many forms" (Duke Ellington). "Jazz is about the only art form existing today in which there is freedom of the individual without the loss of group contact" (Dave Brubeck). "... a feast of everything that lives and breathes ..., a declaration of war on death ...., a refusal to go under, hanging on like a limpet, a paean to the bloodstream, a hosanna to the sweat glands, a hymn to the stomach that aches when it's empty" (Mezz Mezzrow). "Jazz is your death and my death" (Charles Mingus).

"Mellow" was the word most often used when a radio station in a Chicago ghetto invited its audience—its black listeners—to describe black music. "Mellow", the dictionary tells us, means "done to a turn, soft, mature, mild, gentle, juicy, sweet, beneficent, melting, understanding, limpid, joyful, agreeable, sympathetic, tasty", referring to fruit, wine, colours, light, sounds, voices, weather, human beings, and so on.

Gertrude Stein, the friend of Hemingway and herself a literary figure in the Paris of the Jazz Age, as the twenties have been called, gives us the six most beautiful words on jazz: "Jazz is tenderness and great power". This remark embraces all the rest. It oscillates between love and wrath, freedom and togetherness, shit and sweetness, blackness and universality, spirituality and earthiness.

Those who try to describe jazz become involved with paradoxes. Being so many things at once is perhaps the distinguishing characteristic of jazz. But in the jazz world "mellow" and "great power" are less of a paradox than they are in ours. People today talk a lot about European jazz having found its feet and having here and there attained the same validity as American jazz. But the same experience repeats itself over and over. Some American band or other comes on a European tour—unknown musicians maybe, certainly not first-class—and at the drummer's first tap we shrink back before the power, before this mighty force that is none the less "mellow"—tender, sweet and soft. This is what we over here find so difficult to combine—power and mildness. Maybe it is just that in the black world and black music the energy reservoir is disproportionately greater, even if a light and playful touch may make it seem mild, easy and soft. Thus mildness within power becomes possible.

The word "jazz" first appeared in print in San Francisco around the turn of the century, as "jass, jasmo, jismo". Sports reporters in a local paper used it to represent energy, mighty strength, top form. But in fact it is rather older. In black jargon, which certainly never found its way into print, "jass" was an obscenity; like so many technical terms of popular music it had sexual implications. Blues singers used to sing: "Give me your jazz"—or alternatively: "I don't want your jazz".

Right from the beginning jazz has been misunderstood. Those who heard it took it for something quite other than it really was.

In the programme of the Berliner Jazztage 1966 I wrote on the encounter between jazz and other artistic fields: "The same thing happens in the phenomenon of our music. Jazz fans want to keep it pure and look on any form of jazz that is not absolutely purist as a crime. But it is just where jazz has been "impure" that it has made itself felt most—on Scott Fitzgerald and Hemingway in the Jazz Age of the Roaring Twenties, on Debussy and Stravinsky, on Hindemith and Křenek, on Gershwin and Kurt Weill, on Matisse and Klee, on Ballanchine, Jerome Robbins and Maurice Béjart. Experts have proved many times over that all these great personalities of modern art misunderstood jazz. Křenek for instance, with whom I had an argument years ago in the magazine *Melos,* really had music-hall or vaudeville music in mind when he wrote his so-called "Jazz Opera" *Jonny spielt auf.* Matisse had his mind on circus music when he created his "jazz" cycle; but so what—if misunderstandings like this have given rise to the *Histoire du Soldat* or the *Ebony Concerto,* to Ginsberg's *Howl* or Jerome Robbins' choreography in *West Side Story*".

It's not only artists who have misunderstood jazz but the public too. In the twenties and thirties they thought the saccharine-sweet "symphonic" concert music of Paul Whiteman and Jack

Hylton was jazz. Later, mainly in Europe and most of all in Germany, people thought any hit that had a steady beat—as practically every hit does—was jazz. I well remember how in the fifties, when I was going all over Germany lecturing, I could never talk about jazz without first having to explain what jazz *was not*—commercial hits and dance music. It has since struck me that this provides the best evidence of all of the power of jazz—that it has penetrated into so many areas, that it has been misrepresented over and over again and that despite this it is stronger and has a larger public now than ever before in its history. We can demonstrate this point. Never before have there been so many jazz concerts and festivals or jazz records and programmes; and never before have so many musicians made their living from jazz. The jazz scene has become too broad to take in at a glance. Any older fan will remember the time when he could reel off by heart the hundred or so musicians who had made their name in jazz. But who bar the experts can do that today? And it is only in this decade of the seventies, after about 80 years of jazz history, that jazz musicians' records have hit the million mark.

Yet jazz is always being pronounced dead. The first time this happened was in 1921, not long after it was born. Arnold Loyocano, the bass player of the New Orleans Rhythm Kings wrote: "Jazz has died down". From Loyocano in 1921 to *Der Spiegel* of the sixties death notices seem just as much a part of jazz as its most deepseated musical elements like swing or blues.

Jazz was "dead" in the early thirties when the Chicago style gave way to swing. It "died" once again in the early forties when swing ran its course and modern jazz rose sparkling from the ashes. It "died" in giving birth to free jazz—and yet again when free jazz met its end. Despite all this jazz is alive and well and living at a hotter pace than ever, which won't stop the news magazines pronouncing it dead five or six times more before the decade is up.

Those who pronounce jazz dead are mainly people who once belonged to the jazz scene themselves and now want an excuse to get out of it because they think they can do better in other fields of music. They are right beyond doubt. Success-seekers will do better in almost any other form of music, from the subsidized music of the symphony orchestra to the light music of the late night radio programmes and pop.

Usually too jazz is pronounced dead to the benefit of the prevailing pop music fasion. For Arnold Loyocano for instance in 1921, jazz "died" under the onslaught of the dances of that time—the charleston, foxtrot, one-step, quickstep and so on. Nothing changed; in the thirties swing, despite in fact being one aspect of jazz, was said to have taken over. And in the rock era of the sixties jazz was written off in favour of the then-popular "big beat". The media men who were plugging it lead such a hand-to-mouth existence that they never notice how history regularly goes on repeating itself and all these pop fashions die off in a few years, while jazz, which at some point gave birth to them, has as many lives as a cat. It happened again in the seventies with the end of the rock era, which could certainly never have come into being without jazz.

Twist the evidence how you like, jazz has left a stronger imprint on twentieth century sound than any other music. Light music on the radio, background music in hotel lounges and supermarkets, commercial jingles, dance music in bars, discotheques and night-clubs, songs from Marlene Dietrich to Barbra Streisand, hits of the last 80 years of every form and every age from ragtime to rock—all are unthinkable without jazz.

But it is to the very profusion of these fringe and secondary effects and whims of fashion that misunderstandings about jazz relate. Don't tell me that misunderstandings like this are to be found just as much in other fields of contemporary art. In practice other art forms show them only to a certain extent. But in jazz music you cannot use any limiting expression like "to a certain extent". Jazz is unique in having been taken for something quite different to what it really was by most of its audience over most of its history.

Misunderstandings about jazz stem not least from its richness and multifariousness—New Orleans jazz and Free Jazz, Dixieland and Bebop, Swing and Electric Jazz, Cool and Hot Jazz, Mississippi

Blues and Harlem Jump. All these are so different from one another that it is not easy—least of all for the outsider—to spot the common denominator of "jazz" and to sense how they all form an entity. No other contemporary art has spread out in so many directions. You hear new concert music—by Stravinsky or Webern, by Penderecki or Ligeti, and straightaway even the outsider identifies all these sounds as new concert music. In jazz this kind of pinpointing is always fraught with difficulties. Modern art too, say from Picasso to Rauschenberg, can be far better perceived as lying within a single, all-embracing entity. Diversity causes more confusion in jazz than in other modern arts.

The history of jazz is made up of the wealth of diverse jazz phenomena. Every ten years, roughly speaking, there has been a new mainline style with a dozen or two offshoots. Over 70 or 80 years all this has happened with astonishing inevitability and with a regularity that seems inherent in any development process. If I can quote from a book that I wrote 25 years ago and come back to in greater depth in the closing chapter of this present book: "It was Ortega y Gasset who pointed out that the development trends of art—music or painting, literature or architecture alike—must always be repeated in the same sequence and over the same course as long as no fundamental or radical doubt is cast on their validity of expression. On the one hand, once it came into being at all, jazz *was bound* to appear in the same forms that marked the beginnings of the history of music of European and other cultures. On the other hand, having come into being *in our times,* it was bound to adapt itself as rapidly as possible to the forms which are inherent in our epoch. As a form of artistic expression that first made its appearance in the twentieth century it had inevitably to go through everything that European art has gone through over the centuries. This is not a question of syncretism, but of the force of a law which governs artistic development wherever we can observe it".

This trend is repeating itself in our day, at a hotted up pace, with rock, which is currently going through all the different phases appropriate to developments of this kind. Back in 1970 Herbie Hancock, the pianist whose jazz records are now among the million-sellers pointed out: "If rock is an art form which develops and not just a folk idiom which stays still, it must go the same way that jazz went".

The wealth and diversity of these manifestations of jazz calls for specialisation. Hardly anywhere else does the enthusiast for specialisation find such happy hunting grounds as in the world of jazz. But this is the way things are. There are jazz phenomena which can only be understood by immersing oneself completely in them. The person who really wants to get to know New Orleans jazz or ragtime has no time for bebop or free jazz.

American jazz experts—and this is often where they have the edge on us in Europe—can virtually live with the jazz musicians and get their information first hand. In this situation—maybe from a certain conscious or unconscious resignation in face of their American colleagues' advantage—some European musicologists have found common ground in treating jazz "scientifically". But what they have to say is for the most part so detached and has so little to do with any real feeling and commitment for jazz, that the quintessence of jazz, what it is really about, escapes them. As has been shown over and over again—those who do not live jazz cannot write about it.

What then are good jazz books like? In the *The Jazz Book (Jazzbuch)* I tried in four successive editions to depict each of the modern jazz styles at a key moment in its development from a position of direct commitment to it—Bebop in 1950, Cool Jazz and Hard Bop in 1959, Free Jazz in 1968 and Modern Electric Jazz in 1973. In this way the new material in each successive edition came from direct contact with the individual styles and modes—and most of all with those who played them—while the long cool look that resulted from further evolution held its own.

In this book I have used a different approach. Leading European and American experts in the various fields write on the styles and jazz forms which they have experienced, lived through and researched. As far as possible I have called on experts who themselves are or were musicians—Leonard Feather, Reimer von Essen, Ekkehard Jost, Karl

Lippegaus. Apart from a few ground rules on shape and sequence which, as editor, I felt to be necessary there are as many different approaches as there are contributors to the book.

Reimer von Essen's contribution brings out the commitment of a musician who himself plays New Orleans jazz. Manfred Miller is one of the first to look at jazz and blues from the sociological viewpoint. Werner Burkhardt's essay on the Chicago style bears the marks both of his admiration for the young, enthusiastic jazz musicians of those days and of the experience of a successful writer. Dan Morgenstern writes about swing from direct contact with many of the great soloists and bandleaders of the Swing Age. Leonard Feather's contrasting study of the two greatest personalities of jazz—Louis Armstrong and Duke Ellington—bears the mark of his authority as the USA's best known jazz expert. One thing that goes to make his contribution on Bebop so definitive is that, at a time when almost the whole body of jazz criticism was rejecting the newly born modern jazz, Feather was the first expert writer who expressed faith in the new sound and so had a large hand in its success.

The same goes for Ekkehard Jost. From the start his musical and personal life was bound up with the young generation of European free jazz players. Rock jazz was the music which Karl Lippegaus grew up with and in which he goes on growing in stature. It would hardly be sensible to entrust the presentation of a music form which is still barely five years old to anyone other than a young writer who is himself something of a fan.

The diversity of presentation meant that the contributions often overlapped. Where these overlaps were no more than repetitions they were trimmed out. But often they were much more—they complemented and enriched one another. The "blue note" means one thing to Reimer von Essen with his New Orleans music and quite another to Manfred Miller with his sociology of jazz. Ekkehard Jost and Karl Lippegaus see John Coltrane rather differently; maybe only by superimposing the two images can one see the whole man. As was to be expected, outstanding musicians like Louis Armstrong and Duke Ellington burst the bounds of Leonard Feather's contrasting study and spread themselves over the whole book. Likewise a number of swing players started their careers in the Chicago era and so have a place in the chapter on Chicago as well as that on Swing. These are just a few examples. This multiplicity of facets is a great attraction in a work to which several writers have contributed. To this extent the book is not just a kaleidoscope of jazz musicians and style but equally of critics and experts. Each critic has an approach and a style of writing particularly fitted to the jazz style with which he deals and to the things he thinks important. Thus the kaleidoscope of critics has a pleasing sharpening effect on the kaleidoscope of styles. I should like to thank the contributors for having made this possible. I should also like to thank the photographers, who have enriched our kaleidoscope with important photographs, some of them of great historical interest and never before published.

Joachim-Ernst Berendt

Reimer von Essen began his jazz career in 1957 as a clarinettist in Dixieland and New Orleans bands in Frankfurt. Since 1962 he has been leader of the Barrelhouse Jazz Band, a New Orleans combo from Frankfurt that many critics regard as the best trad band in Germany. A teacher by profession, von Essen became in 1963 a founder member of the German *Gesellschaft zur Förderung des New Orleans-Jazz* and its magazine *Hot Jazz*. During a visit to New Orleans in 1968 he received the freedom of the city. He took advantage of an African tour with his Barrelhouse Band in 1971 to run jazz courses for African musicians.

Jazz began in New Orleans. Yet it is not easy to start a book on the history of jazz with the chapter "New Orleans". For over three centuries of prehistory went into the birth of this music.

In between 1618 or earlier and the ban on the import of slaves in 1808, millions of Africans—as many as 4.3 million even by 1786—were transported to America. They brought a rich musical tradition which came naturally to them and was taken for granted by them.

In North America they were by and large forbidden to practise their own music, so right from the start they set about singing and playing the permitted "white" music in accordance with the rules of their own musical tradition. In this way certain basic elements of the old African culture were unconsciously passed on to this Afro-American music as it came into being. This progressive adoption of areas of European music continued up to 1900. It came about through the choice of types of music which had parallels with African traditions, and through the shaping of the chosen music to African musical usage. There resulted a whole series of new Afro-American musical styles.

In the spirituals, the Negroes' Christian religious songs, were to be found elements of African religious rituals. The spirituals provided the first demonstration on American soil of the Negro's ability to bring about ecstasy by musical — and non-musical — means. This ability later found expression in all forms of jazz music.

Riverboats carry jazz from New Orleans to the Mississippi ports. Here we see the Beale Street Jug Band from Memphis. The skiffle craze of the fifties originated from jug and washboard bands.

Blues Music joined Afro-American melody and declamation to simple European harmony.

In Minstrel Music many minor forms of primitive black music were standardized and offered to white audiences as well. In melodic terms most of these kinds of music may indeed have resembled European music, but the rhythm and to some extent the harmony were way outside the European tradition. Their rhythm was characterized by *off beats*—accenting the beats which our European musical sensibilities regard as "weak", and often producing an accent within a beat. The main effect of this form of accentuation, syncopation, is to induce an ecstatic state. Harmonically

the main differences from European music were the *blue notes*—tones from various African scales which deviate from the seven-tone scales of European music. These tones occurred mainly around the third and the seventh. (Later, in bebop, the fifth was also flattened (played flat) to make a blue note; and in the Free Jazz of the sixties there were musicians who played the whole scale blue.) This phenomenon of blue notes is the most important harmonic characteristic of New Orleans jazz and thence of jazz as a whole. Players talk for instance of the "flattened third" or "flattened fifth", meaning a third or a fifth note played flat. This produces a rather characteristic harmonic structure unknown in European music. European musicians have from time to time compared this structure with Debussy's impressionistic whole tone harmony, but this comparison is superficial. It has no bearing on the true nature of this kind of harmony which keeps alive the African sensibility for relationships of weight and function between tones.

By the end of the American Civil War, an Afro-American music rich in forms had been built up. The documented history of this music begins in 1870 in the American Midwest with the birth of ragtime. This most European form of Afro-American music had grown from the application of black techniques of execution to popularized forms of the European Palm Court music of the time. Its godparents must have been mainly piano versions of marches, polonaises,

polkas and quadrilles. What came to be called ragtime remained faithful to these European originals in form, harmony and melody. It was only in the rhythm that the Afro-American influence had penetrated. In some cases this extended to markedly African motifs like those that have lived on in the West Indian isles of the American coast and developed into the Spanish-European rhythms of what we call "Latin American music". This music was *composed;* thus it only became possible after many coloured Americans had undergone an advanced education in European music. Ragtime was mainly played on the piano, occasionally on the banjo. But the Palm Court orchestras of the time also played orchestral arrangements of rags. The home of ragtime was St. Louis and its greatest exponent **Scott Joplin** (1868–1917), who wrote many of the best known rags.

Other great names of ragtime are **Tom Turpin**, and the white men **Joseph Lamb** and **James Scott**. The delightful and technically sophisticated compositions of these pianists usually had three of four parts; they were often written in difficult keys and packed with musical tricks and special turns of phrase. From 1880 up to almost 1920 ragtime largely dominated the field of American popular music. Its dominance was reinforced from 1900 onwards by the popularity of the pianola; many rags were punched onto "piano rolls". In the seventies ragtime has enjoyed a worldwide renaissance, sparked off by

the use of a Scott Joplin track in a film. Suddenly young people everywhere have started playing rags again.

But a more important influence on jazz than ragtime was the street music of the coloured quarters of the small and medium-sized towns of the south, and most of all of course the capital New Orleans. We know of two kinds of such music. On the one hand, alongside begging blues musicians and proselytizing spiritual singers, there was a host of small groups which sang to string and percussion instruments—often homemade. Their repertoire was made up of the hits of the moment and all kinds of folk songs, with a preference for songs with a pronounced sexual content.

The second type of street music that had

16

a decisive influence on jazz was that of the Brass Bands. These had sprung up as early as 1865 or thereabouts in imitation of the white marching bands, but their playing often had a marked Afro-American shape. One instrument used to play the melody, while others improvized rhythmically accented middle or bass parts which by and large had very little to do with the harmonic arrangements of the white originals. There were also small and large drums or—as substitutes—washboards and "jugs". This form of music has come to be known as "Archaic Jazz".

The principal models for these Brass Bands were the French marching bands which, in accordance with the New Orleans' South of France tradition, used to accompany every kind of celebration and community event from beginning to end. We have some of the high-sounding names of these bands: Excelsior Band, Eagle Band, Imperial Band, Onward Band, Tuxedo Band, Superior Band . . . Some of their successors are still playing today. The "best", meaning "most European", of these Brass Bands were the Creoles. This term originally applied only to the white French colonials, but in New Orleans, which was French up to 1803, the word "Creole" took on an extra meaning. From 1724 onwards individual slaves were given their freedom and these naturally tended to be the mistresses of white gentlemen and their children. Up to 1889 they were regarded by the law as white and lived completely within the Creole culture.

Many opera musicians were Creoles—as were many members of dance bands which played from music but played ragtime too, famous among them the band of **John Robichaux** (1866–1939). In 1889 an American law declared these cultivated, coffee-coloured French people "black". From then on most "white" jobs were closed to the Creoles and coexistence with their darker skinned Afro-American neighbours was forced on them. Black musicians who played by ear and improvized and Creole instrumentalists who played "straight" began to join together to form bands. In this way the Brass Bands' improvisation techniques blended with ragtime music. Brass Bands began to play rags in their own way, and dance bands to improvize like the street musicians did. In 1895 the barber, gossip-columnist and trumpeter **Buddy Bolden** (1868–1931) formed a band that was really a black dance band. It played rags and contemporary dance music, but Buddy Bolden played quite differently from earlier trumpeters. There are no records of him, but his style has been very well described in numerous interviews. There can be no doubt that he added to the Afro-American distortions that had already become common a further one—he played like a blues singer, imitating vocal music on his instrument.

This was to be important for many kinds of jazz, far beyond the bounds of New Orleans. Buddy Bolden used to play in a recreation park for the coloured popula-

tion and he played what his audience wanted to hear. When the public were packed like sardines round the bandstand and the only form of dancing possible was "bellyrubbing", he used to shout between numbers: "My chillen's here, I know it, 'cause I can smell 'em". And then he would play songs with lyrics that left ambiguity far behind, like *All the Whores Like the Way I Ride*. He could also play rags and quadrilles but he only really let go with the songs of his "chillen". Then, the story goes, he would blow so loud that you could hear him miles away. And we know from his pupil **Bunk Johnson** (1879–1949) how he used to play—the melody to begin with, then the first cautious variation, then a few more notes thrown in with a few blue notes in between, sharpening up the rhythm with off beats to build up to a climax. But the melody always stayed recognizable. If we can isolate one point in time which divides the prehistory of jazz from its history, this was "King" Buddy Bolden's music.

The most popular bands in the New Orleans of those days were the brass bands with their proud names, and their stars were the cornet players. Buddy Bolden played in these bands too. They were generally made up of: 2–3 cornets, clarinets, 1–2 trombones, 2–4 horns in middle positions (later replaced by saxophones), tuba and large and small drums. They played in this form at parades, on bandstands and for major open-air events. If they were booked for a dance the band was reduced to: 1–2 cornets, clarinet, trombone, one drummer and bass (at first mainly bowed) or guitar or banjo. There were also smaller groupings with 4 or 5 players. All these bands played on request marches, rags, quadrilles and other dances of the time such as waltzes. After Buddy Bolden's great success they began to play blues and the themes of the street musicians too—but as yet this new music remained unnamed.

A first generation of musicians made a name with the new style. We can divide them roughly into Creole musicians with a strong ragtime tradition and signs of a classical European training; and more markedly blues-oriented black musicians. Among the Creoles were the cornet players **Manuel Perez**, (c. 1880–1946), **Peter Bocage** (1887–1967) and **Freddy Keppard** (1889–1933). Keppard was a real cornet virtuoso. His variations were inexhaustible; when he "played it hot", this meant mainly power that seemed to burst forth and fast rhythms. Most of the early clarinettists were Creoles—**George Bacquet** (1883–1949) and **Lorenzo Tio** (1884–1933), the founders of the New Orleans clarinet school, and **Alphonse Picou** (1878–1961) who developed his famous *High Society* solo—perhaps the most imitated solo in the history of jazz—from the piccolo part of a march. Among the trombonists was **Honore Dutrey** (1890–1937) whose sensitive ensemble playing still owed much to the written trombone parts of marches and rags.

Among the best known musicians of the "blacker" style were cornet players **Bunk Johnson** who replaced Buddy Bolden in his band in 1907 when the latter became insane, **Oscar "Papa" Celestin** (1884–1954) with his "silvery" tone, **Puddy Petit** (c. 1897–1932) who is said to have had a crucial influence on Armstrong, and best of all perhaps **Joe Oliver** (1885–1938). Oliver introduced a new phase which shifted more decisively than Buddy Bolden's style towards the blues with their blue notes and their offbeat speech-like rhythm. To bring out these blue notes, he used a whole range of mutes which modified the tone of his cornet until it imitated the human voice. But more important was the relaxed, almost dignified rhythm of his phrases, against which the ragtime rhythm of his predecessors and colleagues seemed almost hectic. A famous tale of those days tells how this style gradually supplanted the older one in the favour of public and colleagues alike. **Richard M. Jones** (1889–1945), the pianist, recalls, "Freddy Keppard was playing in a spot across the street and was drawing all the crowds. I was sitting at the piano, and Joe Oliver came over to me and commanded in a nervous, harsh voice, 'Get in B Flat'. He didn't even mention a tune, just said 'Get in B Flat'. I did, and Joe walked out on the sidewalk, lifted his cornet to his lips, and blew the most beautiful stuff I ever heard. People started pouring out of the other spots along the street to see who was blowing all that horn. Before long, our place was full and Joe came in,

smiling, and said, 'Now that ... won't bother me no more'. From then on, our place was full every night".

Shortly afterwards a manager began to bill Oliver as Joe "King" Oliver.

Although he was a Creole, **Edward "Kid" Ory** (1889–1973) was the main exponent on the trombone of the improvized, highly rhythmic base lines of the black style. Ory's mixture of the pure accompaniment playing of the brass band trombonists and melodic phrases heavily modified in the direction of the blues became the embodiment of the New Orleans trombone.

The pianists were in a class of their own. The best of them played in the distinguished establishments of Storyville, the world famous red light quarter of New Orleans port, where the ladies could be chosen from catalogues which classified them by shades of skin colour and left little to the imagination. The pianists earned so much there as solo entertainers that they were too expensive for bands. The first of these "princes of the piano", who used to compose jazz numbers and play them along with operatic arias, popular hits and rags, was the famous **"Jelly Roll' Morton** (1885–1941). He later claimed to have "invented" jazz in 1902. Certainly he was the first pianist who played his whole repertoire in typical jazz rhythm. This first generation of jazz musicians created the classical New Orleans style. They took off from the turning point of archaic Brass Band jazz and developed it into the ecstatic, expressive, occasionally elegant and virtuoso-like music of the dance halls, cabarets, bars and brothels of Storyville. They created a style of ensemble playing with rare solos. In this most parts were improvized in accordance with precise concepts from the prehistory of jazz, but the melody was dominant and gave the playing its shape. Oliver, Ory and Morton invented the new rhythm which moved away from ragtime to a "swinging" execution.

Alongside and under the influence of this mainline trend, but by and large separate from it, the New Orleans white bands grew up. This movement was already under way before the turn of the century with the brass bands and dance bands of **"Papa" Jack Laine** (1873–1966). These white musicians played mainly from music, but started at an early stage to respond to the influences of the new black music. Many connoisseurs of jazz preferred to reserve the term "New Orleans jazz" mainly for the black and Creole jazz which shows a pronounced African influence, and to refer to the music of the white bands from New Orleans as "Dixieland Jazz". These first jazz players became the idols of the new generation. Anyone born in New Orleans around 1900 could scarcely escape the influence of the new style. So many musicians of worldwide repute grew up in the New Orleans of those times that it is impossible to list them all. The leading figure of this second generation of jazz musicians was **Louis Armstrong** (1900–1971), who is the subject of a special study in this book. His

George Lewis, a leading representative of the New Orleans Revival

19

Far left:
Sidney Bechet and Bunk Johnson

Left:
Albert Nicholas, Sidney Bechet's musical heir in Europe

Right:
King Oliver's Creole Jazz Band in 1924, with Louis Armstrong (second from right), Lil Hardin-Armstrong and Buster Bailey (third from left).

story was that of many a New Orleans boy. Drawn by the new exciting music, they followed their idols everywhere; they disguised themselves in borrowed long trousers to be able to hear jazz in Storyville at night; they somehow or other got hold of an instrument and began to imitate what they had heard from childhood. The main trendsetter was the new style of **Joe Oliver** and his friends. Musicians were growing up who were to carry jazz to the world. A string of trumpeters followed the same models to achieve a style similar to Armstrong's: **Lee Collins** (1901–1960), **Punch Miller** (1894–) and the young **Henry "Red" Allen** (1908–1967).

The clarinet was the instrument in which the distinction between Creole and black styles was longest maintained. The Creoles had as their star the virtuoso **Jimmy Noone** (1895–1944), who later had his clarinet keys gold-plated. Other famous Creole clarinettists were **Albert Nicholas** (1900–1973), **Barney Bigard** (1906–), **Omer Simeon** (1902–1959) and **Darnell Howard** (1892–1966). More strongly influenced by the blues were **Johnny Dodds** (1895–1940), whom his friends ceremoniously dubbed "Toilet" because he "stank of the blues", and **Sidney Bechet** (1897–1959) who was later to blend all the influences—both of Creole (as he himself was) and black clarinettists and also of the cornet players he admired so much—into a completely individual style of his own. The first saxophonists began to appear;

Barney Bigard, who was later to make his name with Duke Ellington, began by playing more tenor sax than clarinet. There were two young New Orleans drummers who left a lasting imprint on the history of jazz—**Baby Dodds** (1898–1959), a drummer of almost magic brilliance in a distinctively African tradition, and **Zutty Singleton** (1898–1975) whose milder style was even then beginning to sound a touch more "modern".

Despite the almost unimaginable abundance of black talent in those early days, it was the numerically and creatively inferior whites who scored the first successes. It will always remain one of the great—and typical—ironies of jazz history, that the first discs of the new music

20

were cut not by black musicians, but by white—by the Original Dixieland Jazz Band in New York early in 1917. They and the New Orleans Rhythm Kings were also the first to bring the new music to the attention of white audiences in Chicago and New York. What the Dixieland band played was really ragtime with satirical touches of jazz, but the NORK—as the New Orleans Rhythm Kings soon became known—had already moved a long way towards the jazz of Oliver's generation.

One of these white New Orleans bands, the trombone player **Tom Brown's** (1888–1958) group, used to maintain that they were the first people to use the word "jazz" in a musical context. To get near to the idiom of the day we should interpret "jazz music" as "bang music". They say that it was on a trip to Chicago that musicians there first used this word derisively of the new music from New Orleans, but the brash young Dixielanders found the notion amusing and incorporated the word in the name of their band. By this time black New Orleans bands too had already gone on tour in the North and West of the United States and made a great impression wherever they went. The bass player **Bill Johnson** (1872–1976) played from 1909 on in Los Angeles and in 1911 organized a tour with a New Orleans band that lasted up to 1918 and played in Chicago and New York. Other bands followed in its path.

Johnson is said to have been the first jazz bass player who stopped bowing his instrument *(con arco)* and took to plucking it *(pizzicato)*. In this way the bass could still play its former part in the harmony and add to this a rhythm function of a very precise kind. And this was what the new music was about—improving the accuracy and depth of the rhythm.

In 1917 after the United States entered World War I the Storyville red light quarter was banned by law. As Louis Armstrong used to tell it: "A lot of people were getting killed there at that time. Some sailors were robbed and killed. The Navy got worked up about it ..." The great centre where so many players had earned their living was no more, and the best musicians moved on. The first headed for San Fransisco, where they failed in fact to spark off anything of great musical significance. In Chicago it was another story.

Bill Johnson set up there in 1918. He sent for **King Oliver** and **Jimmy Noone** and the drummer **Paul Barbarin** (1901–1969). Oliver gradually took the band over and moved up the club market, making his name as he went. Soon his band contained the best musicians from New Orleans. After a trip to San Francisco (1921) he got an engagement at Lincoln Gardens, a well-known dance café. There, playing to six or seven hundred people every evening, he was such a hit that he decided to bring in the young **Louis Armstrong** as second cornet. Now he had a band of a quality that would perhaps never be equalled in the history of jazz—top class musicians, some of them the best on their instrument, moulded together by a great integrating musical personality and by constantly playing together with steadily mounting success. They played the popular numbers of New Orleans, their own compositions and their musical friends' pieces—often demanding works in several sections with some written parts. King Oliver's Creole Jazz Band, as the band was called, started by sticking fairly close to the written original but soon added improvized extra parts. As they went on they brought in more and more of their own variations—they "played it hotter". The rather rare solos were the climax of improvized ensemble playing.

From the historical point of view the nubs of short solos like this were the "breaks". At the end of a part of the piece the rhythm section stops playing its steady beat and pauses before beginning a new part, usually of eight or twelve bars. The figure the soloist improvizes in this pause is known as a "break".

King Oliver was the first musician to make his name with breaks. The showpieces of his band were the precisely improvized two-part cornet breaks which he played with **Louis Armstrong**. Musicians and fans used to puzzle their heads over how it was possible to improvize freely in two-part harmony. The secret was that at the end of the previous number Oliver would blow a phrase to his young colleague,

giving Armstrong until the first break in the next number to work out a matching second part in the right key. When the band stopped at the agreed point and the two cornets burst in with never-repeated two-part breaks, the audience was always overcome with astonishment. Musicians from all over the United States came and listened and were influenced. Interviews give ample evidence of the way that evenings with the Creole Jazz Band were for many musicians the start of their jazz career. But it was the new rhythm of the Oliver band that was the most striking of all. This was characterized by the way in which Baby Dodds struck the bass drum on every beat. In other bands the bass drum came in only on the first and third beats. This marking of the minims gave

The George Williams Brass Band at a New Orleans funeral.

Fats Waller, the pianist and bandleader of the twenties and thirties, had a great sense of humour. ▶

rise to the term "two-beat". Traditional jazz as a whole is often referred to as "Two-Beat Jazz", but it is important to realize that the beginnings of a four-beat rhythm had already made their appearance with King Oliver at this relatively early stage. Generally speaking this four-beat rhythm is taken as the mark of the succeeding style, swing (on which Dan Morgenstern writes in this book). But it is at once remarkable and typical that the ones who really pioneered swing were the great black musicians of the previous epoch—**Oliver**, **Johnny** and **Baby Dodds** and most of all **Louis Armstrong**.

Many other good musicians from New Orleans came and set up in Chicago. A steady stream of creative talent began to

flow from South to North, initiated by the closing of the Storyville red light quarter. In this respect as in others, the black and Creole musicians from New Orleans were the advance guard of a stream of coloured people who flooded from the American South to the North, drawn on by what, in their belief at least, were better living conditions.

It started with the people from New Orleans, then came the blues singers and players, followed later by black musicians of other styles and, as already mentioned, ordinary coloured people, expecting to suffer less under racial discrimination in the North than they had in the South.

This career pattern is typified by *Jelly Roll Morton,* the famous pianist who, by the early twenties, had years of touring as a topline solo star behind him. During this time he had written a series of ambitious compositions which he now began to play with the bigger bands in Chicago. He headed for the new recording business and began to record his compositions with combos specially assembled for the occasion. Unlike Oliver he gave his players little freedom; they had to submit to his direction. But once they had understood what he wanted of them, he gave each of them precisely defined points in the piece where they could let themselves go. This approach made Morton's discs all-time greats as models of artistic unity in jazz; modern musicians were later to study them over and over again with deep respect. From 1926 on his recording

band was called the Red Hot Peppers. Together with Oliver's discs, their music represented the artistic peak of the New Orleans style in its 1920s Chicago phase. In 1924 Oliver's famous band broke up. The Dodds Brothers and Louis Armstrong went their own ways. In the years to come Oliver showed unfailing discernment in bringing in from New Orleans one young cornettist after another. He put his stamp on these young players, made their name and launched them on their careers. The same was true of clarinettists. Apart from Bechet all the great New Orleans style clarinet players passed through Oliver's band. **Johnny Dodds**, another ex-Oliver man as we saw above, joined his brother Baby to found their own band which lasted through the thirties and made its name with an individual blues-slanted style, with heavy accenting of the basic beat in the melody line. Johnny Dodds, perhaps the most vital clarinettist of New Orleans jazz, used to like playing in quartets and other small groups. He would take blues-minded musicians like the pianist **Jimmy Blythe** (c. 1901–1931) into his band or let his brother play "washboard". He also showed his taste for the primitive blues sound in the nature of his own compositions. This style, which originated in the "Black South" of Chicago is also known as the South Side Style; this refers of course not to the South of the USA but to the district of Chicago where coloured people first settled. A few years later this "South Side" would become

The Frankfurt Two Beat Stompers, one of the best known German Revival Bands of the fifties.

America's most important focus for the blues.

The development of jazz followed other paths. **Louis Armstrong** had left Oliver together with the Creole Jazz Band's sometimes underrated pianist **Lil Hardin** (c. 1900–1971), who was later to be his wife, and started playing as the star of other Chicago bands. He met up with **Earl Hines** (1903–) and had a deep influence on the latter's complex piano style. A little later however, from 1924, he was engaged by the New York bandleader **Fletcher Henderson** (1898–1952) and learnt to play in an "orchestra".

In those days every major city of the American East and Midwest had an orchestra of this kind. They were essentially dance orchestras in late ragtime style which also played jazz arrangements. To begin with their rhythm remained that of the old-fashioned ragtime. We can hear the difference between this and the new swinging rhythm from New Orleans very clearly on the first recordings that Henderson made with Armstrong. As long as they stuck to the arrangement, a stiff rhythm dominates; when Armstrong launches into an improvised solo, the music begins to come alive.

Soon the new rhythm began to spread. The new fashion was a stimulating mix of the traditional art of arranging derived from dance music with these new ideas on rhythm from the New Orleans style and individual, sometimes local influences from older Afro-American forms. The first big bands were laying the foundations of swing. The trend was set by bands from Kansas City, from Missouri and later mainly from New York and the East. But it was also followed by New Orleans musicians who had already now and then played in larger combos at home in New Orleans. **Oliver** remained in Chicago and built his band up to a larger orchestra, which moved progressively towards the later swing style. And others, not from New Orleans, added steadily increasing momentum to the development.

Only one band made up of New Orleans musicians succeeded, without losing its essential quality, in finding a style of performance that not only fitted the new

24

trend but in fact had a decisive effect on it. This was the orchestra of **Luis Russell** (1902–1963) who had moved on from Oliver's last Chicago band. It became one of the best known big bands of the new epoch.

But despite all their talents neither he nor Jelly Roll Morton, who was also leading big bands around 1930, could compete with the new form. In fact their New Orleans style which had started out by being so revolutionary now sounded dated to the younger players. It was indeed pianists who led the new bands and did their arranging, but now the most highly regarded piano men were coming from the New York school of the Harlem Stride. This was a piano style with extreme emphasis on off beats which grew from late ragtime and led from **Eubie Blake** (1883–) through his teacher **James P. Johnson** (1891–1955) to **Fats Waller** (1904–1943). What were probably the best of the early big bands were led by Stride pianists such as **Don Charlie Johnson** (1891–1959) and **Duke Ellington** (1899–1974). However Ellington accepted certain New Orleans influences in his orchestra—Creole clarinets, trumpeters with Oliver's stamp on them and the Bechet school represented by the young Ellington star **Johnny Hodges** (1906–1970). In this way most of the key New Orleans musicians were drawn to New York, but their style changed. If they couldn't change their style, they stopped playing professionally or went back home.

Meanwhile in New Orleans the music of those who had stayed at home remained for a time unchanged. It was mainly two bands who upheld the tradition there—the Tuxedo Band with **Papa Celestin** (1884–1954) and **Sam Morgan's** (1895–1936) Band. In addition musicians who had not emerged in the old days were beginning to make their name—trumpeters like **Kid Howard**, (1908–1966), **Dede Pierce**, **Kid Thomas Valentine** and most notably the clarinettist **George Lewis** (1900–1968). Their style was formed partly by the earliest musicians of the pre-Oliver era and partly by turning to their own ends trends from the new epoch and its stars, learnt from concerts, radio and records. Kid Howard for instance started by playing all the well known Armstrong solos of the swing era. This mixture of unadulterated early style and swing rhythms was further enriched by musicians coming home after having worked in New York—among them the drummer **Paul Barbarin** (1901–1969) and the guitarist **Johnny St. Cyr** (1890–1966). Lifelong playing in brass bands—at processions, funerals, carnivals and feasts of every kind—probably imprinted an ineradicable stamp on the style of every local wind player. In any event the New Orleans style was still very much alive in its home town at the end of the thirties. But its development had taken a turn all of its own characterized by the playing of the hits of the swing years along with the backstreet ditties of the Buddy Bolden generation and particular local hits. The other feature was that arrangements, whether of the classical or the ragtime period, vanished into oblivion and gave way to a slicker, wholly improvized style.

In the late thirties jazz critics and record collectors began to show an interest in the origins of jazz. The book *Jazzmen* edited by Frederic Ramsey and Charles Edward Smith, in which Oliver, already dead, Morton and other New Orleans style musicians were given the hero's treatment, focused attention on these origins. For the first time something like "jazz research" came into being. The New Orleans style experienced its first revival. Enthusiastic amateurs discovered **Bunk Johnson** working as a farm labourer in the little town of New Iberia, Louisiana, bought him a new set of false teeth and a new trumpet and took him to New Orleans. There they cut discs with him and those bands they could still find. He went to New York with **George Lewis** and made a hit there. Although the later New Orleans music had little appeal for him—he complained that the members of his new band had learnt their music way out in the sticks—he was soon in great form again and showed that he was more than just a legend. **Kid Ory** was rediscovered in San Francisco and started a second career which was to last around twenty years. **Louis Armstrong** got together a traditional combo. **Bechet** made a series of immortal records with **Tommy Ladnier** (1900–1939) and the Chicago clarinettist **Mezz Mezzrow** (1899–1972) who had gone right over to the old black style. **Jelly Roll Morton** cut

25

a series of discs on his life history for the Library of Congress in Washington.

In San Francisco another aspect of this revival was sparked off. Young white musicians discovered the charms of the old time style and formed bands in which they tried to play the music of Oliver and Morton and the young Armstrong. Prominent figures among these groups were **Lu Watters** (1911–) and **Turk Murphy** (1915–). In this way a new "trad" style was created—the San Francisco style which made countless young Americans addicts of trad jazz.

In Europe too young bands began to turn to the old jazz. Once again the classical style of Oliver and Morton was the model. George Webb and later and more notably **Humphrey Lyttleton** (1921–) started things off in England; after 1945 they were joined by **Claude Luter** (1923–) and others in France. A little later on, **Sidney Bechet** really hit the high spots in his new home of Paris with **Luter, Andre Reweliotty, Rene Franc** and **Michel Attenoux**. In Holland the Dutch Swing College Band was founded. The first combos of this European revival grew into really top class jazz bands. Later groups were less successful and few of them got beyond amateur status. In Germany most bands still belong to the first revival, which in the post-war years up to around 1956 started by playing in the style of the early Armstrong and Oliver records. Two Frankfurt bands made their names—the Two Beat Stompers and the Barrelhouse Jazz Band.

Trumpeter Kid Armstrong with his Preservation Hall Band in New Orleans.

Meanwhile in America things had gone rather dead for the New Orleans style. Bunk Johnson was dead, as were Morton, Dodds, Ladnier and many others. The only trad players to remain popular were the white Dixieland musicians whose jazz was based more on the Chicago style (see Werner Burkhardt's contribution to this book) than on New Orleans. George Lewis was playing again in New Orleans with a band that had grown up over the years with Bunk Johnson. Then a new wave of enthusiasm for trad jazz broke out in England. The English trumpeter **Ken Colyer** (1928–) made his dream come true. He went to New Orleans, where he listened to George Lewis and the other bands, and came back home in 1953 with the message that New Orleans music was now something quite different from the old records. He founded a band and developed it on the basis of records from the first New Orleans revival. His colleagues **Chris Barber**, (1930–) **Monty Sunshine** and **Acker Bilk** soon formed their own bands. But once again, instead of maintaining the old style they developed a new one—this time a highly Europeanized, sophisticated style which nonetheless swept through Europe in a flash and even spread back to America. This was English trad jazz. Scandinavian bands, notable among them Papa Blue's Viking Jazz Band, made their name by following the same trend. And in Germany literally hundreds of amateur bands of this kind sprang up.

By the early sixties this music had become so popularized that it was swept aside by the next fasion, the big beat. Only the leading names of the epoch stayed in business, and they had to change their ways.

But the original also profited from this pursuit of imitation. Dozens of long-playing records with George Lewis and other New Orleans bands were cut. Some of these discs are among the most exciting that the New Orleans style has ever produced. The Lewis Band had reached its peak. Its mix of a very early New Orleans style with its naivety and sentimentality and the swinging, almost rock rhythm of later years, played with the brilliance of originality and the soundness of rich musical experience, is yet another unique contribution by New Orleans to jazz history.

The records stemming from the second revival stimulated a new generation to look towards New Orleans music. These Europeans—and Americans, Japanese and Australians—could see the mistakes of the Colyer generation. Meanwhile air tickets had become cheaper and so it was possible to study the original on the spot in greater depth. Admittedly they did not have the sudden and conspicuous success of their predecessors; but from around 1965 they gradually brought New Orleans music back into the field of vision of a wider public. Once again it was mainly English musicians, most notably **Barry Martin**, who led the way. They lived for a time in New Orleans, studied the style in depth, and where it was still possible sought tuition from survivors of the classical New Orleans period. They recorded the old musicians and their bands and took these records back to the four corners of the earth. With their own bands they slowly made the New Orleans style known in Europe. German bands too followed this trend. The centres of New Orleans jazz in Germany are Hamburg, Berlin, Stuttgart and Frankfurt. In New Orleans the Preservation Hall, a plain room in the old French Quarter, became the focus of indigenous jazz and the meeting point of the new disciples of the old music. To start with the foreign New Orleans bands took individual New Orleans musicians with them on tour in their own countries. Then, as popularity spread, complete New Orleans bands made comprehensive concert tours in Europe, the United States, Japan and Australia. Old musicians started new careers. New stars were discovered in New Orleans, such as the trombone player **Louis Nelson** (1902–) and the incredibly vital alto sax player **"Captain" John Handy** (1900–1971).

This slow-moving painstaking third revival still goes on today. As long as the bands which were and are heirs to the tradition still exist, the history of New Orleans jazz has not reached its end.

Manfred Miller
Blues

Manfred Miller was head of jazz and pop programmes at Radio Bremen from 1969 to 1971, since when he has been freelancing. For two years Miller has been giving a fortnightly series *"Blues Time"* for Southwest German Radio, which has had particularly high ratings. Born in Reichenberg (Czechoslovakia) in 1943, Miller studied musicology, philosophy and sociology at Cologne University. Since 1974 he has been lecturing at Bremen University.

No other kind of popular music has had such a lasting influence on the music industry's output over the past twenty years as has Afro-American folk music—in a word, the blues. With rock'n roll, the blues provided the basis of a new form of entertainment music; since then their various forms have sparked off a whole string of new styles which can be grouped under the broad heading of "rock". It is significant that at European concerts blues men introduce themselves by simply saying: "Everybody knows the blues". True, anyone who has even the most superficial acquaintance with the new forms of popular music "knows" the blues. This does not mean that there are not some extremely vague if not erroneous ideas about what kind of music the blues is.

The specialist literature insists on describing the blues as a particular musical *form*. On this definition "blues" is a song with 12-bar choruses, each subdivided into three groups of four 4/4 bars each. In the melody and lyric the second 4-bar phase is a repetition of the first, usually with variations, and the third is an answering phrase. Harmonically the 12-bar chorus consists of four bars based on the tonic triad, two on the subdominant, two back on the tonic, two on the dominant and a final two bars on the tonic. There are, however, many simple variants of this progression.

Some musicians have supported this formalized definition. T-Bone Walker for instance said: "There is only one blues, and that is the 12-bar harmonic layout".

Being so specific has indeed one thing in its favour—it meets the centrist requirements of European musical analysis which seeks to confine every kind of musical expression within a laid-down form. But it has a great deal against it too—in the shape of numerous Afro-American songs which clearly lie within the blues tradition but in no way conform to the 12-bar blues layout.

Quite apart from countless individual examples which meet the blues definition simply in their 3-phase structure and to some extent in chord sequences but not in metrical development, the current definition excludes two large categories of blues which lack the remotest resemblance to it. The first of these are associative songs which make some use of quasi-modal recitative, sung to a single chord, and often lack clearly formed choruses. Such songs are current in the country blues tradition and are also highly thought of by famous bluesmen like **John Lee Hooker** (1917–) or **Robert Pete Williams** (1914–), because they offer great scope in the shaping of rhythm and lyric. The second category are the blues with 2-part choruses. These belong mainly to four popular extended blues families—"extended" in that variants and offshoots of the four basic rhythmic and melodic models crop up under widely differing titles in the repertoire of every blues musician. The four "family names" are: *Baby Please Don't Go, Sittin' on Top of the World, Someday Baby* and *Slidin' Delta* or *Crow Jane*.

Bessie Smith, "Empress of the Blues"

Big Joe Williams

Clearly the deviations are too numerous and too fundamental to make it any use talking about "the exception which proves the rule". It is the "rule" itself, the "harmonic" definition of blues which covers only one type—one form of blues which was developed under particular conditions and is very commonly used.

The second misunderstanding that gets dragged into most definitions along with that about form relates to the content and expression of the blues. Blues, it says, are "melancholy and plaintive".

Despite its false premises the 12-bar definition does serve some kind of purpose in describing the form of a major group of blues. But the definition of content, also derived from European classification, is sheer rubbish. The way blues people express themselves musically is only seen as "melancholy" or "plaintive" because it strikes a European ear that way. The typical tonality of the blues is based on a seven note scale, of which the third and seventh (occasionally the fifth and sixth too) are not "correctly" intoned but waver between the major and minor third or seventh of the Western scale. An ear schooled in the tradition of European music hears this wavering intonation and perceives the intervals typical of the blues as those of a minor key. And minor keys normally are associated with "plaintive", "melancholy", "sad" or "sentimental" feelings.

For the Afro-American on the other hand these blue notes which have their origin in African musical usage do not in the least represent a melancholy state of mind. He uses them as means of *emphasis,* to indicate a high degree of emotional arousal and excitement. It is worth noting that Afro-Americans also use this floating intonation in everyday speech when they get worked up about something. Those who hear in the wavering blues intonation a similarly unsure melancholy, withdrawn or depressed state of mind are listening with the wrong ears. They are applying the aural responses they have learnt from European tradition to Afro-American forms of expression. This is just about as sensible as an English-speaking tourist interpreting the Italian word "belli" as a reference to his stomach. Admittedly

31

this misunderstanding is fostered by an ambiguity of language. "To be blue" has meant to be "troubled", "melancholy", "down in the dumps" in conversational English since the sixteenth century. In the Afro-American's speech the same word has however acquired considerably more complex overtones.

Things are still further complicated by the blues having made their entry onto the stage of musical history in a form which is to no small extent due to the misunderstandings outlined above. If the concept of "classical" includes the idea of finely sculptured, exemplary shape, the so-called "classical" blues of the twenties were anything but classical. "I can't sleep at night/ I can't eat a bite/ 'Cause the man I'm lovin'/ He don't treat me right". These lines which open *Crazy Blues* also mark the point in time, 10 August 1920, from which the documentation of the blues begins. True, **Mamie Smith's** (1883–1946) *Crazy Blues* was not, as we shall see in a minute, literally the first recording of a vocalist of Afro-American origin. It was not even Mamie Smith's first record, which had been cut six months earlier on 11 February 1920. And well before that there were records of spiritual choirs like the Fisk Jubilee Singers and of black minstrels. What was new about *Crazy Blues* was that it stayed relatively close to the forms of expression of black folk music and that it was aimed specifically at an Afro-American public. The earlier records were nothing but versions of Afro-American music that had been adapted to European

bourgeois musical ideas and sentimentalized. These were aimed at a middle-class, mainly European market.

A double coincidence led to Mamie Smith making her first disc—on the one hand the doggedness of the pianist, composer and producer Perry Bradford, in selling Mamie Smith to the Okeh management; and on the other the fact that Sophie Tucker, the white cabaret singer originally engaged, could not make the recording date. Mamie's first chance record—*That Thing Called Love* and *You Can't Keep a Good Man Down*—sold unusually well, almost entirely in the coloured ghettos of the industrial cities of the American Northeast and Midwest.

Because of this Okeh launched her second record, *Crazy Blues,* with carefully aimed publicity—and with overwhelming success. In the first month after its appearance the record sold at least 75,000, and months later sales were still running at 7,500 a week. The record industry had found a new market—or more precisely, it had stumbled by chance on a new market and still didn't know what to do with it. Victor for instance, one of the largest firms, made innumerable test recordings with singers of the "new music" between 1920 and 1922, of which they published scarcely one. A campaign against the alleged effect on morals of jazz music and its dirty—dare one say "blue"—lyrics got under way at that time and may have contributed to the major record firms' hesitation in realizing the market

possibilities that the success of *Crazy Blues* had revealed.

Only two Afro-American vocalists cut their first discs in 1920, but in 1921 there were twelve and by 1922 fourteen. The real breakthrough for blues—and for black jazz as a whole—came in 1923, when the record industry saw its turnover falling and started looking round for new markets. That year as many as 55 new singers made their first blues records, among them **Ida Cox** (1889–1967), **Ma Rainey** (1886–1939), **Bessie Smith** (1895–1937) and **Clara Smith** (c. 1885–1935), the four all-time greats in the interpretation of "classical" blues. Up to the Depression, a total of over 250 blues artists recorded over 3,200 titles.

The underlying cause of this trend was the migration of Afro-Americans from the agricultural states of the American South to the industrial centres of the North—a migration that grew considerably during World War I. At least 460,000 Afro-Americans migrated from the South between 1910 and 1919, and between 1920 and 1929 the number of migrants rose to some 770,000. One cause of this wave of migration was the wretched living conditions in the agricultural areas—the notorious share-cropping system which to some extent still survives and under which agricultural labour is performed for a share of the crop, against which is offset the costs of lodging, clothing, food, tools and so on. This had simply replaced slavery by the rather more sophisticated condition of serfdom. Secondly the migration enjoyed massive support from the industrialized North in the shape of propaganda and organisation. In this way industry hoped to meet the demand for cheap, unskilled labour that had reached enormous proportions because of the War and the introduction of production line techniques. It is true that the living conditions in the industrial areas were by no means rosy—in fact conditions in the ghettos, which quickly became overpopulated as people flooded in, were and are appalling. But in any event improvements in the average wage sufficed to make the mass of Afro-American industrial workers a potential market for the record industry—and after Mamie Smith's chance recording an actual market too. For the purchasing power to buy records went hand in hand with the need for them. The organisation of working and social life in the industrial cities ruled out the cultural self-sufficiency that is taken for granted in rural communities. Those who wanted to hear music had generally to buy it—either in the form of a ticket for the clubs and variety theatres or on records. As early as the mid-twenties the sociologists Odum and Johnson estimated the annual sales of records made by Negroes for Negroes at five to six million.

Nothing could be further from the truth than the idea, fostered by the tag "classical", that production for this market differed in any real way from the methods used for Tin Pan Alley hits.

Those whose records failed to hit the jackpot first time sank back into the mire. Of the 252 blues musicians—mainly women singers—of the "classical period" whose names appear in the recording lists, 138—or more than half—made only one or two records. It was not just the harsh rules of the market but the equally demanding way the records were made that gave the "classical" blues their character of a musical industrial product. The songs were produced by division of labour, made up generally speaking by professional lyric writers and composers. These were often people who had no contact whatever with the blues tradition and thus understood the blues as a form of music to be exploited in whatever way they chose because of its melancholy content. The women singers "interpreted" these songs in the full sense of the word. Even among the 160 titles of **Bessie Smith's** whole record repertoire, there are only 38 of her own including those for which she obtained copyright protection under her husband's name. And even she, the most successful female vocalist of the time, had no say in the choice of the titles she recorded, most of which were chosen for her by their respective producers. Admittedly not all these titles were, at least in their form, blues; no fewer than 76 follow the usual hit-song form. In addition mixed forms were often used in which the blues, already reduced to its 12-bar layout, was treated as no more than a particular form of chorus.

The "classical" blues ought then to be called vaudeville blues, for they represent nothing more than a commercialized form of blues folk music which grew up in the vaudeville theatres from 1900 onwards. Bessie Smith's *Frankie Blues* of 1924 typifies the resulting mixture in two main ways. Formally it begins with an introduction, as was usual in hits of the time, the first 12 bars of which in this case match the conventional blues harmonic sequence. Then comes a blues chorus followed by a hit chorus, which is finally repeated with a variant of the lyric from the middle part onwards. (This is another common practice in Tin Pan Alley songs, probably due in the first place to the limited playing time of records. Later with the chorus vocals of the swing bands it became a stereotype.) The second respect in which *Frankie Blues* is typical is its relationship to the blues tradition. The material for the piece, comes in part from the traditional ballad *Frankie and Johnny* reworked by one E. Johnson. This is true both of parts of the melody and of whole lines of the lyric: "Frankie was a good fellow"; "He know' he's done me wrong". Yet a third reason is the structure of its content. The introduction depicts a scene which serves in fact to trigger the whole song.

In other words the mixed form of the vaudeville blues presupposes the existence of two different traditions—that of the blues and that of the stage song. It is above all in the introduction that the part played in vaudeville blues by the theatrical tradition can be seen over and over again. These introductions set a dramatic scene for the song and—often explicitly—make the singing of it the acting of a part. Generally speaking acting was very important in vaudeville blues, both in the presentation and in the assumption of a different identity. In the description of one of **Clara Smith's** appearances we read: "She makes her entrance through the steel blue views of the background. She is wearing a black evening dress trimmed with white fur. She doesn't come right downstage, but hesitates, turns her side to the public and starts singing. As the song goes on her tone becomes more and more pathetic. Tears roll down her cheeks. Finally her voice seems to die away in grief and she buries her face in the curtain".

In assessing the place of vaudeville blues in the history of the blues a critical distinction must be taken into account—the respective conditions of production and reception. It makes a big difference whether the presentation of blues takes place for friends and neighbours on street corners, in bars and at bucolic celebrations, or on the stage of a theatre. Many of the features of vaudeville blues which run markedly counter to the blues tradition may also be attributed to the fact that it is a stage performance, an interpretative art. It is not entirely without significance that **Ma Rainey** was already an experienced and successful singer in minstrel shows, a form of theatrical entertainment, when in 1902 she was the first to introduce blues into her show. Quite a few of the

"classical" blues singers worked in the twenties for Broadway revues and musicals, and nearly all of them toured theatres for the Theatre Owners' Booking Agency founded in 1909. Because of bad working conditions and wretched fees the acronym T.O.B.A. soon came to be interpreted as "tough on black artists", or more expressively "tough on black arses". The importance of these tours for the spread and popularisation of the blues has often been emphasised; but such comment is remarkably apt to overlook the way in which the stage-oriented form of presentation inevitably has consequences for the music too. Even the "classical" style of singing with its sustained melodic spans may in large measure be due to the need for the singer to make herself understood from the stage of a large hall without the later electrical aids.

This does not mean that vaudeville blues should be completely excluded from the history of the blues proper. On the one hand, whatever one may think about it, it did much for the standardization of the blues form. On the other, even if they were exceptions which conquered the way they were made, some of the blues in this idiom could justifiably be dubbed "classical", in that they caught the essence of the incorruptible realism and steadfast will to live of blues folk music. The roots of the blues go right back to the music of the slave era. Their immediate progenitors are on one side the dance tunes that these forced labourers brought over from Africa and

used to play at their Saturday night get-togethers, and on the other the worksongs with which they co-ordinated their labour and the field hollers or musical calls by which they communicated in the fields. The liberation of the slaves and the resulting new way of life with free, individual wages ended the development of these forms of musical expression. Worksong and field holler, whose function was by definition restricted to collective labour and living, were transformed by the new sharecropper's isolated way of working into field blues. This was an individual form of expression which brought together the antiphonal structure of worksong and holler in a single, generally freely associated song line. Features of this

Robert Pete Williams

Sunnyland Slim

open form with its freedom from regular strophic structure are still to be found on records like the 1927 *Levee Camp Moan Blues* of **Texas Alexander** (c. 1880/90–1955).

Despite a rather unpromising experiment with the guitar-playing singer **Ed Andrews** in the Spring of 1924, from the end of that year more and more record companies began to record country blues (i.e. folk music) alongside the stage-oriented vaudeville blues. It was not that the firms had suddenly awoken to a sense of cultural responsibility and decided that documentation was their duty. The simple fact was that after 1921 the American record industry went through its first serious crisis. In that year over 100 million discs were sold, and the overall turnover of the firm of Victor alone reached 51 million dollars.

In the following years this turnover fell to 44 million dollars (1923) and only 20 million in 1925—a trend typical of the period. The only line to show a growth rate (and an enormous one at that) was what were known as race records—records that made Afro-American music available to the black working class that was still steadily pouring into the industrial cities from the South. Their musical needs could not be met entirely from records of city vaudeville artists, even if the best-known of these cut a new disc every month, and less known freelance women singers might have records published under six or seven different labels in the course of a year. At this time Paramount shared the lead in the race records market with Okeh Columbia. In its 1924 catalogue there appears the following advertisement: "What would the public like? What do you want? If your favourites aren't listed in our catalogues, we will make them for you, for Paramount must please the paying public. There is always room for more good material and more talented artists. Any suggestions or tips that you have to offer will be very gratefully received by the manager of our race artists line, J. Mayo Williams".

Shortly after this **Sam Price** (1908–   ), himself later to become a well-known blues and jazz pianist but then working in a music shop in Dallas, Texas, drew Mayo Williams' attention to an itinerant Texan musician. Paramount brought him to Chicago to record and his records made him one of the most popular musicians in the history of the blues—**Blind Lemon Jefferson** (1897–1930).

Understandably enough the first musicians to get this kind of recording contract were those who already had a name outside their own region—people such as **Blind Lemon**, **Papa Charlie Jackson** (c. 1900–), **Blind Arthur Blake** (c. 1890–1931) or **Lonnie Johnson** (c. 1889–1970). These were musicians who had learnt their way around maybe as barkers in medicine shows and had learnt how to reduce manifold regional variations of style to a common denominator. Since their style was not local, their records could be sold outside their home regions. Musicians of this kind offered the musical commercialisers an absolutely ideal link between folk roots and professionalism. Not that all the rest of the blues people of those times would have lacked the relative musical skills—what they lacked, as some still do, was motivation, the professional approach needed to respond to the quintessence of their music and shed the close ties with its local rules and usages. Up to a point they could make their living from music within a regional context. On the other hand in the theatres the vaudeville blues were trend-setting and pure country blues would have been out of place on a stage. And no blues musician could make a living from recordings alone in those days any more than he can now. Royalties, which would have linked the musicians' rewards to the sales of their records, were not on offer: the record companies bought the rights to the recordings with a single down payment. They paid between 10 and 30 dollars, 50 at the outside, for each title they accepted. Even someone like Blind Lemon Jefferson could only just earn over a thousand dollars a year from his records—less than half the officially calculated subsistence income.

Unimpaired country folklore on one side, and an admittedly very profitable but organisationally naive exploitation of Afro-American music on the other. Those were the conditions that from 1924 onwards gave rise to an abundance of records which, despite being cut for

T-Bone Walker in a Southwest German Radio television production of the American Folk Blues Festival in 1964. He died in 1975.

Big Bill Broonzy

commercial purposes, can still be regarded as a true reflection of the modes of country blues. The record industry simply recorded what there was to record—often using mobile equipment on the spot. It was rare that the musicians had to work to guidelines, the record industry was still far from market-oriented musicmaking. When the chips were down the musicians had no choice but to sing blues as the most marketable form of black folk music, with the result that other types of musical expression are unrepresented on commercial discs and that blues, rather than the broader-based repertoire of songsters, gradually came to be accepted as the dominant musical idiom. Another point is that producers wanted as far as possible, to record "new" pieces. This admittedly led to a significant enrichment of the body of traditional verse, but it also resulted in the mechanical churning out of lyrics which no longer had any real roots in experience. There can be no doubt that the incessant demand of the music industry for new songs of this kind radically changed the way in which new country blues verses came into being and spread. People who record a hundred titles in five years, as Blind Lemon Jefferson and others did, are under pressure for innovation which just does not exist for the country blues musician operating outside the tension of commercialisation. Examples of this pressure are opportunistic titles like Blind Lemon's *Christmas Eve Blues* and *Happy New Year Blues;* this certainly would

never have happened without the pressures of the market. But in fairness one must say that commissioned works like this are very rarely to be found even in the repertoire of the busiest blues people. As to publication, commercial interests certainly had a prominent place in the picture—mainly maybe as censors—cleaning up the lyrics to make sure that they did not shock the microphones of the white recording team.

Another factor was that in the twenties no record company as yet had a monopoly. It is true that the invention of electrical recording in 1926 resulted in a certain process of concentration; the firms with less capital could not afford to invest in new equipment, and the inferior quality of the old acoustic system put them out of the running. But there were still a good dozen firms competing in the Afro-American market—as is shown by no fewer than 3,655 titles by 411 country blues artists being published between 1923 and 1933. As Sam Charters has remarked, "These titles have preserved almost every style of southern blues singing".

One of the most expressive, highly developed and influential of these regional styles is the Mississippi Blues, as they are generally known. Their characteristic is the contrasting of strong bass figures and chords struck offbeat with riffs in the upper part, which either provide counterpoint to the melody line or double it in octaves. In line with the African tradition of "talking" instruments, these riffs can also be substituted

for individual words or complete lines. This idiom came into being, probably around 1912 and certainly earlier than 1920, in the Yazoo Delta, the fertile plain south of Memphis and north of Vicksburg, which is flanked by the Mississippi on one side and the Yazoo River on the other. We can pinpoint it more closely—the birth must have taken place near the little township of Drew, Mississippi. At the end of the nineteenth century Will Dockery and Jim Yeager had founded two large cotton plantations in the neighbourhood of Drew. They offered relatively good working conditions, renouncing the sharecropping system which amounted in effect to the slavery of debt. They employed agricultural labour for really good wages and not just seasonally. The result was that the Dockery and Yeager plantations provided a very attractive contrast to the general situation of the black rural working classes of the South. Large-scale migration to the Yazoo Delta began before the turn of the century, so that this area had an unusually high density of Afro-American population even by Southern standards.

With them came musicians. Around 1912 there were living on Dockery's Plantation or elsewhere round Drew: **Charley Patton** (1887–1934), **Tommy Johnson** (c. 1900–1955), his brother **LeDell, Willie Brown, Roebuck Staples** (founder and guitarist of the family gospel group **Staples Singers**), **Chester Burnett** (1910–) (later to be known as **Howlin'Wolf**, who claimed that Patton

38

taught him the guitar), **Jake Martin, Dick Bankston, "Cap" Holmes** and quite a few other less well-known musicians. Subject to individual variations, they all made the style mentioned above their own.

It would be fair enough to call this style "Dockery Blues" or "Drew Blues" instead of "Mississippi Blues". For it was rooted in a local idiom, even if this later spread widely through the movements of its musicians and then through records. A striking motif of this local tradition was used over and over again, and in the early fifties became the basis of Chicago blues. This is "rolling and tumbling" which features under a variety of titles in the repertoire of blues men like **John Lee "Sonny Boy" Williamson,** (1921–48) **Sleepy John Estes** (1904–), **John Lee Hooker** (1917–), **Muddy Waters** (1915–) **Elmore James** (1918–1963), **Big Joe Williams** (1903–), **Howlin' Wolf, Sunnyland Slim** (1907–), **Furry Lewis** (1900–) and **Charley Patton**. It crops up again even among the rock bands (Yardbirds, Cream, Livin' Blues) and as Roll and Tumble Blues, first recorded by **"Hambone" Willie Newborn** in 1929. "Hambone" Willie embodies the statistical average of the country blues musicians who were recording in 1929. He cut six titles. (In that year 150 musicians had a total of 856 titles, or around six each). He did his recording in one of the mobile studios with which the record firm made regular trips to the South. (Between 1927 and 1930 a good third of all blues records other than vaudeville blues were cut in this way—a proportion never reached before or later). And his name disappeared from the record catalogues in the Depression. (Of the blues musicians who had records published between 1923 and 1942, only one in ten made records both before and after the Depression).

These data and the comparative figures evidence the shattering impact that the years of the great financial crisis had on the production of blues records. Most of the firms which had been strongly competing before the Depression for the Afro-American music market, and had thus contributed to the completely disorganized but historically fruitful abundance of records, either went bankrupt in the crisis or were taken over by competitors who could call on larger capital. By 1934 this ruthless thinning out process had left two groups of a monopolistic nature. On one side was RCA Victor with its Bluebird race record label. On the other were the combined forces of Columbia-Okeh, Brunswick-Balke-Collender (with the Brunswick and Vocalion labels) and American Record Company (A.R.C.) (Perfect, Oriole, Romeo, Banner, Melotone), which in 1938 were bought up by CBS. In addition there was an American subsidiary, founded in 1934, of the British firm of Decca. These giants were no longer interested in making small quantities of records for limited markets—the way in which a good proportion of the pre-Depression race records had come into being. Their production was aimed at the national market, so that they recorded by and large only musicians who had completely freed themselves of local tradition and thus had coast-to-coast appeal. On top of this they tried to extend the star system of hit production into the blues field too. They no longer recorded new material by new musicians regardless, but went to considerable length to build up specific musicians with a whole string of records. Between 1934 and 1942 considerably fewer musicians cut considerably more blues discs than between 1923 and 1933. On the average every recording blues-man after the Depression achieved almost twice as many published titles as his predecessors of the twenties. Before the slump firms had been prepared to go on making numerous recordings of country blues with their archaic charm, which they themselves described in their publicity as "weird". The big groups of the thirties concentrated mainly on technically competent musicians with an execution that was sophisticated and polished in harmony, rhythm and form alike—pianists like **Leroy Carr** (1905–35), **Roosevelt Sykes** (1906–), **Peetie Wheatstraw** (1905–41) (promoted under the sobriquet "The Devil's Son-in-Law") and **Walter Davis** (1912–64); guitarists like **Josh White** (1908–70), **Bo Carter** (Bo Chatman), **Blind Boy Fuller** (1903–40), **Bumble Bee Slim** (1905–) (Amos Easton), **Lonnie Johnson, Tampa Red** (1960–) and **Big Bill Broonzy** (1893–1958).

Trains, the transport which carried the Negros in their migration from South to North, are much featured in blues lyrics.

These musicians had over 100 titles published in 1942—in the cases of Broonzy and Tampa Red over 200 even. It is surely no coincidence that these were not exponents of regional traditions but preferred a sophisticated, refined, swinging blues style.

Production took place almost entirely in the studios of the music industry centres of Chicago and New York. In the thirties field trips to record blues out in the sticks played a very secondary role. Frequently the accompanying group was made up from an unvarying clique of studio musicians, among them not only Broonzy and Tampa Red but the pianists **Joshua Altheimer**, **Black Bob** and **Blind John Davis** and the bass players **Ransom Knowling** and **Alfred Elkins**.

In a word the broad trend in the making of blues records was coming to resemble the industrialized production of other forms of entertainment music. Yet the blues, unlike these other forms, did not go down the primrose path of commercialisation. They succeeded in preserving their vitality and in conserving a musical expressiveness that only very seldom showed signs of the monotony inherent in the way they were made. This was because the blues of the music industry could always fall back on the uninterrupted and continuously developing tradition of blues folk music.

It is important to realize that the country blues musicians and the pianists who played blues in the bars of lumber camps and the working-class joints of urban ghettos may have earned their living with their music—or at least tried to—but were not in the narrower sense of the term professional musicians. The musical ethnologist David Evans has suggested the term "folk professionals" for them—musicians who play professionally music rooted in folk usage and thus serve to crystallize the musical activity of a group. They are specialized producers working in a field in which unity of production and consumption is still by and large conserved. They are performers living under the same conditions as their public, playing pieces and singing songs which tell it the way it was and seek to transform shared experiences. Even the stars were unable to break out of this setting completely; they could not divorce themselves from the experiences of their people.

In practical terms they could not do so because the earnings even from frequent recordings were too slender to ensure a stable existence. To pick two examples among many, even a man like **Broonzy** had at least sometimes to depend on the support of the Roosevelt Administration's WPA Program; even a man like **Roosevelt Sykes** got most of the money he needed to live on from selling bootleg whisky.

At the personal level they could not do so because their music put a caste mark on them. In the social hierarchy of musical idioms the blues took bottom place, as the "raw" music of the lowest social class, the black working class and incompetents. It would be decades before a man could climb out of this class on the blues ladder; in the thirties he faced the choice between social climbing and the blues.

It was harder for a "guitar picker" or "piano tickler" to enter the kingdom of even the black lower middle class than for a camel to pass through the needle's eye.

The exploitation of the blues, which became the dominant black idiom in the commercial and folk music framework alike, was grounded on this continuing tradition of the "folk professionals". It was provoked entirely by the interest of the Afro-American public, which found its social and cultural identity mirrored in the blues with considerably more precision than in the songs from the minstrel and ballad tradition which had formed the early repertoire of the itinerant players. Blues discs were a hot commercial property just because they didn't intrude on the territory of the hit of the moment. What is more they brought into play the specific experiences of the black working class and specifically Afro-American culture, thus relating directly to the experience and needs of Afro-Americans. It was **Robert Johnson** (1898–1937) who brought the regional style from the Yazoo Delta to its fully mature form, at the same time passing it on to the generation which developed the Chicago blues. In his *Walkin' Blues* Robert Johnson did not sing of any kind of "fateful compulsion to migrate"—although even today we sometimes read rubbish like this. He sang of the life of the black agricultural labourers, of migration as the only possible individual response to intolerable living conditions.

From the beginning of their commercialisation the blues can only be understood in terms of tension. Pulling one way was the need to be a marketable commodity subject to the interests of the music industry. Pulling against this ran the powerful current of a living folklore which the Afro-Americans used to communicate about their living conditions and to conserve their ability to act in face of these.

Werner Burkhardt
Chicago

Werner Burkhardt was born in Hamburg
in 1928. His contributions to *die Welt* and
the *Süddeutsche Zeitung* have made him
one of the best known of German jazz
critics. He translated Billie Holiday's
autobiography *Lady Sings The Blues* as well
as *Hear Me Talking to You* edited by
Shapiro and Hentoff, and novels by Jack
Kerouac. He is jazz consultant to the
Teldec record firm and produces jazz
programmes for North German Radio,
Bavarian Radio and Southwest German
Radio.

Looking back on the Chicago of the golden twenties we see a rather hazy picture from which certain broad outlines stand out. We see gangster joints and moonshine liquor, the beetling cynicism of the tales of Scott Fitzgerald and the rather heady fashions of the time. We hear the charleston and we hear jazz—jazz from large orchestras and small groups, jazz of shirt-sleeved warmth and high sophistication, jazz from whites and jazz from blacks.

It was in Autumn 1925 that **Louis Armstrong** came back to Chicago from New York. He had hit the jackpot in the metropolis, but was homesick for the familiar bars, the colourful life of the South Side—that exciting black ghetto of the city on Lake Michigan. And there was longing for his wife Lil, who had stayed back home, to draw him too. The fact that we are talking about a homecoming when Armstrong was actually born in New Orleans is a matter of historical and social fact, of the epoch-making migration of coloured people from the rural South to the great cities of the North. That is why the dark-skinned jazz musicians felt at home in those days in Chicago with its host of lucrative engagements.

They achieved fame as well as fortune. What had been taken for granted and regarded as just grassroots folk music on the banks of the Mississippi now hit the headlines, carrying a wide public with it and enthusing not only the white drinkers in the bars but the young white musicians too.

Lil Armstrong (née **Hardin**) had done her homework well and landed for herself and her husband a dream job in the Dreamland Café.

There Louis Armstrong made something more than jazz history, he made a deep impression on the young white middle-class people who quickly became fired with enthusiasm for this new music. **Muggsy Spanier** (1906-1967), later to become one of the most laconically expressive cornet players of that era, recalls the year 1925: "I knew the owner of the Dreamland and was allowed to sit in a dark corner of the balcony to listen to the music. I was only 14 then, still not old enough to be allowed in a public dancehall, but as long as I heard the music, conditions didn't matter. The band played from 9.30 to 1a.m. and after hours they played the Pekin Café, one of the worst gangster hangouts in Chicago, which has now been turned into a police station. In summer the Pekin kept its windows open, so I'd sneak from home just about every night and sit outside on a kerbstone listening to the music. Sometimes the goings-on would get rough inside, then you'd hear the flash of forty-five calibre revolvers trying to fire with a beat. Before I knew it, I'd be running home as fast as my feet could take me. But the next night would always find me sitting on the same kerbstone. I thought the music well worth running the risk of getting shot by a stray bullet". This young white hope of the musical world, who came from a good family and was swept up in the vitality of black music; this gesture of grateful respect for the great trendsetters whose creative power had yet to gain the public recognition it deserved; this boy, sitting on the threshold figuratively too, full of longing and envy—you could hardly have a clearer picture of the way things were then. It was the way things had to be, the way the jazz played in Chicago was transformed into Chicago jazz. It's a true enough picture, except that everything falls into place too pat. For the foundations of what was to become the Chicago style had already been laid a few years earlier.

It was not just coloured musicians who laid them. The black jazz of New Orleans interacted with the white jazz of Chicago. There were really two bands that handed on the torch, bringing the dark flame from the Mississippi to Lake Michigan—the Original Dixieland Jazz Band and the New Orleans Rhythm Kings. Both bands came direct from New Orleans.

With all the bitterness and cantankerousness of a sad old age, **Nick LaRocca** (1889–1961), the cornet player of the Original Dixieland Jazz Band, maintained right up to the fifties: "It was me who invented jazz. Those niggers pinched my music". A claim like this comes of course simply from the disillusionment of one who was tragically underrated; there was no question of black men stealing his music. Yet Nick LaRocca has been robbed. Oversimplification stemming from a single-minded effort to credit the birth of jazz solely to

The Wolverines with Bix Beiderbecke (third from right) in 1924

coloured musicians denied him the recognition he deserved. For LaRocca's five-man band had had a great success in the gangster city of Chicago as early as 1916 and went on to better things in New York with its famous appearances at the Café Reisenweber to reach its first peak on 26 February 1917. That was the day the band, still calling itself the Original Dixieland Jass Band, went into the RCA-Victor studios and cut the first ever jazz disc—*Livery Stable Blues* on one side and *Dixie Jass Band One Step* on the other. Their repute became world-wide and a European tour followed. Of course it is unfair, and a terrible reflection on the social position of the coloured musician of those days, that it should be white men who first penetrated the

recording studio and carried the jazz gospel across the Atlantic. But despite the vaudeville presentation with paper hats and wild gestures, despite the sometimes rather stupid imitations of animal sounds, this band did not make bad music.

Half forgotten as they may be, they are worth plucking from oblivion; their effect on the Chicago scene cannot be overestimated. Even the New York groups fell under their influence at this time—the musicians who in the late twenties were still playing hot jazz in small combos, before the swing era either plunged them into darkness or drew them into the big bands that were becoming fashionable. The trumpeter **Red Nichols** (1905–1965) and the

trombone player **Miff Mole** (1898–1961) were just as much a part of this as the brothers **Tommy Dorsey** (1905–1956) and **Jimmy Dorsey** (1904–1957), whose star really rose only in the swing epoch.

With their less riotous and more sensitive music, the New Orleans Rhythm Kings had an even more direct influence on the jazz that was being played in Chicago. Headed by the clarinettist **Leon Ropollo** (1902–1943), one of jazz's first truly lyrical musician and also one of its first drug victims, the players were worshipped like demi-gods and—much more important—provided musical models whose language had to be learnt. On these three pillars—the Original Dixieland Jazz Band, the New Orleans

45

Rhythm Kings and of course the group formed round great coloured musicians King Oliver and Louis Armstrong, The Creole Jazz Band—the edifice later to be know as the *Chicago style* was raised. When all the arabesques and trimmings were cut away, this style centred on the music of one great personality and one deeply committed group—the cornet player **Bix Beiderbecke** (1903–1931) and the band of music-crazy school kids known as the Austin High School Gang. The term school kids sparks off some far-reaching and highly irrelevant trains of thought here. Somehow Bix Beiderbecke, a musician of genius, seemed all his life to remain the eternal happy-go-lucky student. And the music of the **Austin High School Gang** seemed like an eternal class reunion which never came to an end and seldom overstretched the limits—like a collection of old boys decades after they had left high school. There is nothing to be done for those to whom that seems a bit too romantic. They fail to see that in the context of the development of jazz the word Chicago represents not just a historical phase but an aura, an atmosphere of searching, adventurous youth, kicking over the traces without sparing itself and without wanting to know that this state of enchanted wildness would have to end one day. **Bix Beiderbecke** is a legend. He came into the world on the 10th March 1903, and that may well be the least probable and credible part of his legend. The smile on his charming, rather crumpled baby-face seems to bridge the darkest past with our present reality. We can hardly tell any more which parts of his biography are fiction and which fact—and yet, as I write this now, he would have been six years younger than my father, who is quietly mowing the front lawn of his house in Hamburg. You could scarcely have a sharper contrast between "time counted and time lived". On top of this Bix Beiderbecke's origin does little for his legend. He didn't come—as did most black jazz musicians of those days—from the deep, mysterious South but from Davenport, Iowa in the cool Northwest. His musical homeland was not the Gospel Church but the college campus danceband. He came not from some fascinating ruin of a parental home but from an established upper middle class family. He didn't have to yield to his love of music clandestinely and behind the back of unsympathetic relations; his parents and brothers and sisters were very musical.

It is the name Mississippi that strikes the first surprising note of the legend. Right up in Iowa, far from the marshes of Louisiana, those who travel across America are baffled even today when they cross a river that they thought lay much further south. They have forgotten that up near its source "Old Man River" was once a small stream, however full of promise. And young Bix Beiderbecke in his little boat must have rowed far out on this river to get as close as he could to the paddle-steamers where they played roulette, poker and hot black jazz. Young Leon Beiderbecke, as his parents of German stock called Bix, must have lurked there full of enchantment and devotion, and his closest friends or their sons—those of them that are still alive or have put pen to paper on this subject—still argue who he heard most often—King Oliver and Louis Armstrong, or Nick LaRocca. What we do know is that his first notes on the cornet were played not in a band but in his parents' drawing room. When the family went out, Bix stirred himself from his morning lie-in, went downstairs in his pyjamas and played his responses to records of Nick LaRocca's improvisations in *Tiger Rag*.

But no matter whether it was the white or the coloured trumpeters from New Orleans who influenced Bix Beiderbecke, one thing is clear. He too never learnt to read music. Later, when he was very well known, his colleagues always used to send him out of the room for a quiet smoke at rehearsal and only let him in again when the arrangement was firm and he only had to be told *when* to play his solos. No-one ever needed to tell him *how* to play his solos. And when he was the celebrated star in **Paul Whiteman's** (1890–1967) world-famous orchestra and had to sit behind a music stand for the sake of appearances, Bix, they say, always used to have a whodunnit on his stand.

His musicality must have been some kind of natural event, but not one that came in a flash. It crept in gently—first when he went to high school in Davenport and played for dances in the school band; again when in 1921 he went to the Lake Forest Academy on the north side of Chicago and was always going down town to listen to jazz and maybe even to find himself a seat in a band. He never played trumpet, but the much more expressive cornet, with its resemblance to the human voice. That was the instrument of King Oliver and the young Louis Armstrong, but the tales that Bix had to tell on his horn were quite different ones.

What he was putting together in his first Chicago period was not rooted simply in the blues. It had a quite different, more lyrical and singing design which contrasted with the thumping vehemence of the coloured musicians. His music was completely personal; it did not hark back to ancient African techniques of call and response, but swung into the air in great leaping bounds of light. It was shy and bristling at one and the same time.

Anyone who lives only for his music as Bix Beiderbecke did will quickly form a band as if it were the most natural thing in the world. It was towards the end of 1923 that the **Wolverines** played for the first time in the Stockton Club, a way-out roadside joint near Hamilton, Ohio. And the literature of the history of jazz passes judgement with astonishing unanimity—this was the third significant white jazz band, and the first made up entirely of non-New Orleans men.

The boys started to make their name in the Ohio and Indiana countryside and became big fish in the small pond of university dances. But they didn't have to stay in the provinces for long. The first recording offers came as if from nowhere; but in 1925 it was all up with the Wolverines. They were a wild enough bunch but they were idle, and people didn't want to hear the same pieces over and over again. Bix went into hiding in a commercial orchestra run by a man called Charly Straight and found himself playing alongside pretty mediocre musicians. On the other hand he had time on his hands, was able to stay in Chicago and could now really enjoy and go to work on the music that King Oliver and Louis Armstrong were blowing in the coloured bars on the famous South Side. The tale is still told today of how on the evening Bix Beiderbecke first heard Bessie Smith, he threw his week's wage packet at her feet just to hear her sing again.

But in September of the same year we find that restless young man on his way again. He got himself a booking in St. Louis and played for a year in the Arcadia Ballroom in the band of the sax-player **Frankie Trumbauer** (1900–1956).

This year, at first glance a job like any other, left deep marks on Bix Beiderbecke's cultural development. It gave him the opportunity to formulate more clearly the European, one might say the middle-class ingredients of his music; for St. Louis was then not just the gateway to the wide plains of the West or the town famed in W.C. Handy's Blues. It also had

48

Tommy and Jimmy Dorsey with their parents

Pee Wee Russell

a symphony orchestra of wide renown, and Bix, who even as a boy had revelled in the impressionistic Debussy sound, put his time to good effect.
Pee Wee Russell (1906–1969), the clarinettist, recalls that year: "Bix had a miraculous ear. As for classical music he enjoyed little things like some of those compositions of MacDowell and Debussy—very light things [sic.]. Delius, for example. Then he made a big jump from that sort of thing to Stravinsky and stuff like that. There'd be certain things he would hear in modern classical music, like use of the whole-tone scale, and he'd say 'Why not do it in a jazz band? What's the difference? Music doesn't have to be the sort of thing that's put in brackets!' Then later it got to be like a fad and

49

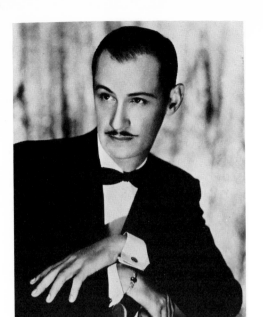

Frank Trumbauer

everybody did it, but they wouldn't know what the devil it was all about. We would often order the score of a new classical work, study it and then request it from the St. Louis Symphony Orchestra. And we'd get ourselves a box for those concerts when they did a programme we all liked. It would be Bix, Hassler (a tenor sax man who did quite advanced arrangements) and I. We'd haunt them to play scores that we wanted to hear. Stuff like the *Firebird Suite* [by Stravinsky]".

It was no legend then that the whole-tone scales in Beiderbecke's cornet improvisations came from Western music, from the French impressionists. Or again how truly the young musician felt himself at home in this world of mixed shades and floating chords—anyone who has heard Bix Beiderbecke playing the piano can tell that. His famous *In A Mist,* recorded without a rhythm group and as if in a reverie, could well find a place among Debussy's Preludes.

His career was still prospering, for the bands in which Beiderbecke played got bigger—as did the fees. From Trumbauer he went to **Jean Goldkette**, (1899–1962) from Jean Goldkette to **Paul Whiteman**. But in some strange, paradoxical and yet inevitable way the upward trend in his career went hand in hand with his artistic downfall and—as is so often the case with jazz musicians—his downfall as a man too. Back in the days when Beiderbecke was still at school there was often a bit too much gin around when they were playing. And in the hot days in Chicago with their wonderful ways of making up for Prohibition, this hero of a cornet player found he couldn't walk on the water without getting his feet wet.

But it was playing with Paul Whiteman's orchestra that put paid to his health. It was such a big organisation, with such strict discipline. Much too much music had to be played for a public that loved its shows and was interested in more than just the music—sentimental ballads, overtures, pot-pourris. Jazz was just a layer in the sandwich, a little blue joke. Bix suffered. Today we should say he felt frustrated.

Those who have little chance to play solo have plenty of time to reach for the bottle. Whiteman, who was far from being a petty man and certainly not the slavedriving boss that the prejudices of the jazz ideology like to make him out, sent Bix to be dried out. Even when Bix was away, Whiteman made a point of leaving his favourite musician's chair empty on the stage. But to no avail.

The body of this man, whose brief cornet solos even today burst forth like a ray of sunshine in the old-fashioned, sonorous arrangements of the Whiteman band, had become so frail that a cold turned into a fatal attack of pneumonia. On 6 August 1931 Bix Beiderbecke died. His life was over but his legend was just beginning. Story upon story was woven round the head of the man who had died young, and he soon found a place in literature too.

Dorothy Parker wrote her novel *Young Man with a Horn* as a thinly disguised biography of Bix Beiderbecke, and Hollywood was quick to turn it into a real tearjerker of an epic.

Bix Beiderbecke was the great individualist, the lone wolf, even in the swirl of conviviality of his times. But it was a group that came to the fore alongside him—the Austin High School Gang had made its entrance.

It all began in 1922. Five kids from Austin High School out on the west side of Chicago started a schoolboy band. When they first came together they were still wet behind the ears. **Jimmy McPartland** (1907–), the cornet player, was only 14, and the oldest, their bassist **Jim Lanigan** had no more than 17 summers to his name. McPartland's brother Dick played banjo and guitar. Then there was **Frank Teschemacher** (1906–1932) and **Bud Freeman** (1906–); in those days Frank was still playing the smoochy C melody sax, while Bud Freeman played guitar. Before they found the instruments with which they broke into the history of jazz—clarinet and tenor sax—they used to play the popular middle-class music of the day. But when they changed their instruments they changed their tune. From being pleasant boys who played dance music in a detached kind of way at every possible opportunity, they went jazz-crazy. Jimmy McPartland tells how it happened:

"Every day after school Frank Tes-chemacher and Bud Freeman, Jim Lanigan, my brother Dick, myself and a few others used to go to a little place called the 'Spoon and Straw'. It was just an ice-cream parlour where you'd get a malted milk, soda, shakes, and all that stuff.

But they had a Victrola there, and we used to sit round listening to the bunch of records on the table. They were Paul Whiteman and Art Hickermann records, and so forth. And Ted Lewis. He was supposed to be the hot thing, but he didn't do anything to us somehow.

This went along for two or three months; we'd go in there every day, and one day they had some new Gennett records on the table, and we put them on.

They were by the New Orleans Rhythm Kings, and I believe the first tune we played was *Farewell blues*. Boy, when we heard that—I'll tell you we went out of our minds. Everybody flipped. It was wonderful. So we put the others on—*Tiger rag, Discontented blues, Tin roof blues, Bugle call rag,* and such titles. We stayed there from about three in the afternoon until eight at night, just listening to those records one after the other, over and over again. Right then and there we decided we would get a band and try to play like those guys".

It took them a while to get there. To begin with their enthusiasm outmatched their skill. Like Bix Beiderbecke, these young white jazz musicians too started their career with the help of records. The devotion they put into it, the

Jimmy McPartland

Sidney Bechet with the Chicago clarinettist Mezz Mezzrow

Bud Freeman

fanaticism with which they tried to master this exciting, new, difficult language—again we can hear McPartland talking about it and describing how they used to learn a piece:

"What we used to do was put the record on—one of the Rhythm Kings', naturally—play a few bars, and then all get our notes. We'd have to tune our instruments up to the record machine, to the pitch, and go ahead with a few notes. Then stop! A few more bars of the record, each guy would pick out his notes and boom! We would go on and play it. Two bars, or four bars, or eight—we would get in on each phrase and then all play it. But you can imagine it was hard at first. Just starting, as most of us were, we'd make so many mistakes that it was

horrible on people's ears. So, as I say, we'd have to move around because the neighbours couldn't stand it too long". A few months out in the sticks and the school kids learnt how to play nine or ten pieces very well. This wild horde from the Austin High School quickly built up a faithful body of fans, a clique of young people which followed wherever they went. Naturally they almost always played at charity functions and for various high school engagements—in the afternoon that is. They couldn't get into the joints at night. When they wanted to name their band they called it the **Blue Friars**—a sign of gratitude and loving homage. For "Friar's Inn" was the name of the spot where the New Orleans Rhythm Kings made their music.

Soon the boys were playing for dancing too. They hired themselves a hall for a few dollars and their young public came flooding in—in the idiom of the time "they went crazy". But this school class did more than just make its own name; there were new enrolments too, and plenty of them. To be serious, in the mid-twenties the Austin High School Gang must have had such charisma that it became a crystallisation point of jazz in Chicago. Musicians came from all around drawn by the new music and infected by the wild pleasure with which these young people played. A boy in shorts, 15 at the outside, looked in one day, took up his clarinet and played 16 choruses of *Rose of the Rio Grande,* a particularly complicated piece.

53

Everyone's mouths fell open. His name was **Benny Goodman** (1909–). He was very happy to find himself a seat now and then with the types from the Austin High School, but he never joined them. Among those who did was **Dave Tough** (1908–1948), the drummer, who was then still a student and whom they met at a university ball where they were playing. Dave Tough became one of the hottest drummers of the Big Band era. The way his drums drove on Woody Herman's **First Herd** was unforgettable. Many more big names in music got some experience under their belts in the joints of Chicago and put it to good use a decade later in the ballrooms of New York and other cities.

But they never made the hard core of Chicago jazz. That was made up of musicians for whom jazz meant and still means playing in small groups, the classical 6 to 7-man combo; of individuals, often half-crazy freaks who couldn't knuckle under to the discipline of a large orchestra even when public demand for small groups fell off and fashion came to favour the beat of the larger orchestras. Then a jockey suddenly came on the Chicago scene—no, not a disc jockey but a real one who rode horses. But what he liked to ride best of all was his hobby-horse by the name of jazz. He never mastered a proper instrument. He could sing a bit and blow up a tune on the comb, and when he went into a shop to buy a suitcase it didn't mean he was going away but that he was forming a new band. The fact is that he had a

fixation on the sound you get from banging an empty suitcase with all kinds of sticks. Many a time he nearly found himself inside; the salesmen in the leather goods shops got mad when the customer asked to see one suitcase after another just to bang on it and test its tone and pitch. But this character **Red McKenzie** (1899–1948) did a gread deal for jazz—not, it is true, as a musician, but as a kind of Mr. Fix-it who was always gathering new groups round him, finding jobs for people, cultivating contacts with recording companies or arranging and supervising recording sessions.

In his circle we now find **Eddie Condon** (1905–1973) who came from Goodland, Indiana and moved to Chicago with his parents in 1915. He taught himself the banjo and started going the rounds with any dance orchestra that offered until one day he got too close to the Austin High School types and finally got bitten by the jazz bug. Suddenly he seemed to be all over the place. There are still a few eye-witnesses living who claim to have seen him sober. His ancestors came from Ireland and he combined—typically but to an almost ridiculous extent—Irish musicality, humour and head for drink with a certain dourness. He stayed faithful his whole life long to his particular kind of jazz and never allowed himself to be deflected by modern developments from doing his own excellent thing. Right into the forties and fifties he arranged concerts with the mature heroes of the old days and saw to

it that the old melodies from that hectic age were not quite forgotten. He also propounded numerous rules of life well worth taking to heart—among them the immortal prescription: "For a particularly bad hangover, take the juice of two bottles of whisky". We also owe to him the characteristic delineation of the Chicago style, preserved for us on record.

That was in December 1927—late enough in the day. It took the school kids a few years to learn their lessons properly and grow up to be a band. Of course they didn't go on always playing together, but on those winter days the whole set would meet up again in the studio. **Jimmy McPartland** blew his cornet. **Frank Teschemacher** played clarinet and did the arranging. **Bud Freeman** played tenor sax and **Jim Lanigan** bass. Round this hard core came **Mezz Mezzrow** (sax and clarinet) and pianist **Joe Sullivan** (1906–1971) and another very young man who sprang into the breach when **Dave Tough** was taken ill. His name was **Gene Krupa** (1909–1973). And then of course there was **Eddie Condon**.

Jazz historians have never found it altogether easy to come to grips with what the Chicago style really is. Jazz lovers have argued endlessly whether there is really enough shape and body to these often whimsical or even amateurish imitations of New Orleans jazz to justify calling them a "style". True, a lot of the music made there could be described as titillation rather than

Eddie Condon

passion, fever rather than temperament. And yet the people in the Austin High School Gang circle have a sound of their own. Their music contains hallmarks which make those who hear it say that these young people made a real contribution to the development of jazz music.

New Orleans jazz was always mainly music-making in groups. In metropolitan Chicago improvisation by ensembles tended more and more to take a back seat. The individual musician could let his individuality blossom forth in a far more uninhibited way and play solos much more often. In place of the raw polyphony of trumpet, clarinet and trombone, there appeared more and more frequently the written arrange-

ment for a melody group—and more and more frequently with the tenor sax in the lead. Up to the Chicago days the saxophone family's role in jazz had been for the most part a thankless one; it was rare for them to be taken out of the showcase and put under the spotlight. In Chicago the saxophone arrived and quickly became the musicians' favourite instrument. These two factors—the new importance of arrangements and the lead part for the tenor sax—show the extent to which this Chicago music is a music of transition. On the one hand it drinks deep at the wells of tradition; on the other it points an unmistakable finger towards the future—the swing era. In the thirties, the day of the swing bands, the arrangement would make or

break a band and it was to be the tenor sax that would characterize the tone colour of an ensemble.

Records like *Nobody's Sweetheart* and *China Boy* are pretty representative examples of how they played then. They convey at the same time something of the heady wildness of the epoch and of a much higher degree of refinement in structure and approach. A typical trick was for the wind instruments to start playing softer and softer just before the end of the piece to lull the listener into a sense of security and then to go into the riproaring finale with a surprise burst on the percussion. "Explosion" the boys used to call it—an old trick of the trade but just as effective now as it ever was. But the peculiar magic of those years doesn't repay clever musicological analysis. It is the aura that matters—how the players recall those fabulous days in those fabulous joints . . . **Al Capone** and his henchmen, and the gangs which steadily wiped each other out. A musician led a much more dangerous life then than he does now—as drummer **George Wettling** (1907–1968) recalls: "We would see those rods come up—and duck. At the Triangle Club, the boss was shot in the stomach one night, but we kept working. After that he walked sort of bent over".

Bass players had a relatively safe existence; when minor skirmishes broke out they could always take cover behind their instruments. But between all the reminiscences which have taken on a dream-like quality as the years go by,

55

Jack Teagarden, one of the most important trombone players of traditional jazz

there is one story which **Jimmy McPartland** tells again here and which gives valuable insights into the psychology of the criminal:
"At one place we worked, Al Capone would come in with about seven or eight guys. They closed the door as soon as he came in. Nobody could come in or out. Then he gets a couple of hundred dollar bills changed and passes them around to the entertainers and waiters. His bodyguards did the passing. We got five or ten bucks just for playing his favourite numbers, sentimental things".
Interesting what delicate souls these kings of the underworld have when the day's work is done. But very soon the word "depression" stopped meaning a sentimental gangster's worries. At the

end of 1929 the economic life of the nation crashed to the ground. The great Wall Street slump brought ruin and poverty almost overnight to a flourishing society whose wealth had made it too arrogant. In 1933 the number of unemployed rose to 13 million. No, the Depression was a very public matter—a catastrophe that threatened the existence of the jazz musicians too. In those hard times people didn't want to hear anything exciting but soft, soothing sounds. The jazz age, as Scott Fitzgerald called it and lived it, seemed to have come to an end.

The life of the great coloured musicians ended in loneliness for King Oliver, in embitterment for Jelly Roll Morton; likewise many gaps appeared in the ranks of our friends, the erstwhile young whites of Chicago. It wasn't just Bix Beiderbecke who died young. **Leon Ropollo**, the New Orleans Rhythm Kings' clarinettist, drugged his way to madness; he used to sit in the open countryside and improvise round the thrumming chords of the telegraph wires. He died in a mental hospital. The clarinettist **Frank Teschemacher**, another typical Chicago figure with his air of abandonment to his mad world, was killed in a car crash.

The Austin High School crew had moved to New York. As Marshall Stearns tells it, they lived "off baked beans and salt and peper sandwiches", living in a downtown hotel. They took on whatever work they could get. **Jack Teagarden's** (1905–1964) song on a record called

Makin' Friends says a great deal about how jazz men felt in those days:
'I'd rather drink muddy water,
sleep in a hollow log,
Rather drink muddy water, Lord,
sleep in a hollow log,
Than be up here in New York treated like a dirty dog.'

And here we must leave for the moment the musicians of Chicago jazz. It was the end of an epoch, but even this end carries within it the germ of a new beginning. We shall meet them again, these crazy men of the first wave of white jazz. We shall meet them in the swing bands of the thirties, in the security of a large orchestra. But not everyone wanted to find safety in numbers. Many of them remained adventurers—and their adventuring took what seemed to be a paradoxical form. The adventurers stood their ground; and in the forties when trad jazz found a new public among the young, there they all were again, or at least all of them who had survived—another class reunion for these grown-up school kids from Chicago.

Dan Morgenstern

Swing

Dan Morgenstern. Born in Vienna in 1929 and brought up in Denmark, Dan Morgenstern has lived in the United States since 1947. A great-nephew of Leopold Sonnemann, founder of the leading German newspaper *Frankfurter Allgemeine Zeitung,* he has edited the three main American jazz magazines. Editor of *Metronome* in 1961 and of *Jazz* and *Bop* for the two years following, he moved in 1964 to *Down Beat,* first as a New York editor and then, until 1973, as editor. He produced the series of summer concerts, *Jazz in the Garden,* at the Museum of Modern Art. Morgenstern translated the American editions of J.E. Berendt's *The Jazz Book.* Since 1968 he has served as consultant on the Jazz Committee of the National Endowment for the Arts. In 1973 he was awarded the "Grammy" for the year's best record sleeve.

The Jazz All Stars of 1940: (left to right)
Tex Benecke, Buddy Rich, Benny Carter,
Toots Mondello, Coleman Hawkins, Artie
Bernstein and Benny Goodman

Jimmy Lunceford

*It don't mean a thing if it ain't got that
swing:* The title of this song written and
recorded by Duke Ellington in 1932 was
prophetic.

Officially, the Swing Era began in 1935,
when **Benny Goodman's** band scored its
first big success and brought about a
decisive change in popular dance music,
first in America, then the world. But it
had really started long before.

To understand Swing with a capital
"S"—the name of a musical style—we
must first attempt to define swing with a
small "s"—a key concept in jazz as a
whole, at least until recently. Such a
definition is not easy, and even learned
musicologists have failed to formulate it
clearly. That is because swing is a feeling,
a rhythmic impulse, that cannot be
notated. It is the unique pulse, the
heartbeat of mature jazz, and like so
much else having to do with the
maturing of jazz as an art, it was brought
into the music by Louis Armstrong
(whose contributions are discussed in
detail elsewhere in this volume).

It was as a member of **Fletcher
Henderson's** (1898–1952) band in
1924–25 that Armstrong made his first
big impact on jazz, and to hear the solos
he recorded with this band and compare
them with their musical surroundings is
to realize what swing is and is not. But his
most gifted colleagues learned quickly
and well from Louis. Among them was
the band's arranger the saxophonist **Don
Redman** (1900–64), who developed the
arranging style that became the foundation for the Swing of the next decade.
Redman conceived what was then
considered a large jazz band (3 trumpets,
1 trombone, 3 saxophones doubling
clarinets and other winds, and a rhythm
section of piano, banjo, tuba, and drums)
in terms of "sections". He used the
call-and-response patterns that had
originated in Africa and survived in
black American work songs and church
songs and later in the blues, pitting
trumpets (and trombone) against reeds.
He used the brass to punctuate melodic
passages scored for the reeds, the reeds
to play harmonic backdrops to a trumpet
solo, and so on. For maximum effect, he
would deploy the brass and reeds as a
massed choir.

These basic principles were adhered to

as the size of the standard jazz-flavoured dance band grew. When Redman left Henderson in 1927 to become musical director of McKinney's Cotton Pickers (which he made into one of the best bands of the period), Fletcher himself began to write arrangements, and soon mastered the Redman method to such a degree that it has become known as "Fletcher Henderson style"—perhaps because Fletcher's band always had the greatest soloists.

The relationship between arrangement (what is written) and solo part (what is improvised) is another key concept in Swing. The arranger who best understood the creative process involved in the inventive play of the great soloists, and made use of it in the writing of his scores—not only in the sense of giving his soloists ample opportunity to play, and devising attractive and inspiring backgrounds for them, but also in the sense of writing for the sections as if they were "soloing", that is to say, in the idiom of the improviser—was the most successful in jazz terms. Behind every Swing band stood at least one gifted arranger, as well as gifted soloists and rhythm players—a fact that has sometimes been overlooked by critics and historians.

As the twenties moved on, both the music and the technology that was so important to its dissemination and growth became increasingly sophisticated. Armstrong set new standards for brass players in terms of range and technique, and not only for brass players: he had disciples on every instrument. Radio broadcasts by bands became increasingly popular as demand for arranging increased in proportion with the growth of the medium, and since music on the radio sounded so much better than the still primitive, acoustically recorded gramophone music, the electrical process of recording had to be adopted by the recording companies from 1926 on. Among other things, this vastly increased the communicative power of jazz recordings.

The influence of the gramophone record on the development of jazz is almost inestimable; suffice it to say that without this medium, jazz might well have remained a regional "folk" music. In jazz, the record is the material for study used by the learning musician. It is the counterpart of the score in classical music, since notation can give no accurate idea of what a jazz performance sounds like. In the Swing era, records played a tremendous role, as we shall see. We must also understand that at least up to the late '40's and the advent of bebop, most jazz was dance music. Even when the musicians began to be able to play for audiences that also listened to the music, the primary source of employment was playing for dancers. This was especially true of the big bands: Jazz or no, they were dance bands, by definition. Though the twenties is the decade known as "The Jazz Age", that application would be much better suited to the thirties. This was the decade during which jazz and popular music, for the first and so far only time, were by and large synonymous.

This great popularity would have been impossible without the dance as the vehicle for the music, and it was among young dancers, weaned on the "jazzy" sounds of the '20s, that big band Swing first took hold.

The band that made the first important breakthrough is largely forgotten or dismissed today. It was the Casa Loma Orchestra, and though it included no really important soloists, it did have a very important arranger, guitarist **Gene Gifford** (1908–70). Gifford in a sense streamlined and mechanized the Henderson-Redman style. He used in abundance the "riff"—a short, propulsive phrase, rhythmic rather than

61

melodic, that lends itself to constant repetition. Contrasting riffs by brass and reeds were a key feature of such Gifford pieces as *Casa Loma Stomp* and *Wild Goose Chase*. The band played these pieces with great precision and speed, to the delight of practitioners of the Lindy Hop and other fast, semi-acrobatic dances. The Casa Loma balanced this with romantic ballads excellently played (all the reed players were expert doublers on such then uncommon instruments as flute, oboe and bass clarinet), and their "crooner", Kenny Sargent, was quite popular. By 1932, even the Henderson band was playing Gifford's arrangements and commissioning Casa Loma-styled works from others. The earliest recordings by the important **Jimmy Lunceford** (1904–47) band are in this style, and Benny Goodman's early band flirted with it as well. (The Casa Loma continued with moderate success throughout the thirties and into the mid-forties, but with Gifford's departure in 1934, the band had lost its originality).

This was the year in which **Benny Goodman**, a 25-year-old clarinettist who was doing very well as a studio musician in New York (that is to say, he participated in commercial recording and radio work and also played in theatre pit bands), decided to form a big band dedicated to playing good, jazz-flavoured dance music. It did not do well in its first engagements and its early recordings were not successful. It managed to remain alive by landing a

spot on a nationally broadcast dance programme, sharing the three-hour show with a Latin band and a "sweet" (non-jazz oriented) dance band. Goodman had commissioned Fletcher Henderson and his talented younger brother **Horace Henderson** (1904–) and other black writers including the eminent **Benny Carter** (1907–) (who had taken Redman's place with Henderson and become a master at writing for saxophones) to do arrangements for his band—not only of original jazz pieces and jazz standards, but of popular tunes of the day.

In the summer of 1935, the Goodman band went on a cross-America tour, working their way from New York to California. Such road trips had been common for dance bands from the mid-twenties on and continued to be routine through the Swing Era. The less established the band, the more so-called "one nighters" (i.e. engagements lasting a single night) it had to play; the best jobs were those that had a regular broadcast outlet, such as most of the better hotels in larger cities.

The Goodmanites soon discovered that their new brand of music was not much appreciated by ballroom customers or owners. They were asked to play more waltzes and slow numbers, and were nearly fired a number of times. Greatly discouraged, they pulled into Los Angeles, the final stop of the tour. At the Palomar Ballroom, to their astonishment, they found a packed house waiting. Not only that, but the dancers

knew the band's repertoire, and requested the best and "hottest" pieces. The band was a sensation.

What was the explanation? In California, which is in a different time zone from other parts of America, the Goodman portion of the radio programme had been heard at a time when young people were listening; in other states, they had been on the air too early to have an effect.

Before examining the consequences of Goodman's success, we must clarify another aspect of the American scene. The Goodman band, of course, was white, and dance music—not only in the south, but almost everywhere in the States—was a segregated business in 1935. While the history of jazz up to this point showed many instances of inter-racial influences, and personal contacts, clearly there were no opportunities for black and white musicians to play together regularly. On the other hand, quite a few black bands regularly played for white dancers, among them Fletcher Henderson's, which from 1924 to 1931 spent most of its time at the Roseland, the biggest ballroom in New York City's theatrical district. And as we have noted, black arrangers were writing for white bands—a practice that had begun in the twenties and would increase greatly from 1935 on.

Despite such overlappings, differences between black and white music were often crucial. Black dancers were always far ahead of their white counterparts; the Lindy Hop, introduced in Harlem in

Benny Carter

1927 (named for "Lucky Lindy", the transatlantic flier Charles Lindberg) wasn't very different from the jitterbug dances adopted by whites almost 10 years later. Consequently, black bands could play a much more flexible and swinging music for their audiences while white orchestras were still struggling with sedate fox trots and the English waltz.

The impact of Goodman cannot be understood without such facts. Goodman played "blacker" than almost any white band—certainly any successful white band—had before. To be sure, his band played the works of Henderson and other black writers much more "correctly" than black bands did (perhaps with the exception of Benny

Artie Shaw with his orchestra

Count Basie and singer Jimmy Rushing

Carter's and Don Redman's, which had very high conventional standards of intonation, section blend, etc.). But the essential characteristics of the music were retained by Goodman.

By 1935, standard instrumentation for big jazz bands had grown to 3 trumpets, 2 trombones, 4 reeds (five if the leader, such as Goodman, Carter or Redman was a reed player) and a rhythm section of piano, guitar (instead of banjo), string bass (instead of tuba) and drums. The relative harshness of banjo and tuba had been exchanged for the softer, more supple guitar and bass, in keeping with the more legato character of jazz rhythm following Armstrong's breakthrough.

With the larger brass section, the importance of the lead trumpeter grew.

His phrasing and tone determined, by and large, the punch and volume of the band. The two other key men were the lead altoist, whose phrasing and intonation had to be compatible with the lead trumpeter's, and the drummer, whose ability to swing and inspire the band was crucial, and who paced the rhythm section. Without good men in these three positions, a band, no matter how good otherwise, had to suffer. As the number of bands playing in a jazz-oriented manner grew, so did the demand for capable lead men and drummers.

But the soloists attracted most of the attention among the fans, and from a jazz standpoint, they were indeed the most important men in the band.

Swing fans were a new breed, interested

as much (if not more) in listening as in dancing. By the late thirties, they would know the important players in each band, read about them in the Swing magazines (*Down Beat, Metronome*), collect the records, and listen to their broadcasts. The top band leaders were becoming national figures on a scale with Hollywood film stars (and most of them did appear in films).

A number of important bands sprang up in the wake of Goodman's success, among them that of his arch-rival and fellow clarinettist **Artie Shaw** (1910–   ). A year younger than Goodman, Shaw had also been a successful New York studio musician, but unlike Goodman, he had not grown up in the rich jazz environment of Chicago in the twenties,

having spent his learning years touring with more or less obscure "territory bands."

The territory bands, both black and white, were orchestras without a national reputation who worked in specific geographic areas. The midwest and southwest regions of the U.S.A. were particularly rich in such bands, and it was here, in the mid twenties, that the seeds of a style that would eventually supersede Henderson's were sown.

Kansas City, the centre of these musical trends, was ruled during the prohibition years by "Boss" Pendergast, an amiable crook who let nightlife and its vices flourish uninhibitedly, which, of course, resulted in ample employment for dance musicians.

Bennie Moten (1894–1935) had the most successful band in the city, and it performed in a blues-based style characterized by a rolling bouncing rhythm already implying swing. In 1930, Moten swallowed up most of the key men of **Walter Page's** (1900–1957) Blue Devils, a musically brilliant but commercially inept band, including leader Page on bass and tuba, **Count Basie** (1904–   ) on piano, trumpeter **Hot Lips Page** (1908–1958), altoist and arranger **Buster Smith** (1904–   ), and singer **Jimmy Rushing** (1903–   ). Already with Moten was the gifted trombonist, guitarist and arranger **Eddie Durham** (1906–   ), and a bit later tenor saxophonist **Ben Webster** (1909–   ) also joined.

By 1932, Moten had the best band of his career, and its recordings, among them

the famous *Moten Swing,* announce the coming of Kansas City Swing style, with its smooth, driving rhythm, inspired soloists, and flexible, swinging riff patterns. The style was perfected by Basie, who came to the attention of jazz enthusiast and connoisseur John Hammond, who in 1936 secured a booking agency contract and recording deal for Basie, and brought the band to national attention.

Hammond had also been instrumental in getting Goodman's band into shape (it was he who recommended Fletcher Henderson to Benny and had procured for it the services of a young Chicago-born drummer, **Gene Krupa** (1909–73). It was Krupa who made the drum solo an obligatory (and not always

artistically fortunate) component of every Swing band appearance. Krupa's talent, energy and good looks made him one of the first (and lasting) popular heroes of the Swing Era.

Some bands that had preceded Goodman's also benefited from his success. They included pianist **Earl Hines'** band (active from 1929 to 1947), and those led by the **Dorsey Brothers**, alto saxophonist-clarinettist **Jimmy** and trombonist **Tommy**, who for a while had co-led the Dorsey Brothers Band, whose chief arranger was a man named **Glenn Miller** (of whom more later). Both Dorseys became top Swing bandleaders, but Tommy's was the musically more significant band.

First, it played in a Dixieland-flavoured

Drummers of the Swing era: (left to right)
Buddy Rich, Jo Jones, Gene Krupa

Stan Kenton

style (its personnel included Chicago jazzmen **Dave Tough**, drums, and **Bud Freeman**, tenor saxophone, and for a while, the inspired ex-Goodman trumpeter **Bunny Berigan** (1908–42)), contrasted with the leader's smooth, tastefully melodic trombone in ballads. Then, in 1939, Tommy hired the arranger **Sy Oliver** (1910–), who was one of the architects of the Jimmy Lunceford style, and steered the band in a Lunceford direction. The addition of a young singer named Frank Sinatra brought the band to its peak of popularity; the presence of a drummer named **Buddy Rich** (who had already played with Bunny Berigan and Artie Shaw and was—and is—perhaps the technically most gifted of all jazz

Lester Young (centre) with Teddy Wilson and Jo Jones

percussionists) did no harm either. Tommy and Jimmy Dorsey died in 1956 and 1957 respectively; a few years before they had once again joined forces to co-lead a band.

We have made several mentions of the **Jimmie Lunceford** band. Born in 1902, Lunceford was an instructor at Fisk University, one of the foremost black colleges in the United States. Not an outstanding player himself, he had leadership abilities, and the band he formed in the late twenties (consisting mainly of Fisk students or graduates) made its first breakthrough in 1934 at New York's Cotton Club, where Duke Ellington had gained early fame.

The Lunceford style was based on a unique rhythm that combined four beats with two, the two-beat feeling being the dominant one. It was also based on very disciplined ensemble playing and inventive, unconventional arranging touches. Sy Oliver, who also played trumpet in the band, **Ed Wilcox** (1907–1968), the band's pianist, and later **Billy Moore Jr** (1916–) and **Gerald Wilson** (1918–) were the chief arrangers. The band was also famous for its showmanship (the trumpet section members for instance would throw their instruments in the air, clap their hands, and catch them again while keeping perfect time) and for its solo, trio and quartet singing, all of it done by musicians in the band.

The Lunceford style influenced not only Tommy Dorsey but also, a bit later on, the pianist and arranger **Stan Kenton** (1912–), who became one of the few successful big band leaders of the late forties and beyond.

The Cotton Club had also launched the fame of **Cab Calloway** (1907–), a spectacular singer and entertainer, who fronted a band known as The Missourians before it adopted his name. A midwestern band not unlike the earlier Bennie Moten orchestra, it contained many excellent musicians in the early '30s but didn't graduate to the first rank of big bands until about 1939, when Calloway featured the brilliant tenor saxophonist **Chew Berry** (1910–41), **Cozy Cole** (1909–), one of the greatest Swing drummers, and a young trumpeter named **Dizzy Gillespie** (1917–), who a few years later would become one

of the founders of the new jazz style called bebop.

When Berry—one of the most gifted disciples of the great **Coleman Hawkins** (1904–) (who was justly called "father of the tenor sax" and the supreme soloist on Fletcher Henderson's band until 1934)—joined Calloway, he had already sparked the bands of Teddy Hill and Fletcher Henderson.

In both bands, his close musical and personal companion had been trumpeter **Roy Eldridge** (1911–), nicknamed "Little Jazz". Eldridge, inspired by Louis Armstrong, was the creator of the most influential Swing style of trumpeting, based on a brilliant technique (particularly in the realm of speed and high notes) and a very sophisticated harmonic

69

Billie Holiday in Frankfurt 1954

sense (influenced in no small way by the playing of saxophonists Hawkins and Benny Carter).

Berry and Eldridge, who also made important small-band records together, were representative of the new breed of musician that shaped the Swing era. In firm technical command of their instruments and solidly grounded in musical fundamentals, they were "modern" in outlook, always on the alert for new sounds and new ideas, experimentally inclined (though not yet willing to break out of the framework possible for a working jazz musician in the thirties nor able to do so in any radical sense) and self-assured, extroverted soloists able to dominate, even within the collective atmosphere of big bands.

Berry's career was cut short by a motor accident—the nemesis of many a travelling musician. The man whose place he had taken with both Henderson and Calloway, **Ben Webster** became, in the Ellington band, the undisputed leader of the Hawkins school (after the master himself, of course). Eldrige, who led his own bands, big and small, from 1936 to 1940, became a social as well as musical pioneer in 1941, when he joined Gene Krupa's band, becoming one of the first black players in otherwise all-white bands.

Here, the first breakthrough had also been made by Goodman. In 1935, he recorded with black pianist **Teddy Wilson** (1912–) in a trio setting, and in the following year Wilson became a regular member of the Goodman entourage. However, he performed in a trio setting only, not with the whole band. A bit later, **Lionel Hampton** (1909–), a brilliant black vibraharpist (who also plays drums and piano) made the trio a quartet, and while there was occasional unpleasantness when the band played in the south, the prestige and popularity of Goodman (and Krupa, the other white member of the quartet) was sufficient to prevent any serious attempts by racists to interfere with performances.

When Krupa left Benny Goodman to form his own band, Hampton sometimes played drums with Goodman's big band, and when Fletcher Henderson gave up his own big band temporarily in 1939, Goodman hired him as his band pianist. In that same year, a young Texas guitarist, **Charlie Christian** (1916–1942), discovered by John Hammond, joined Goodman as member of a new small group, the sextet, which also included Hampton.

Aside from Henderson, whose role in the big band was quite inconspicuous, the black Goodmanites had mainly functioned as members of special small groups, so-called "bands within the band". It was Goodman rival Artie Shaw who was first to hire a black musician to sit in the band alongside the others as a regular member. This was trumpeter and singer Hot Lips Page (whom we met with Bennie Moten), but before Page could really establish himself with Shaw, the clarinettist decided to break up his band, something he frequently did. Page's tenure with Shaw only lasted six months.

Eldridge, on the other hand, was with Krupa for almost two years (he later also worked with Shaw and again with Krupa in 1949) and succeeded in breaking the ice as far as integrated bands were concerned. (Singers also pioneered here: **Billie Holiday** (1915–1959) was with Shaw in 1938 but couldn't take the stress; black singer Bon Bon Tunnel was with Jan Savitt, a good white band, for many years, and June Richmond sang with Jimmy Dorsey).

Today, it is difficult to realize how much patience and courage the first black musicians in white bands had to muster up to endure the hardships and indignities of prejudice (and sometimes outright hate). It is important to remember that jazz, not sports, was the arena in which the first public battles for racial equality were fought—and won. This is the Swing Era's proudest extra-musical achievement.

Krupa, in 1938, was the first Goodman sideman to form his own band—fittingly, since he was the most acclaimed. He was followed in 1939 by the trumpeter **Harry James** (1915–), who had joined Goodman in 1936 after playing with Ben Pollack's band—drummer Pollack (1903–) had been one of the most prominent band leaders of the twenties and then his sidemen had included young Benny Goodman.

James, like Krupa, had Goodman's blessing and financial help in forming a band. Getting a big band under way was no easy task: there had to be a musical library, which meant buying arrangements and paying for having all the individual parts copied; there had to be music stands and uniforms; there had to be a band bus, rented or bought; a band "boy" (usually a grown man) to handle the packing, unpacking and setting up of the music stands, instruments, etc.; a road manager to handle reservations in hotels (if there was time between one nighters to sleep, other than on the bar), deal with agents and ballroom operators, handle the cash and so on—not to mention lawyers, accountants, insurance men, managers, publicity agents and whatnot. Being a bandleader meant much more than standing in front of the band and playing or conducting, and it

Lionel Hampton

can well be claimed that it was (and is) one of the hardest jobs in music.

Other Goodman alumni who started bands were Teddy Wilson (1939—a fine, musical band without much else than music to offer, and only short-lived) and Lionel Hampton (1940, with much more to offer than music, and with great and long-lasting success).

Initially, both James and Hampton had bands that aimed for good jazz, but these shrewd and successful men soon discovered that, by 1940 or so, this was no longer enough. Goodman, aside from Krupa's natural showmanship, had not offered any "show" or diluted his music, but the Swing era had now reached a stage of incipient decadence.

James's trumpet playing, basically inspired by Armstrong and Berigan, had also in it a touch of the theatrical, the melodramatic, the schmaltzy, and this is what he exploited—along with his considerable virtuosity and the more and more important singers, male and female. The James band, moving further away from jazz but still retaining some elements of it, added a big string section by 1943, and became the commercially most successful big band since Paul Whiteman's in the twenties. James made many Hollywood movies, married Betty Grable, and had countless imitators (none of any musical significance). He also hired alto saxophonist **Willie Smith** (1910–67), one of the best soloists of the Jimmie Lunceford band, and **Juan Tizol** (1900–), the Latin trombonist who had spent years with Duke Ellington and composed *Caravan,* one of the Swing Era's lasting hits.

Hampton, himself a showman with great energy, endurance and enthusiasm, discovered the potency of the two-tenor saxophone formula. It was the Basie band that started the two-tenor "battles", but the great **Lester Young** (1909–59) and his section mate and rival, **Herschel Evans** (1909–39), a Hawkins disciple, were natural protagonists and Basie never exploited their rivalry, which stemmed from different musical aesthetics. Young founded a new and extremely influential style of tenor playing, moving on from the rhapsodic Hawkins sound, with its characteristic vibratos to lyrical melody lines played cool.

Hampton, on the other hand, used **Illinois Jacquet** (1921–), a gifted but sometimes exhibitionistic player, and later **Arnett Cobb** (1918–) (followed by a host of lesser talents) to generate excitement by using high, squealing notes, honks, growls and physical gyrations. Hampton himself also liked to pound on the drums, jump on top of them, and perform other semi-acrobatic feats, and his biggest hit, *Flying Home,* would sometimes conclude with the re-iteration of the same simple riff, played at mezzoforte, to the point of exasperation.

Perhaps such antics—which, it must be noted, were always interspersed with excellent music, not least from Hampton himself on the vibraharp—were a direct offspring of Goodman's greatest hit, the famous *Sing, Sing, Sing,* featuring virtuoso cadenzas and high notes from Goodman and what then seemed "wild" drumming from Krupa. This routine had been perfected by 1938 and was a highlight, in terms of public reaction, at Goodman's famous concert that year in Carnegie Hall, a milestone in terms of acceptance of jazz (Swing) by the cultural establishment.

Swing, even at its artistic peak, was always a music mixed with entertainment. When the emphasis moved from dancers to listeners (though the former still provided most of the daily bread), the normal environment was not the concert hall but the stage of a cinema. (Most first-run American cinemas in the thirties—and well into the forties—had

stage shows, a hangover from the days of silent films and vaudeville, and by 1936, a "name" Swing band would be the centre of such shows more often than not). Thus, Goodman's zenith of popularity is symbolized by his band's 1937 engagement in New York's Paramount Theatre, when queues of young people began to form outside in the early morning hours, growing larger throughout the day. All attendance records for the theatre were broken.

In a sense, it is something of a miracle that so much good music did survive within Swing under such circumstances. Musical inspiration continued to come from bands and musicians that were relatively unencumbered by show business trappings, and it was the problems of being musically and personally famous that caused Artie Shaw, a dedicated musician *and* a man who wanted success, to break up his band more than once—always when things were going well.

The black bands did not often have such problems, and this worked for the benefit of the music. Even so, they had to make concessions, too. The band of **Erskine Hawkins** (1914–), for example, derived its commercial viability from the leader's unpleasant high-note playing and the modest talents of its singers. Yet, it was an excellent band, first in the Lunceford mould, then developing its own "Harlem" style during a long stand at the famous Savoy Ballroom.

Harlem was the homeland of Swing in more ways than one. We have mentioned

The Woody Herman Orchestra playing in a performance of Stravinsky's Ebony Concerto in New York's Carnegie Hall, under the baton of Walter Hendl

the Cotton Club as the proving ground for the bands of Ellington, Calloway and Lunceford. It was a nightclub, with elaborate stage shows catering to white audiences. The Savoy was a ballroom, with no show other than that put on spontaneously by the dancers—considered the best in the world. Perhaps the most popular of the many great bands who played here was that of **Chick Webb** (1909–39). The Savoy was Webb's home ground, and here he played many "battles of the bands"—one of the most famous against Goodman.

A tiny hunchback who suffered from—and was killed by—tuberculosis of the spine, Webb was the Swing drummer *par excellence*, a master at driving a band through an up-tempo number, or guiding it smoothly through slower pieces. His beat was as solid as a metronome but without any stiffness, and he knew how to shade and guide each phrase of band or soloist with a variety of sounds. "I was never licked by a better man", said Krupa after the battle.

Webb's popularity with the dancers at the Savoy was unshakable and didn't depend on commercial considerations, but Webb had a difficult time keeping the band alive until he hired a teenaged girl singer in 1935. Her name was **Ella Fitzgerald** (1918–), and she set the style for Swing band singers. After Webb's death, she fronted the band for a while, then moved into a career as a solo singer that, as even the least informed layman knows, led to enormous success. Singers were often a problem to the serious Swing fan. Ella was an exception, of course, and so was **Billie Holiday**, the other great female Swing voice, who sang with Count Basie as well as Shaw before starting her solo career. But the average band singer was no Ella or Billie, even though the girls were more musical and adaptable, in general, than the male singers.

An exception was Basie's **Jimmy Rushing**, the ideal voice for this most swinging of all big bands, at home in the blues as well as in popular songs of the day. For a while, Basie also had the services of **Helen Humes** (1913–), a superior singer with a style compatible with Rushing's.

Another fine band from Kansas City, **Andy Kirk's** 12 Clouds of Joy, rode to popularity on the high tenor voice (a near falsetto) of Pha Terrell, whose style was a forerunner of such things as the Ink Spots, and later The Platters. Jazz fans had little use for it, but without Terrell we might not have been able to savour on many records the first-rate arranging and piano playing of Mary Lou Williams (1910–), the Kirk band's guiding musical spirit. The band excelled at medium-tempo swing, and was one of the most consistently tasteful. Its chief soloist was tenor saxophonist **Dick Wilson** (1911–41), who like his colleagues Chew Berry and Hershel Evans, died young.

Another consistently tasteful band was **Benny Carter's.** In fact, there were many Carter bands—the one he led before the Swing era got under way; the one he formed after his return from several years in Europe, in 1939; the one he led in the forties, which gave valuable experience to such bebop stars to be as drummer Max Roach and trombonist J.J. Johnson. None of Carter's bands was commercially successful, all of them were musically so. No lead altoist could match Carter for purity of sound, mastery of phrasing, and perfection of intonation. His scoring for saxophone quintets (a more fitting term here than "section") belongs among the outstanding achievements of the period.

If Carter's bands were marked by the saxophone sound, Count Basie's band was—aside from its richness in soloists—characterized by its peerless rhythm section. Consisting of Basie himself at the piano, **Freddie Green** (1911–) on guitar (unamplified), **Walter Page** at the bass and **Jo Jones** (1911–) on the drums, this unit became the model for swinging. The essence of its time conception was the feeling of 4/4, and the four men worked together, breathing as one. The rhythm came first, then the sound. Jones, one of the earliest drummers to move the centre of timekeeping from the bass drum to the cymbal (the first, says Jo himself, was Fletcher Henderson's Walter Johnson), had a sound "like the wind", and it blended perfectly with Basie's crisp, delicate piano sound (and economy of notes), Page's springy, deep but never booming bass tones, and, at the core of it all, Green's rock-steady, lilting guitar.

This was the carpet upon which Lester Young unfolded some of his greatest creations, upon which trumpeter **Harry Edison** (1915–) placed his sly, unexpected sequences of notes, fellow trumpeter **Buck Clayton** (1911–) stepped delicately and tastefully, the master trombonist **Dickie Wells** (1909–) displayed his wit. The classic Basie band (1936–41) was the epitome of Swing.

(In today's Basie band, all that remain from that era are Basie himself and Freddie Green. The style of the band has changed greatly, but it still has the most perfect tempo and the most perfect swing of any big band).

The only other bandleader still active in

1974 who can approach Basie's longevity is clarinettist-alto saxophonist-singer **Woody Herman** (1913–), who was elected leader of a co-operative group of musicians from the Isham Jones band in 1936.

At first, the Herman band was known as "The Band That Plays the Blues"; not the Basie kind of blues, but a rather Dixielandish sort, similar to the style of the **Bob Crosby** (1913–) Band (which had in it key men from New Orleans: drummer **Ray Bauduc**, clarinettist **Irving Fazola** (1912–1949), tenor saxophonist **Eddie Miller** (1911–), guitarist **Nappy Lamare** (1907–), and the robust trumpet of **Yank Lawson** (1911–)). As a singer, Herman was influenced by **Jack Teagarden** (1905–64), one of the greatest trombonists in jazz, who spent the key Swing years (1934–39) buried in Paul Whiteman's cumbersome band, and never achieved much success with the Dixielandish big band he led from 1939 until 1947, when he joined Louis Armstrong.

The Herman band gradually changed its style towards mainstream Swing. By 1945, it had become the most vital of new bands (new because it had changed style drastically and consisted mainly of young players) and was rivalled only by Ellington for creativity and fire. The arrangers who helped shape its sound were pianist **Ralph Burns** (1922–) and trumpeters **Neal Hefti** (1922–) and **Shorty Rogers** (1924–), and its key soloists were trombonist **Bill Harris** (1916–), trumpeter **Sonny Berman**

Mel Lewis, co-leader of the Thad Jones-Mel Lewis Orchestra

(1920–1947), and tenor saxophonist **Flip Phillips** (1915–). But the story of this Herman "Herd" and its successors belongs to the story of bebop rather than Swing.

The story of **Duke Ellington**, told elsewhere in this volume, straddles the story of Swing. The work of this genius, of course, had profound effects on many of the prominent Swing bands—hardly any arranger in jazz could remain untouched by Duke—but none was more directly influenced than **Charlie Barnet** (1913–), whose main instrument was the tenor saxophone (he also played alto and soprano) and who formed his first band in 1933. Some of the band's best arrangements were written by trumpeter **Billy May** (among them its theme,

Cherokee). Barnet was also a pioneer in integration, and such black musicians as trumpeters **Peanuts Holland** (1910–), **Howard McGhee** (1918–) and **Clark Terry** (1920–), the former Lunceford trombone star **Trummy Young** (1912–) (one of the most influential Swing stylists on his instrument), and the great bassist **Oscar Pettiford** passed through his ranks.

America's entry into World War II had profound effects on the music scene. Many musicians were drafted or volunteered for military service, and the Swing bands lost one key man after the other. Suddenly, musicians still in their teens found themselves in demand if they could play at all well. Many who were to become stars of the new, post-war jazz began their careers in big bands, some as young as 15.

The war also brought psychological changes that reflected themselves in popular taste. The singers, who had already begun to become more popular just before the war, now found themselves at the centre of attention. Frank Sinatra is perhaps the prototype; after singing with Harry James and Tommy Dorsey, he became a solo attraction in 1942. Big bands added string sections (James, Dorsey, Krupa), not least because they made the singers sound better. But this also made the bands bigger and more expensive, and petrol shortages cut down touring possibilities. The success of **Glenn Miller** (1904–44) was an indicator of changes in taste to come. A trombonist who had played with

and arranged for Ben Pollack and Red Nichols in the twenties and the Dorsey Brothers in the early thirties, he repeatedly tried and failed as a big band leader until, in 1939, he finally found a formula for success. This included a clarinet (rather than alto saxophone) lead voice for the reed section, giving it a distinctive sound on slow numbers, a clever mixture of jazz externals (drum solos, riffs, tenor battles) and show elements (vocal groups, comedy singing, instrument juggling à la Lunceford), and a sure sense of what the public wanted. It was Miller's aim to have the most versatile of all dance bands, and up to his joining the U.S. Army in 1942 his popularity grew steadily, until it eclipsed even the "King of Swing", Benny Goodman, and his closest rivals.

The period that had given America (and the world) perhaps its most artistically significant popular music—since jazz and popular music were practically synonymous—had come to an end. Swing and its big bands lingered on, but they were terminal cases. After 1945, there was room only for the very best of big bands—those who, like Ellington above all, had something to offer that transcended periods and styles.

At its peak, Swing and its bands incorporated both past and future. There was room in their ranks for the best players from older traditions and the most gifted young players who were shaping styles to come. The variety of big band music that could be heard was staggering; each band strove for, and

many achieved, an identifying sound and style; each player of more than routine ability tried for, and often achieved, a personal voice.

The Swing era—and it was by no means an era of only big bands—has been called the Golden Age of Jazz. We have mentioned the great players who worked in the big bands: Roy Eldridge, Chew Berry, Benny Carter, Lester Young, Charlie Christian, Ben Webster, Trummy Young, Bunny Berigan and many more. Some we haven't mentioned such as the wonderful drummer **Big Sid Catlett** (1910–1951) simply to stop this chapter becoming a catalogue of names and nothing else. Some we haven't mentioned because they did their best work outside the big bands. One of these was violinist **Stuff Smith** (1909–1965), one of the true jazz originals, whose driving inventiveness was almost a definition of swing. Another is the great Belgian Gypsy guitarist **Django Reinhardt** (1910–1953), the only non-American musician to exert an influence on jazz in America in the thirties. And still another is the phenomenal pianist **Art Tatum** (1910–1956), who worked mainly as a soloist and influenced almost every jazz musician, regardless of instrument, with his chromatic harmonies and virtuoso technique.

There were also important small bands which, unlike the loosely organized jam combinations heard on New York's 52nd Street (Swing Street), where every other door led to a nightclub featuring jazz, developed a style and approach that was unmistakable.

The most original and inventive of these was the **John Kirby Sextet,** also known as "The Biggest Little Band in the Land". Led by a former Fletcher Henderson bassist, and featuring the arrangements of trumpeter **Charlie Shavers** (1917–71), it developed a unique ensemble sound and performed a repertoire including light classics adapted to jazz with wit, skill and swing.

Wit was also a key feature of **Fats Waller** (1904–43) and his Rhythm, a quintet led by the ebullient pianist-singer-composer. Fats was so swinging a pianist that some musicians said they perferred his left hand to most rhythm sections. His quintet included trumpeter **Herman Autrey** (1904–), clarinettist-tenor saxophonist **Gene Sedric** (1907–1963), and the splendid guitarist **Al Casey** (1915–). They made hundreds of records, and on and off formed the nucleus for big bands organized for tours.

The bands within bands, small groups culled from big bands and featured as a change of pace, included some of the Swing Era's best. We have mentioned the Benny Goodman trio and quartet; the Goodman Sextet of 1939–41, with Charlie Christian, and first Lionel Hampton, then **Cootie Williams** (the ex-Ellington trumpeter who later formed his own big band) was perhaps the greatest of all Goodman small groups, mainly due to Christian's inspiring presence. The Kansas City Six, from Count Basie's band, was only a recording group but produced some of the most memorable Lester Young music of all time. Bob Crosby's Bobcats was one of the era's best Dixieland bands, second only to Muggsy Spanier's Ragtime Band. Artie Shaw's Gramercy Five, with the gifted **Johnny Guarnieri** (1917–) on harpsichord, and later with Roy Eldridge, reflected the musical intelligence and restlessness of its leader. And the small groups from the Ellington band were a microcosm of Duke's music, a fascinating workshop for his ideas.

The Swing Era was ended by a combination of political, social, economic and psychological factors—plus the advent of television and the decline in ballroom dancing. It was not, as some modernist critics would have it, killed by musical inertia. Its legacy remains in an abundance of recordings, in the work of its many still active survivors, and in the work of those who have learned well from it and added something new while retaining the best of the tradition, such as the brilliant Thad Jones-Mel Lewis Orchestra.

When you hear his band at its best, the old Ellington adage still holds true: "It Don't Mean A Thing If It Ain't Got That Swing!"

Leonard Feather

Louis Armstrong and Duke Ellington

Leonard Feather is the author of the *Encyclopedia of Jazz* among many other works including *Inside Bebop* and the *Book of Jazz.* He has held chairs in the History of Jazz at the University of California, the Marymount-Loyola University and other colleges, and is known throughout the word of jazz for his articles in magazines like *Down Beat, Melody Maker* and music periodicals in France, Sweden, Germany, Japan and other countries. Feather, who comes from England, went to school in Berlin and lives in Hollywood, and has been recognized for thirty years or more as the USA's leading authority on jazz.

Hundreds of his compositions have been recorded by Louis Armstrong, Cannonball Adderley, Aretha Franklin, B.B. King, Ella Fitzgerald, Sarah Vaughan and others. It was Feather's *Evil Gal Blues* that launched Dinah Washington on her career to become Queen of the Blues.

Side by side, the two names seem somehow incongruous. It would be difficult to find two figures whose image, significance and contribution to jazz history have been more obviously antithetical.

The similarities are only superficial. Louis Armstrong and Duke Ellington both were black Americans, born around the turn of the century, died early in the 1970s. Both achieved success on a global scale, and material wealth, as the consequence of a lifelong dedication to music. For all practical purposes the resemblance ends here.

Yet the very differences in their personalities, their roles and the legacy they have left us makes for a logical combined study, for between them these two men represent the ultimate achievement in their respective fields. Armstrong was the father figure of improvised jazz, Ellington the supreme nobleman of composition / arrangement / orchestra-leading. Their paths overlapped rarely; when they did, as on the couple of occasions when they recorded together, it was done for the novelty value and the combined impact of their names rather than for any reason grounded in logic, or any expressed desire on the part of either man.

Louis Armstrong's influence can be traced more directly than Ellington's. It has been said a thousand times, but will always bear repeating, that both as trumpeter and singer he showed the way to everyone, and that for all his immense popularity as a result of his vocals, it was

as an instrumental genius that he first made his mark; only second and secondarily did he become the beloved show business figure who could charm the world with *Hello Dolly* while record collectors hurried home to pull out their old copies of *West End Blues* and the other definitive masterpieces.

Ellington was less directly influential, for a reason that was calculated and deliberate on his part. The old cliché is that the instrument he played best was his orchestra; and the manner in which he played it, the particular talents of members of that orchestra, were secrets to which very few men were privy, and which for all practical purposes went with him to his death. André Previn once made a much-quoted remark to me: "Stan Kenton can stand in front of a thousand fiddles and a thousand brass, give the downbeat, and every studio arranger can nod his head and say, 'Oh yes, that's done like this'. But Duke merely lifts his finger, three horns make a sound, and nobody knows what it is!"

The disparities between Armstrong and Ellington as men were related almost entirely to their backgrounds. For Armstrong, born dirt-poor in a New Orleans slum, consigned during his early teens to a waif's home where he first learned the cornet, married in his late teens to a prostitute, life was a continuous battle. For Ellington, the product of a middle class family in Washington, D.C., life was relatively easy. While it is not possible to take at face value the totally optimistic accen-

tuate-the-positive attitude of his autobiography *Music Is My Mistress,* nevertheless it is true that he suffered far less from the automatic penalties of blackness, and only once in his life, during a brief and unsuccessful first fling in New York, did he really know the meaning of poverty.

Armstrong received a limited education; he could read and write fluently but his grammar, spelling and punctuation were his own. He read music only fairly well; it might be safe to say that though he could have held down a chair in Duke Ellington's brass section had fate decreed it that way, he would have retained the job only because, as in the case of Rex Stewart and others in Ellington's band, his individuality of style would have

Duke Ellington in the twenties

Louis Armstrong in the thirties

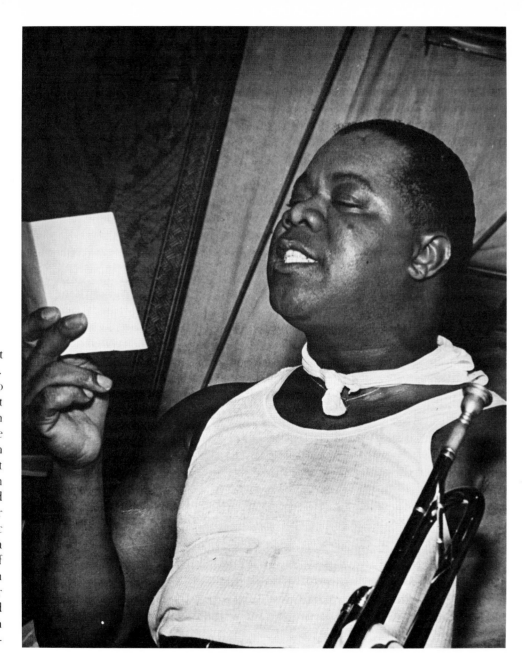

compensated for the extra time it might have taken him to learn an arrangement. Ellington, though he never went to college and was all but self-taught musically, was a sophisticated youth whose desire to acquire knowledge impelled him from a very early time in his life. I can well remember the contrast between the reaction to Armstrong, on his first visit to London in the 1930s, and the impression created just a year later by Ellington on his maiden Transatlantic voyage. To some journalists and to a large segment of the public, many of whom had never seen a black man before, Armstrong seemed like an utter primitive in his speech, his manner and his music. The shock of finding in Ellington a black American so completely poised, urbane, witty and articulate, whose orchestral genius reflected these qualities, left some observers confused. To this day it is possible to find, among older Europeans, a great deal of misunderstanding about the black American, all of it grounded in foolish generalisations based on an encounter with either Armstrong or Ellington.

An examination of the chronological evolution of both men shows that Armstrong, though only a year Ellington's junior, had no real interest in music until the waif's home period, in 1914. That was the year when Ellington wrote his first composition, *Soda Fountain Rag.*

During the next few years both were at one time or another involved in extra-musical activities, but whereas Armstrong was hauling loads of coal, Ellington was painting signs, eventually refusing the chance to study under a scholarship to Pratt Institute in Brooklyn where he could have prepared for a life in the world of visual art. By the time the offer came he was too deeply involved in music. Like Armstrong, he was married before he was out of his teens, but unlike him, he soon became a father with the birth in 1919 of Mercer Ellington, and for a few years had a relatively stable family life.

The pivotal year for both Duke and Louis was 1923, when Louis, at the bidding of his mentor and "inspirator" (his word) Joe King Oliver, left home to join the Creole Band in Chicago. Around the same time Duke, who had made one short and unhappy foray into New York, returned, this time to score an immediate success at Barrons's Club in Harlem and the Kentucky Club on Broadway.

While Ellington was gradually building up his band and strengthening his scope as a composer-arranger, Armstrong worked with several bands, spending most of a year in New York with Fletcher Henderson before returning to Chicago, where one of the groups in which he played was led by his second wife, Lil, a more knowledgeable and educated musician than himself.

It seems to me significant that whereas Ellington from childhood had a considerable ego and sense of identity, Armstrong allowed himself to be buffeted by the winds of fate. It was predestined, by the very innate character of the man, for Ellington to be a leader. Louis Armstrong might have remained in comparative obscurity as a sideman had it not been for the urging of Lil, who was constantly helping him to advance himself.

Whereas Ellington knew exactly what he wanted from his musicians and had an uncanny feeling for selecting them, Armstrong never quite had the knack for leadership and often allowed himself to be surrounded by inferior men whose frailties showed up even more glaringly in the light of his own fast-growing brilliance. Faced with the harsh realities of the American business world in the gangster-dominated Prohibition era, Armstrong in attempting to handle money was a failure. In 1927 he and Earl Hines and the drummer Zutty Singleton tried to operate their own night club in Chicago, but the venture was short-lived. So were many of the bands Louis Armstrong fronted. The word "fronted" is appropriate, because he almost invariably delegated the real authority of leadership to someone else.

Around the same time when Armstrong made his unfortunate attempt to become a businessman, Ellington, who had acquired a slick and resourceful manager in Irving Mills, opened at the Cotton Club in Harlem. It was the beginning of a long tenure, and of a period that would catapult him to international renown. Armstrong, though still primarily a local Chicago figure working with bands led by Clarence Jones, Carroll Dickerson and others, began to make an impression in New York in 1928, when he spent four months at Connie's Inn, another of the mob-controlled Harlem night spots.

More significantly, both Armstrong and Ellington were beginning by now to gain acceptance abroad, as serious harbingers of what students outside America acknowledged as an important and exciting new art form.

The contrast between these two towering figures and the music to which they devoted themselves in those early years is well pointed out in two representative records both stemming from 1928. In that year Louis Armstrong's Hot Five, at that time only an occasional recording

Earl Hines, who brought Armstrong's style to the piano

group that varied in personnel, made the historic *West End Blues.*

Armstrong's introduction is a masterpiece of carefully built tension, composed mainly of one long upward-moving phrase and another that falls just as gracefully and logically as the other one rose. His purity of tone was perhaps his most admired asset; others were the warmth of his sound, his control of what was considered in those days to be the upper register, and the complete confidence with which the two main cadenzas were constructed. From this introduction he moved into a chorus based on the theme by King Oliver. Later he sings a wordless obbligato to the clarinet solo, in the guttural, intimate voice that was always at its most affecting in a slow blues

number. The final chorus, too, is immaculately carried off, with Louis holding a high C for four bars, then gradually weaving his way down again both in register and volume; and in contrast to the applause-milking high note climaxes of later years, he ends very simply with a repeated low tone. Earl Hines' piano solo, driving and intricate, shows that he was the only man in this group who was a match for Louis; the other musicians were pedestrian—but at that point in time it was not easy for Louis to find a group of his peers to support him. He had few, if any peers, as *West End Blues* made very obvious.

By 1928, Duke Ellington had transcended the simplistic 12-bar form. Despite the three minute limitation of

the old 78 rpm records, he fashioned out of many early works a multi-layered expression of what the Afro-American idiom meant to him. *Black and Tan Fantasy, Creole Love Call* and others that were to remain in the band's repertoire throughout his entire lifetime involved changes of mood, the use of two or more themes, and even the incorporation of the human voice, used wordlessly as though it were a horn. Typical of this early Ellington phase was *The Mooche,* with a vocal along those lines by Baby Cox. The first theme is minor, the second major, with an orthodox blues passage later on.

The soloists in *The Mooche* were **Bubber Miley** (1903–1932) on trumpet, the pioneer in the much-imitated "growl"

85

style; saxophonist **Johnny Hodges** (1906–1970) who was then as much admired for his dazzling technique as for his beauty of sound; the clear-toned New Orleans clarinet of **Barney Bigard** (1906–) and a guest soloist, **Lonnie Johnson** (1889–1970) on guitar.

By the late 1920s Armstrong and Ellington were both firmly established as bandleaders. Coincidentally both made their first California appearance in 1930: Louis to play at a cabaret, Frank Sebastian's Cotton Club, Duke to appear in an Amos and Andy comedy movie. The band only played two numbers, but was treated with reasonable dignity by the Hollywood standards of those days. Their reasons for fronting large orchestras was sharply contrasted. Louis took on the role because this was a necessity for a big night club, and because many of his dates were played for dancers. Of course, heading a big dance band in those days was also a sort of status symbol, a sign that he had entered the big time of show business. For Duke, however, his participation as entertainer was secondary. He led a band because it was an extension of himself, the only medium through which he could fully express his creativity. Louis listened to the so-called "legitimate" white trumpeters such as B.A. Rolfe, and to the already successful Guy Lombardo orchestra. He idolized Lombardo, occasionally sat in with the band, and tried to get his own saxophone section to emulate the Lombardo sound.

So in Armstrong's case the orchestra often was a detriment to the authentic presentation of his phenomenal musicianship, whereas in Duke's case the orchestra had become a dazzling array of unprecedented harmonic textures, swinging ensembles, and powerfully influential solos such as those heard on *The Mooche,* as well as **Tricky Sam Nanton** (1904–46) on plunger-muted trombone, **Harry Carney** (1910–74) on baritone sax and clarinet, and several others, among them the trumpeter **Cootie Williams** (1910–), who replaced Bubber Miley and was still carrying on the tradition in 1974, when Mercer Ellington took over leadership of the orchestra after his father's death.

Although his early recordings often were based on the blues and specially written instrumental themes, the advent of success for Louis went hand in hand with a transition to the world of popular songs. By 1931 he had enjoyed a substantial measure of success singing Tin Pan Alley products; he was singing the tunes in a melodically loose style, taking liberties that gave the results an improvisational feeling. For example, in his memorable version of Hoagy Carmichael's *Stardust* he stripped the melody of all inessentials. The band is a plodding, uninspired bunch; Louis swings not because of them but in spite of them. You'll even hear, just before the vocal, a passage of that Lombardo saxophone blend, somewhat out of tune. The strength of his performance lies in Louis' gradual manner of building beyond the melody, without ever losing sight of it.

The year of that recording was 1931, a year that was relatively uneventful for Armstrong on the musical level. He recorded a rather trite melody, with Uncle Tom lyrics, called *Sleepy Time Down South*—written, ironically, by black-men—and it became his theme song. Eventually, under pressure, Louis stopped using the derogatory word "darkies" which was heard twice in the original version.

On the personal level, however, it was a dramatic year. In Los Angeles Louis and a friend, the white drummer Vic Berton, were arrested for possession of marijuana and spent ten days in the county jail. A rather innocent man capable of becoming a pawn of acquisitive businessmen, he was involved in serious managerial problems and scuffles with gangsters. But that summer he was in residence back home in New Orleans, for the first time since his elevation to fame. Local newspapers ran stories about the former waifs' home inmate who had returned in triumph to his native town. Still it was not easy to steer clear of white harassment, and soon after he left New Orleans, when the band bus pulled into Memphis, Louis and most of his musicians were arrested on trumped-up charges. The real reason was resentment that his white manager's wife was sitting in the same bus with them, and chatting with them as if they were equals. It was no wonder that by the following year Louis felt the need to

The Ellington Band's saxophonists in 1940: (left to right) Barney Bigard, Johnny Hodges, Ben Webster, Otto Hardwicke, Harry Carney

escape from this smothering environment and took off for England, where he was treated like visiting royalty.

Ellington was kept more or less shielded from such problems. When his band toured the South, his manager hired two entire sleeping cars, so that in case no hotels or restaurants were open to them, they could sleep and eat on the train. And Ellington by the early 1930s was showing his determination to emerge from the night club and dance band mould, to express himself on a broader canvas. His *Creole Rhapsody,* which in its revised version ran some eight minutes and covered both sides of a 12-inch record, was a milestone. An orchestral masterpiece, it incorporated several themes, frameworks for soloists, and

changes of mood. This was in 1931; a year later, Ellington was belatedly acknowledged as a concert artist, giving his first such performance at Columbia University.

On his maiden voyage to Europe, Ellington's gracious manner and articulate personality enabled him to enlist the friendship and admiration of everyone from serious classical composers like Constant Lambert to the Royal Family. One evening the Prince of Wales sat in with the band on drums. Still, a BBC broadcast caused considerable controversy. The *Manchester Guardian* called the music "pathetically crude". This concerning a programme that included *Mood, Sophisticated Lady, It Don't Mean A Thing* and a dozen other gems! But the

Harry Carney, a member of the Ellington Orchestra from 1926 up to his death in 1974

general response was favourable, and soon afterward the band gave two concerts. One reviewer commented: "Ellington is no mere bandleader or arranger, but a composer of uncommon merit, probably the first composer of real character to come out of America". That an English musician—Constant Lambert—made that statement in 1933 is particularly significant in the light of the fact that 40 years later, American critics of so-called "serious" music were still refusing to qualify Ellington's monumental library of great works as either classical or serious. Their idea of a black composer is someone like William Grant Still or Ulysses Kay, who write in the conservative tradition for orthodox symphonic instruments and without the use of any improvisation.

During the next two or three years there was a rare constancy in both Ellington's music and the personnel of his orchestra. Duke always knew exactly for whom he was writing, because the same men stayed in the same chairs. Meanwhile Armstrong stood at the helm of this and that band, relying more and more on his own reputation to maintain his popular success. His new image as a lovable, laughable personality was reinforced when he went back to Hollywood for a major acting and playing part with Bing Crosby in the film *Pennies From Heaven,* made in 1936.

That was the year of significant breakthrough for Duke Ellington. After several experiments with orchestral forms transcending the limitations of the dance band and night club worlds, he began to write miniature concertos built around a single member of the orchestra. Jazzmen on most records until that time had been lucky to get one or two choruses of a familiar tune on which to express themselves; but Ellington now fashioned a series of works around the particular styles of men like Cootie Williams, Barney Bigard and Rex Stewart. One of the best, and best remembered, is *Clarinet Lament*, which was originally titled *Barney's Concerto,* co-written by, and featuring Barney Bigard.

By the time he recorded his first concertos, Ellington's career had encompassed eight main phases. He had begun by playing dance dates back home in Washington during World War I.

Second came the night club era; then a lesserknown and generally more frustrating medium in which real success always eluded him, the writing of music for the legitimate stage. As far back as 1924 he wrote the score for a revue called *Chocolate Kiddies.* It enjoyed a long and successful engagement in Germany, but was never seen in the United States. Similarly his *Jump for Joy,* for which he helped assemble the cast in addition to writing music and special material, had a brief *succès d'estime* in Hollywood in 1941 but never reached Broadway. Two or three other shows, such as *Beggar's Holiday* in New York and *Turcaret* in Paris, engendered only modest success.

The 1920s also saw Ellington's conquests of the recording world, of radio and theatres. It was not until the thirties that he made any impact in films and, somewhat later, the concert field. The years of greatest advancement for the orchestra were those in which, with the recording of the works built around soloists, the band became more than ever a showcase for the greatest array of individual talents in jazz.

The swing era was well under way; the bands of Benny Goodman, Artie Shaw, Woody Herman, Count Basie, Jimmy Lunceford and Bob Crosby brought national fame not only to the leaders but later to a number of sidemen who went on to form their own bands. Harry James, Lionel Hampton, Gene Krupa and Teddy Wilson for example, all left Goodman to branch out as leaders. Although he was caught up in the

maelstrom of this swing fever, Ellington was never deflected from his path. While others devoted much of their repertoire to pop jazz standards and conventional songs, he continued to paint his musical portraits with an ever-broader palette, enabling him to display fully the improvisational traits of his unique pantheon of sidemen. Moreover, such was their loyalty to the band, and their respect for his ability to set them off to full advantage, that any musician who ever left Duke, with few exceptions, either returned sooner or later or lapsed into relative obscurity.

It is odd, and regrettable, that the paths of Armstrong and Ellington crossed so rarely. Louis did perform with Duke's band at a one-night stand in Chicago in the mid thirties, but their next joint venture was a brief one, almost a decade later, when they both won gold awards in the *Esquire* poll and played in an all-star recording band, composed of some of the winners. Somewhere during those years, when he was writing pieces like *Trumpet in Spades* or *Boy Meets Horn* to feature Rex Stewart, or *Concerto for Cootie* and *Echos of Harlem* showcasing Cootie Williams, Ellington could have upgraded the course of Armstrong's career immeasurably by arranging for his appearance as guest soloist in a few similarly tailored works. Instead, Satchmo busied himself recording dreary arrangements of songs like *Shoe Shine Boy, The Skeleton in the Closet* and *Jeepers Creepers.* He was even teamed with a Hawaiian steel band for a couple of

Ellington wears the cape of the honorary doctorate awarded him in 1973 by the University of Columbia

Armstrong with his wife Lucille

sessions. If he had any conception of what he really represented to students of music, he kept this awareness strictly to himself.

In a sense, each man had what the other needed. Louis was passive about the guidance of his career, always doing just what he was told would be best for him. Duke, on the other hand, was active in the pursuit of excellence and progress; he broke with Irving Mills in 1939 after Mills had expressed the belief that the Ellington style was becoming too advanced for the public to grasp. And if Duke, for all the brilliance of his sidemen, lacked a soloist of Armstrong's monumental stature, it was true also that Armstrong lacked a composer-arranger of Ellington's calibre who could have provided him with the kind of setting he needed.

Just as Armstrong underestimated himself as a pure artist, so did Ellington deal rather summarily with his own gifts as a pianist. Actually he was a fluent and insightful soloist, capable of great harmonic explorations, oddly tongue-in-cheek note-intervals, and occasional "stride piano" moments that reflected the early inspiration of his old friend Willie "The Lion" Smith. But Ellington seldom featured himself extensively. He always referred to himself in the third person, a little sarcastically it seemed, as "the piano player", almost as if he were a minor adjunct to that more important instrument, the one he most liked to play, the orchestra itself.

The 1940s opened up a new era that was to bring Ellington to what many observers still feel was his peak, in terms of the number and quality of great new works and the strength and consistency of his soloists. The band had two vitally important new members in **Jimmy Blanton** (1918–1942), the youngster who revolutionized the concept of bass playing by making a melody instrument out of what had been essentially a functional rhythm vehicle; and **Ben Webster**, the warmth and gentle force of whose tenor saxophone was brilliantly captured as Ellington framed it in such masterworks as *All Too Soon, Conga Brava, Just A-Settin' and A-Rockin'* and the faster challenge of *Cotton Tail.*

No less important were the frequent contributions to the library of **Billy**

Strayhorn (1915–1967), the sophisticated young man from Pittsburgh who by 1939 was composing and arranging for the band. Strayhorn's writing dovetailed so perfectly with Duke's that even members of the band could not tell where the work of one man left off, and the other took up, in a collaboration between the two. From Strayhorn's pen came the Ravel-tinged *Chelsea Bridge,* the languorous ballads *Day Dream* and *Passion Flower,* both feature numbers for Johnny Hodges' mellowest moods; and of course *Take The A Train,* which soon became the band's signature tune.

After a second European tour in 1939, during which he played a number of concerts, Ellington became increasingly aware that the time had arrived for him to express fully, in an extended work, his thoughts about his people, their lives and folkways, their history, their part in American society. The suite that evolved, *Black, Brown and Beige,* was sub-titled "A Tone Parallel to the History of the American Negro". It was decided to present it at Carnegie Hall, that sacrosanct refuge where nobody, with the exceptions of Paul Whiteman and Benny Goodman, had ever been permitted to offer a jazz recital.

The new work was introduced in January of 1943 at a black-tie affair, a charity concert, with a distinguished list of honoured guests. The première of *Black, Brown and Beige* was more, of course, than a prestigious milestone in the career of its composer. It demonstrated the potentialities of a musical idiom that had been tied down for decades as a prisoner of the three or four minute record, and of the demands of jitterbugs in dance halls or pop music fans in theatres and clubs. Ellington, more than anyone before or since, revealed the true meaning of jazz as serious concert music. Throughout the fifties and sixties he gave frequent recitals, annually at Carnegie Hall for the first eight years, later at the Metropolitan Opera House where he premiered the *Harlem Suite,* and subsequently at the Newport and other jazz festivals.

Almost every year would bring a new, long concert piece. Most of them were eventually recorded: *The Liberian Suite, The Perfume Suite, Tattooed Bride* and *Night Creature,* first played in conjunction with the Symphony of the Air at Carnegie Hall.

For all his pride of ancestry, Ellington never wished to confine himself to writing what would now be called black music. To use a phrase he often liked to apply to others, he was "beyond category". One of his extended compositions was inspired by characters from the works of John Steinbeck. He and Strayhorn collaborated on jazz versions of Tchaikowsky's *Nutcracker Suite* and Grieg's *Peer Gynt Suite.*

One of the most successful ventures along these lines was *Such Sweet Thunder,* an LP comprising a dozen thematic vignettes inspired by characters from Shakespeare. Typical of the stimulus Ellington and Strayhorn found in this source is a work depicting a scene from the third act of *A Midsummer Night's Dream,* in which the various couples—Demetrius and Helena, Lysander and Hermia, Oberon and Titania—were constantly being manoeuvred into awkward positions by Puck, who just stood on one side and laughed. The "couples" heard are **Jimmy Hamilton** (1917–) and **Ray Nance** (1913–), clarinet and violin; **Russell Procope** (1908–) and **Paul Gonsalves** (1920–), alto and tenor saxes; **Johnny Hodges** (1920–) and **John Sanders**, alto sax and valve trombone, with **Clark Terry** on trumpet playing Puck. The title is *Up and Down, Up and Down.* The closing phrase is Clark Terry imitating Puck's famous phrase, "Lord, what fools these mortals be". Other movements in *Such Sweet Thunder* show a more luxuriant and elegant aspect of Ellington, such as *The Star Crossed Lovers,* a poignant melody with Johnny Hodges playing Juliet to Paul Gonsalves' Romeo. Coincidentally, Louis Armstrong also had a brief brush with Shakespeare. He played the role of Bottom, with Maxine Sullivan as Titania, in a swing-era modernization of *A Midsummer Night's Dream.* I saw it at the Centre Theatre in New York in 1939. It was unique and unprecedented, with the Benny Goodman Sextet featuring Charlie Christian, and an Eddie Condon combo, playing from boxes on either side of the stage. But the show received bad reviews and Armstrong's first and last chance for an acting career on Broadway was aborted after eleven nights.

In fact, the swing years failed to bring the genius of Armstrong into proper perspective. His image as an eye-rolling, handkerchief-waving figure continued to overshadow his accomplishments as a giant of the trumpet. Similarly the encumbrance of a mediocre big band, complete with a fat girl vocalist who did comedy dance numbers and a boy singer who handled the commercial ballads, strengthened the public belief that the beloved Satchmo was first and foremost an entertainer.

Three years after Ellington's Carnegie Hall debut, Armstrong still had never appeared there. When it was possible to produce a Carnegie recital with him in 1946, he seemed to take the occasion less than seriously, but reluctantly agreed to use a small band for half the show. However, despite promises to the contrary, he brought along the singers, told blue jokes and let his fat lady do the splits. He just couldn't ever forget that he was in show business. Music by now was second nature to him; pleasing people was his life; and he saw no separation between the two functions.

But the deterioration of the big band situation found Armstrong carrying a 16-piece orchestra and playing one-nighters for a pitiful few hundred dollars. This, and the growing demands to hear him under more suitable conditions, soon led to the inevitable. A few months after the filming of *New Orleans,* for which he was surrounded by a small group composed mostly of veteran New Orleans buddies like Kid Ory and Barney Bigard, Louis' manager, Joe Glaser, who had done much of the hiring and firing for him over the years, decided on a permanent combo setting. So in 1947 the Louis Armstrong All Stars were born. As Louis himself said years later: "It was Joe Glaser's idea. He gave the orders and nobody else mattered to me".

Rather than dwell on the wasted years when he was tied down to the swing era format, it is better to point to the accomplishments Louis was able to achieve once he had shed himself of the excess baggage. Flanked by men who were virtuosi in their own right—**Earl Hines** (1902–) on piano, **Jack Teagarden** (1905–64) on trombone, **Bigard** on clarinet, **Sid Catlett** (1910–51) or **Cozy Cole** (1909–) on drums, **Arvell Shaw** (1923–) on bass—Louis once again was in his element. The spirit that had sparked his Hot Five records in the 1920s began to re-emerge. During the next decade he made some records that far eclipsed anything he had achieved in the big band years. Not the least of these were the LPs dedicated to the memories of W.C. Handy, who composed *St. Louis Blues,* and Fats Waller. A highlight of *Satch Plays Fats* was a new version of a song he had first recorded in 1929 and invested with new life in 1955—one of the most famous of all Waller's compositions, *Ain't Misbehavin'.* Louis' colleagues on *Ain't Misbehavin'* were **Trummy Young** (1912–) on trombone, **Bigard** on clarinet, **Billy Kyle** (1914–66) on piano, **Arvell Shaw** on bass and **Barrett Deems** (1914–) on drums. The Armstrong renaissance that had begun with the formation of the All Stars took on new dimensions in the late 1960s, when he made one of his better Hollywood pictures, *High Society,* and was starred in a film and record album commemorating his travels in Africa, *Satchmo the Great.*

Hollywood's treatment of both Armstrong and Ellington was so casual, and so completely ignorant of what they represented, that it was not until 1959 that Duke was finally assigned to write the score for a film; and it was in a non-Hollywood film, *Jazz on a Summer's Day,* made at the Newport festival by a cinematographer jazz fan named Bert Stern, that Louis was allowed to let his musicianship take priority over his value as a comedy actor. To the average movie producer Louis and Duke both were black entertainers who could be inserted in a production arbitrarily, most often without any suggestion of social mixing with other members of the cast, in order to avoid offending the deep South.

During the 1960s Ellington wrote a few more film scores, but only one, *Paris Blues,* filmed partly in Paris and featuring Louis in a significant role, was of much musical interest. By now any confluence of the two giant talents took on the significance of a political Summit Meeting, and for two record dates in 1961 Duke sat in as guest of honour with the All Stars. If the results were only pleasant and less than world-shaking, it

Billy Strayhorn, Ellington's *alter ego*

was because both men by now were so firmly set on paths they had trodden for so many years that the crossover was not quite natural to them. Louis felt more comfortable playing *for* royalty than *with* royalty. And to Duke it was just an amusing gag, momentarily taking his mind off weightier matters such as the new stage production he was planning. This was *My People,* which was presented in 1963 as part of the Negro Emancipation Centennial celebrations in Chicago, and was a mixture of parts of *Black, Brown and Beige,* some new songs with lyrics and music by Duke, and performances by a "second Ellington band" composed mainly of past members, with Billy Strayhorn supervising, and sharing the conducting chores with Jimmy Jones. This was socially Ellington's strongest statement to date, a profound reflection of joy in his black ancestry, coinciding with the emergence of black pride and the civil rights movement.

This was a bold venture for Ellington. One quality he and Louis had in common was their social and political conservatism. Duke was a guest in the White House of every president from Truman on, but the man he respected most was Richard Nixon, and not just because Nixon held a big 70th birthday party for him. He really believed in the work ethic, in the theory that if you tried hard enough you would overcome all obstacles. As for Louis, he was a totally non-political person; whatever convictions he held surfaced only rarely, as when he once attacked President

Eisenhower for failing to take bold action in the school desegregation crisis. During the final decade of his life Ellington realized a goal that was the most meaningful of all to him—his series of sacred concerts, a celebration of his deeply held religious beliefs. He staged them in churches and cathedrals and synagogues from London to Beverly Hills, using guest singers and choirs and narrators and dancers. To some observers the sacred concerts seemed to steer off the main path of Ellingtonia into a sideway that did not reflect the essence of the man and his music; but then, for most of his professional life Ellington had been accustomed to enduring the advice of people who thought they knew who was the real Ellington.

The real Ellington, of course, was anybody he wanted to be: a suave charmer for the many ladies whose paths crossed with his, a smooth talker for audiences in Las Vegas lounges, a sincere believer for congregations who had come to hear him praise the Lord. He was a grand and grandiloquent man who knew of his own greatness, and who by the same token knew that modesty was a necessary quality for all great men to show—so he outwardly made protestations to indicate modesty.

He was a genius who was determined to let nothing in life disturb him to the point of interrupting his creative train of thought. I worked for him for five years, and watching him close to, I could see that under the surface all manner of irritating problems were gnawing at him; yet he refused to accept the fact of their existence. Reading his book, *Music Is My Mistress,* you would think nothing unpleasant had ever happened to him, and that he had never met a less than admirable human being in his life. In a sense Louis had some of that same affirmative attitude, though I found it easier to break down his facade of total optimism.

Toward the end of their lives, all the honours that should have accrued to them decades earlier finally caught up with Duke and Louis—honorary college degrees, freedoms of the city, medals and awards from all over the world. In 1969, on his 70th birthday, Nixon gave Ellington the highest civilian award of the United States, the Presidential Medal of Freedom.

For Louis, I suspect the greatest honour, the one that meant the most to him, came in 1964 when he enjoyed enormous success with a hit record, something that just didn't happen to jazz artists. *Hello Dolly* represented the kind of commercial triumph that was meaningful to him. For Ellington, simply taking his orchestra into a recording studio to set down some of his thoughts was accomplishment enough in itself; whether the records ever came out or not was almost irrelevant.

The passing of Armstrong in 1971 and of Ellington three years later was widely interpreted as the twofold end of an era. But the respective eras they represented, the images they had established—Louis as the uncontested Titan of traditional instrumental jazz, Ellington the master of an unequalled orchestral ensemble—these eras, these images have survived. They live on in the legacy of recordings, and most of all in the performances of young men today. The lineage may be hard to trace, but somewhere in the playing of any soloist, no matter what new idiom he may represent, you will hear a little of what Louis left us; and somewhere, in whatever ideas may flow from the pen of a composer who has dedicated himself to this unalterably American art form, the ghost of Ellington still lives.

Louis Armstrong ... Duke Ellington. Somehow, as we look back at the memory of the world they enriched, and the years they dominated, the names don't seem so incongruous after all.

Leonard Feather

Bebop, Cool Jazz, Hard Bop

Musical history, like the evolution of any art form, requires that we examine it in the longest possible perspective. At the time of developments that are turbulent, perhaps apocalyptic, we often tend to be less than completely aware that they are taking place, and are certainly not fully conscious of the role they will ultimately be assigned in later evaluations.

Thus, those of us who were very close to the bebop scene and were even actively involved in it could not possibly predict that **Charlie "Bird" Parker** (1920–1955) would in due course be acknowledged as one of the half dozen creative giants of jazz, and would achieve legendary status as a cult hero; or that **Dizzy Gillespie** (1917–) would move from the periphery of jazz to a position in the Establishment so firm, and a contribution so universally acknowledged, that eventually he would become the first American musician to be sent overseas as an official envoy of the US State Department. (The mere idea that any jazzman would be used in this manner by the Government, let alone a bebopper, was beyond our wildest dreams in 1945, when bop was first in flower).

Today, looking back over 30 years of violent change in society, in art, in music, we see that bebop, despite its odd sounding name and its controversial origins, represented a crucial turning point. It is extremely significant that a book which appeared in 1966 under the title *Jazz Masters of the 1940s*, by Ira Gitler, on closer inspection turned out to be not a complete panorama of that hectic decade in jazz, but rather an examination of those musicians who, during that period, were formulating or at least emulating the revolutionary bebop art.

There are many other valuable musicians besides the boppers who came to prominence during the 1940s, and other styles of jazz that were practised. Some represented hangovers from the New Orleans and swing eras; others, like the Woody Herman orchestra with its superb soloists, had an individual sound and style with traces of the bop influence, but were basically an extension of earlier big band concepts.

Nevertheless, in retrospect our ears tell us, just as the historians confirm, that the most durable contributions of that era were made by those pioneers whose innovations at first were known as rebop or bebop and finally just bop.

There has been a tendency, in recalling the manner in which bop took shape, to focus on a few individuals, mainly Parker and Gillespie, and to imply that the new movement sprang fully fledged from their imaginations and collaborations. Yet over the years evidence has gradually come to light that bop in its various manifestations, as a harmonic, melodic and rhythmic outgrowth of what had preceded it, was a logical and perhaps inevitable extension; possibly it would have happened along largely similar lines without the existence of Parker or Gillespie.

Heretical though this view may seem, it has been asserted, and in my opinion shown beyond a reasonable doubt, that other musicians simultaneously were arriving at the same conclusion as Dizzy Gillespie and Bird Parker without having been aware of each other's existence. To take a well known example, there was the first meeting of **Sonny Stitt** (1924–) and Parker, who said to him: "Hey, Sonny, you sure sound like me". Stitt has always insisted that he was playing in his own style before he had ever heard of Parker, and didn't even hear the latter's recorded solos with Jay McShann's orchestra until 1943. He had heard about Parker, however, and on arriving in Kansas City with Tiny Bradshaw's orchestra, looked him up and played with him for an hour at a night club jam session.

By the same token, **George Wallington** (1924–), the white pianist who played with the Dizzy Gillespie-Oscar Pettiford group on 52nd Street in New York before bebop even had a name, was a fully developed bebop pianist at that time and claims that his style had evolved without any exposure to the innovations of Bud Powell. In fact, Wallington had only heard of Powell through a guitarist friend, who had told him: "This is someone who thinks along the same lines you do".

Similar situations existed among the drummers. **Kenny Clarke** (1914–), using the bass drum for accents rather than for emphasis on the regular beats, shifting the essential timekeeping job to the top cymbal, apparently incorporated a process that may already have been

Charlie Parker

taking shape in the minds and performances of **Art Blakey** (1919–) and
even such younger newcomers to the
bop clique as **Max Roach** (1925–).
This "kindred souls" theory applies
equally to the man who wrote rather
than played the new jazz. **Tadd
Dameron** (1917–65), the young composer in Cleveland, Ohio, was not simply
someone who was told by Gillespie how
to write for his band. As Ira Gitler
observed in his book, before Dameron
ever heard Gillespie and Parker and
Monk, his thinking had begun to move
along the same lines. In fact, such
compositions as *Good Bait, Lady Bird* and
Stay On It, which he would later arrange
for the bands of Gillespie or **Billy
Eckstine** (1914–), were actually writ-

ten in 1939, before he had ever come to New York. Harlem thus became the melting pot into which were tossed all these diverse elements by men from varying geographical and social backgrounds. In short, the characteristics that went into the distillation of bebop were drawn from the natural resources of jazz and could not have been created out of whole cloth. Rhythmically, there was a move away from the steady four beat time that had dominated all prior jazz, an obliqueness of statement. In some respects it is possible to draw an analogy between the changes represented by bop and a comparable alteration in the English language. It was as though someone who had been limited to a vocabulary of a few hundred words, all confined to short sentences, later developed a capability for employing thousands of words, incorporating them into much longer and more complex phrases; and, no less important, began to use adjectives where previously only adverbs had been considered permissible, spoke in even cadences instead of an abrupt stop-and-go manner, and had a predilection for sentence structures that were not officially approved in any grammar book.

Thus we had Gillespie, Parker and their fellow rebels weaving their improvisations in longer and more subtly constructed lines than their predecessors; they used flattened fifths, which were notes that did not seem to many ears to belong in a given chord and thus were condemned by less sophisticated

listeners as "wrong notes"; and they often employed smooth passages of eighth notes, even at tempos where this would have been a technical impossibility for older jazzmen.

The most important precursors of the beboppers, in terms of their feeling for time, were **Lester Young** (1909–1959) and **Charlie Christian** (1916–1942). Lester, as I observed in the book *Inside Bebop,* was a radical in that he symbolized the gradual change from hot jazz to cool jazz. To those who measured the value of a jazz solo by its degree of intensity or hotness, Young's relationship to jazz seemed strangely platonic. His tone sounded dull and flat when contrasted with the big, rich sound of Coleman Hawkins, who had dominated the tenor saxophone scene until Young's influence became preeminent.

Lester Young rejected the harshness and blatancy of some earlier jazz styles in favour of a new relaxation and restraint. Similarly Charlie Christian, the young guitarist raised in Oklahoma City, had a sense of time that would sound modern even today. By the time Benny Goodman brought him to New York to join his sextet in 1939, Christian was using the electric guitar, a novelty in those days; had mastered rhythmic devices that would soon be picked up—or developed coincidentally—by Parker and Gillespie; and was working with augmented and diminished chords in a manner that was simply beyond the aural capabilities of most of his contemporaries, musicians and laymen alike.

Thus a new approach to tone, and to time, was the contribution of Young and Christian. Simultaneously, new ideas for rhythm were conceived not only by the drummers but also by the bassists, most notably **Jimmy Blanton** (1918–42) in the Duke Ellington orchestra. Blanton has not been classified as a bebopper, yet he was the first bass player to turn the instrument into a vehicle for melodic improvization along lines comparable with those of a horn solo, and although what he played did not have all the intrinsic idiosyncrasies of bop, it is noteworthy that the first bassists in bop groups, particularly **Oscar Pettiford** (1922–60) in the first Gillespie combo, were clearly inspired by Blanton.

It was Charlie Christian who indoctrinated **Kenny Clarke** into some of the mysteries of the new music. One night Clarke was playing around with a ukulele when Christian took it out of his hand and said, "Look, Kenny, you can make all the chords you want to on this if you just stretch your fingers right". He showed Clarke, handed back the ukelele, and Clarke began experimenting. According to his own story, he got an idea that sounded good, later showed it to the trumpeter Joe Guy (1920–) of the Cootie Williams orchestra. The tune was later known as *Epistrophy* and evidently **Thelonious Monk** (1920–) was present on that occasion, since his name appears as co-composer. Whatever the division of credit should be, this tune was an early example of phrases and intervals that sounded a little odd and eccentric by the

Dizzy Gillespie

standards of 1942, when this record was made by Cootie William's orchestra with **Joe Guy** in the featured role.

Joe Guy, the trumpet soloist on that record, was a frequent visitor to Minton's, the Harlem club where so many of the early boppers held experimental "after hours" sessions during the incubation period of the new music. Again, it becomes impossible to state categorically that Guy found no avenues on his own, or that he and Gillespie and the others did not draw from one another. Certainly his solo on *Fly Right,* recorded at a time when Gillespie's own bop style had just barely matured, fortifies the theory that bebop was a product of many bright, sharp young minds working both individually and collectively.

Bud Powell

Kenny Clarke

Unquestionably, though, Gillespie was the trumpeter in whose hands and through whose mind bebop would develop most decisively. It is futile to draw comparisons between the value of his contribution and that of Parker. Some experts cling to the belief that Parker's was more essentially the creative mind while Gillespie's importance lay primarily in his ability to document the music. The fact is that although Parker was more inclined to create original works spontaneously and was somewhat lazier about writing them down, the two men had much in common both before and during their collaboration.

Gillespie spent his formative years as sideman in a series of big bands. His first recordings show that he was greatly

indebted to **Roy Eldridge** (1911–), whose trumpet sound was the dominant new voice after that of Louis Armstrong in the 1930s. The first records featuring a Gillespie solo, with Teddy Hill's band, reflect this Eldridge influence, but before long Dizzy Gillespie was to break out of that mould, just as surely as Eldridge had found his own identity after Armstrong originally inspired him. It was Gillespie who took a popular hit parade song in 1940, called *How High The Moon*, and changed it from a slow ballad to an up-tempo instrumental; but it was Charlie Parker, with some help from a trumpeter named Little Benny Harris, who introduced an entirely new melody, retitled *Ornithology*, based on the same chord patterns as *How High*

The Moon. Parker was also responsible for taking other popular songs that included a challenging chord sequence, and investing them with new themes: for example, Ray Noble's *Cherokee* became Charlie Parker's *Ko-Ko*. Similarly Cole Porter's *What Is This Thing Called Love?* became Tadd Dameron's *Hot House*, recorded by Gillespie, and *Whispering* became Dizzy's *Groovin' High*.

This doesn't mean that the beboppers were dependent entirely on Tin Pan Alley; however, some of the better tunes happened to make a convenient point of departure, and in their bebop renovation took on what was virtually a new identity.

At the same time when they were borrowing hit tunes from the commercial music world, the early boppers were composing harmonic and melodic structures of their own. Some of them were based on the blues, others simply on a repeated rhythmic figure, and a few others, such as Thelonious Monk's *Round About Midnight*, qualified as ballads with attractive chord patterns and were later equipped with lyrics.

An early illustration of Gillespie's gift for finding new melodic contours in an old playground was his version of a song long associated with the swing era trumpet player Bunny Berigan, *I Can't Get Started*. Dizzy recorded it in January 1945 and there are phrases in it that he uses to this day and have been used not only by other trumpeters all over the world but by saxophonists and pianists as well as composers and arrangers.

Gillespie's masterful way with a ballad proved that there was much more to bebop than merely playing fast and frantically. Even the countermelody devised by Dizzy to accompany him in the first chorus was based on a harmonic conception that was daringly different by the standards of those days; and in the "tag" at the end of the last chorus he uses notes that are unpredictable, in keeping with the definition of jazz as "the sound of surprise". Of course, in today's light the adventurous spirit of the beboppers seems quite conservative. Although what they did was new on several levels, certain norms of jazz were still adhered to; for instance, everything was still in 4/4 time; even jazz waltzes were almost unheard of, in fact I wrote and recorded what I believe was the first bebop waltz in 1949, quite late in the day. Also, the bop soloists used the conventional scales and harmonies; such ideas as modes and atonality, or departure from the orthodox metre and beat, which came with the advent of John Coltrane and Ornette Coleman, were still well over a decade into the future.

It is interesting to conjecture what Charlie Parker would have been doing had he come along at a time when jazz was ready for these later departures. For all his genius, his allegiance was to the blues in various tempos and moods; to the *I Got Rhythm* patterns, and to the regular 32-bar tunes, which between them constituted 99 per cent of his repertoire until the day he died.

Nevertheless, Parker intellectually and

creatively was so far ahead of his time that it was a rare happening for him to find a musician capable of thinking as he did. Ironically, the immense contribution he made might never have seen the light of day had it not been for the humiliation he suffered as a teenager in Kansas City, when he tried to sit in at a jam session. His alto saxophone playing at that time was so limited that the drummer Jo Jones, as a signal of disgust, threw a cymbal all the way across the dance floor. After its deafening crash, Parker said: "All right you guys—just you wait and see!"—and promptly went off to a mountain resort with a band whose guitarist told him all about chord progressions.

Parker learned assiduously. Among other things he studied Lester Young's recorded solos until he could play them note for note. Three months later, when he returned to Kansas City, he was a new man. He not only could keep up with his colleagues in terms of speed, but also was able to devise melodic lines in which every improvisation became instant composition.

One of his earliest compositions was a piece he wrote during his tenure in the Jay McShann orchestra, probably as early as 1939. Although it had no title then, and McShann never recorded it, almost a decade later **Gil Evans** (1912–) wrote an arrangement of it for the Claude Thornhill orchestra, featuring Lee Konitz on alto saxophone and Red Rodney, who was later to spend three years as a member of Parker's own quintet, on trumpet. By then it was known as *Yardbird Suite.*

The Thornhill orchestra, though known mainly as a popular dance band, had several Parker compositions in its books and was one of several white ensembles that had incorporated some of the elements of bop. The first big bands to embrace the new music were those in which Gillespie and Parker themselves played at one time or another—first **Earl Hines',** then the **Billy Eckstine** orchestra which was a unique cradle of bebop, and soon afterward Dizzy Gillespie's first big band. But during that time Dizzy also played briefly with a forward-looking, predominantly white band led by **Boyd Raeburn** (1913–66); and he was a strong influence on the **Woody Herman** orchestra, whose members included such bop-inspired trumpeters as **Neal Hefti** (1922–), **Conte Candoli** (1927–) and **Shorty Rogers** (1924–). The part played by whites in bebop has been strongly disputed. It has become a cliché in critical circles to state that in jazz, an art form of indisputably Afro-American origin, black men accounted for all the completely original developments while the whites were all imitators. Like so many generalizations, this calls for a couple of qualifications. Certainly the first half of the statement is correct. Bop was the child of Parker, Gillespie and a handful of others. But to dismiss **Red Rodney** (1927–) or **Lee Konitz** (1927–) is equivalent to ignoring the contributions of the great black trumpeter **Howard McGhee** (1918–)

or the alto saxophonist **Sonny Criss** (1927–), simply because they were carrying forward, rather than initiating, a vital and durable tradition.

Legend has it that the black boppers played complex harmonies and rhythms in order to confuse the whites and keep them off the bandstand. The truth, however, is that this hostility simply did not exist. **Stan Levey** (1925–), a white drummer, worked for Gillespie as early as 1941. **George Wallington** (1924–) and **Al Haig** (1923–) played piano with Gillespie and Parker. **Shelly Manne** (1920–), one of the first drummers to absorb the essence of bop, played on one of the first Gillespie record dates. These whites were not pioneers; just like certain black musicians, who became involved with the new movement, they were first-rate artists who followed up what someone else had originated.

There were at least two white musicians who, in the opinion of Miles Davis who was among their champions, had something meaningful of their own to say. They were the pianist and composer **Lennie Tristano** (1918–), and the alto saxophonist Lee Konitz, who was featured on the Thornhill record. In the late 1940s Tristano became a sort of Svengali to a group of young white musicians, first in Chicago, then in New York. His ideas took off along a route largely independent from those of Gillespie and Parker. In fact, Tristano, along with Konitz and a small combo of kindred souls, was responsible for the very first jazz recordings, *Intuition* and

(Left to right) Billy Bauer, Lennie Tristano and Eddie Safranski with Charlie Parker

Digression, ever made in which no key signature was used and the musicians were left to improvise without harmonic restrictions, a full decade before "free jazz" became a definition for an accepted new genre. This was considered so outlandish that the record company for many years held up the release of Tristano's works. But meanwhile, Tristano and his disciples played in a cool, often contrapuntal, seemingly unemotional style ("cool jazz") that nevertheless was not incompatible with the qualities of bebop. In fact, he and Konitz and the guitarist **Billy Bauer** (1915–), also a Tristano student, all took part along with a brilliant array of boppers in a 1950 session featuring winners of *Metronome* magazine's annual

105

Lee Konitz

John Lewis and Miles Davis at a German
Radio (SWF) Jazz Session, Freiburg 1955

readers' poll. The composer was Pete Rugolo, arranger for the Stan Kenton Orchestra; the solos are by Bauer, Tristano, **Serge Chaloff** (1923–57) on baritone saxophone, Konitz, **Buddy de Franco** (1923–   ), the first and foremost bebop clarinettist, **Kai Winding** (1922–   ) on trombone, **Stan Getz** (1927–   ) on tenor sax, Dizzy Gillespie, and later on **Ed Safranski** (1918–74) on bass and **Max Roach** (1925–   ) on drums. This was called *Double Date.*

The music on *Double Date* sounds valid by today's standards, and of course, it no longer seems as progressive or venturesome as it did to many observers in its day. The popular acceptance of bebop was very slow in coming. In fact, for several years it tore the jazz world apart, dividing musicians and aficionados alike into two warring camps. On the left were the boppers, the so-called radicals, and a rather small cadre of enthusiastic fans who believed in what they were doing. They were supported mainly by *Metronome* magazine, the only American publication that went out on a limb for them. On the right were the traditionalists, who amassed their support behind Bunk Johnson and George Lewis. These two elder statesmen from New Orleans were discovered, brought out of retirement in the 1940s, and helped by such supporters as Orson Welles, who gave them national exposure, and by a diehard group of old-time jazz lovers, for whom every forward step meant, in their opinion, the suicide of their beloved art form.

The opposition was strong wherever bebop was heard. Travelling in the south with his big band, Dizzy Gillespie found that even black audiences were so unsympathetic that he had to simplify his music for them and just play some basic blues.

The media for a long time ignored the existence of bop. When recognition belatedly came, it took the form of tasteless, condescending articles in *Time, Life* and other major magazines, concentrating on such external manifestations as the beboppers' ostentatious clothes, their goatees and horn-rimmed glasses and comedy vocal solos, instead of on the serious and significant music that was presented, for example, when the Gillespie orchestra made its first concert appearance at Carnegie Hall, sharing the bill with Charlie Parker and Ella Fitzgerald.

The Gillespie orchestra, whose members then included **Milt Jackson** (1923–   ) on vibraharp, **James Moody** (1925–   ) in the saxophone section and **John Lewis** (1920–   ) at the piano, that night presented the premiere of a brilliant composition by Lewis, *Toccata for Trumpet and Orchestra,* as well as a two part work entitled *Cubano Be and Cubano Bop,* by **George Russell** (1923–   ). This latter brought to the forefront an important side-venture with which bop had become involved; the incorporation of Afro-Cuban rhythms and of bongo and conga drums. A member of the Gillespie band who took part in presenting this work was a musician

from Havana named **Chano Pozo** (1915–48), whose chanting and percussion lent a colourful flavour that took bop one step beyond the limitations of normal American four-beat jazz.

By 1948 Gillespie and bebop had at last become nationally known, and as has happened with so many new movements in music, there was an immediate attempt by opportunists to jump on the bandwagon. Disc jockeys who had strongly opposed bop and favoured Dixieland jazz suddenly became ardent supporters of a music that had unexpectedly become a commercial force. One record company, after four years of totally ignoring bop, began a sudden man-hunt for bop talent. One healthy outcome was the signing of a nine piece band led by **Miles Davis** (1926–   ), a group composed partly of established black boppers and partly of men borrowed from the Claude Thornhill orchestra, notably Gil Evans, Lee Konitz and **Gerry Mulligan** (1927–   ). Although the Miles Davis sessions were ultimately released under the title *Birth of the Cool,* the dividing line between bop and cool jazz at that time was extremely hard to determine. In fact, the band's only public appearance was made at a club on Broadway called the Royal Roost, which was nicknamed "The Metropolitan Bopera House" because it was New York City's most prominent showcase for bop musicians. In any event, what had once been stigmatized as a music that was "ruining jazz" now gained international recognition as the

108

J.J. Johnson

harbinger of an entire new musical generation. In the winter of 1947–8 **Terry Gibbs's** (1924–   ) bebop quintet and Gillespie's big band both visited Sweden. In May '49 Charlie Parker, Miles Davis and other leaders of the movement were heard at a jazz festival in Paris. (Ironically, this was five years before America staged its first jazz festival).

For a long time there was resistance to the word "bebop" or "bop" among promoters, night club owners and record companies. When Gillespie recorded for RCA Records, the first major company to show any interest in helping the new music, the sides produced were supposed to be released in an album to be entitled "Bebop". (Actually this was nothing more than an onomatopaeic word derived from a two note phrase frequently played by the boppers). However, the company baulked at the term, and although the music of course was the same and provided its own definition, the album was called *New 52nd Street Jazz,* named for the midtown Manhattan street where many clubs featuring bebop flourished in the mid-1940s.

Businessmen were afraid of bebop because for them it represented a voyage from the safety of their old established values into an ocean of the unknown. But many musicians also feared and resented the music because it represented too great a challenge to their imagination and to their technical facility.

The best-remembered instance of this is the case of the bop trombonists. Bebop at times called for the kind of music that seemed too hard to play on a slide trombone. When **J.J. Johnson's** (1924–   ) first records were released, some musicians were incredulous, swearing that he must be playing a valve trombone to move around so fast.

Though Johnson was the preeminent bebop trombonist, commercially he found it difficult to make a living in music and for a while he quit, taking a day job. In 1956 he and another bop trombonist, the Danish born **Kai Winding,** formed a quintet. Toward the end of this period Johnson extended the idea to encompass six trombones. One of his most successful products of this concept

109

was Johnson's arrangement, featuring his own incomparable solo work, of the early Gillespie composition *Night In Tunisia*. In deference to Dizzy's penchant for exotica, an Afro-Cuban flavour was ensured by the presence of the Cuban drummer Candido.

It is important to note that this record was made in 1956, more than a decade after the recording of the first bebop session, and a year after the death of Charlie Parker on 12 March 1955. When Bird died, although the graffiti on the subway walls proclaimed: "Bird Lives!", the true feeling of many musicians at that point was that this represented the end of an era, and that the music he had fought for might perish with him.

Nothing could have been further from the truth. No valid new movement in any art form dies with the passing of any one of its great masters. This applied also to earlier movements in jazz, as we can see by examining what had happened to pre-bop forms during the years when bop was in full flower.

Many of the important big bands went through some hard times during the late 1940s, but this had to do more with economics than with artistic validity. The Duke Ellington orchestra, which was touched hardly at all by bebop until much later, went on its way under the guidance of a maestro who had no desire and no need to incorporate outside elements into his music. Count Basie used a few bop sidemen from time to time, but essentially he too retained his swing era individuality.

110

The Modern Jazz Quartet: (standing) Connie Kay (drums) and John Lewis (piano); (seated left to right) Milt Jackson (vibraharp) and Percy Heath (bass)

Thelonious Monk with Kinny Dorham

Woody Herman started a new band in 1947 that was more bop-oriented that his previous group, using the famour "Four Brothers" sax section which had clearly come under the influence of both Lester Young and Parker. **Stan Kenton** charged through the jazz world with his various slogans, notably "Progressive Jazz", making extensive use of the Afro-Cuban rhythms in California around the same time Gillespie was introducing them in New York.

As the forties ended and the fifties began, the scene became increasingly dominated by small combos, all of which in some measure mirrored the impact of bop, and the many directions in which its characteristics could take off.

Four members of the Dizzy Gillespie

111

Gerry Mulligan

band in the late 1940s began to work together extensively as a unit, or as the nucleus of other groups. They were **John Lewis,** whose piano style was a gentler and more understated outgrowth of what he had learned from listening to Bud Powell; **Kenny Clarke,** still the senior and most respected member of the bop drum generation; **Milt Jackson,** who had been brought to New York by Gillespie in 1945 and soon established himself as the first vibraharpist to play bop effectively; and finally **Ray Brown** (1926–), one of the few bassists capable of carrying on the tradition of the late Jimmy Blanton. Ray Brown was later replaced in this group by **Percy Heath** (1923–), and the four men, with Lewis as their mentor, began to formulate a sort of chamber music jazz that represented a refined extension of bebop. Under the name The Modern Jazz Quartet, they made their first recordings in 1952, and two years later were able to go out on the road as an organized unit. In 1955 **Connie Kay** (1927–) replaced Kenny Clarke, and with this personnel—Lewis, Jackson, Heath and Kay—the group invested everything from blues to baroque music with the stamp of its uniquely elegant personality. The Modern Jazz Quartet disbanded in 1974, but its continued existence in virtually unaltered form for almost a quarter century gave eloquent testimony to the fact that bop was subject to various mutations and ingenious disguises.

Other combos of the early 1950s that were at least lightly touched by bop were the George Shearing Quintet, whose leader in his earlier more jazz-oriented moments showed a strong Bud Powell influence; the Dave Brubeck Quartet, in which the bop influence was minimal and mainly detected in the alto sax of **Paul Desmond** (1924–), who had come up in the era of Parker and Konitz; and the Gerry Mulligan Quartet, notable as the first jazz combo to achieve a satisfactory group sound without either piano or guitar. Mulligan, always on the periphery of bop, seemingly had been closer to it when he became involved in the Miles Davis *Birth of the Cool* venture. Davis himself, during this entire period—the years following the short-lived *Birth of the Cool* experiments—had

continued to lead a small combo whose values stemmed directly out of bop. By 1956 he had hired a young tenor saxophonist named **John Coltrane** (1926–1967) who at that time was in the so-called hard-bop or post-bop style. Three more years would elapse before Coltrane went out on his own to find a direction as new in its way as bop had been when Gillespie and Parker found theirs. Supporting Davis and Coltrane was a rhythm section whose members had all seen service with the bop pioneers: **Red Garland** (1923–) on piano, **Philly Joe Jones** (1923–) on drums and Paul Chambers (1935–69) on bass. Miles at this point was still turning for his materials to men like Tadd Dameron, whose *Tadd's Delight* was the basis for a 1956 recording.

Although bebop had reached its peak of creativity in the mid forties and its only substantial measure of popular appeal a couple of years later, its status in the years that followed was by no means that of an obsolescent fad or fashion. On the contrary, this vital music, for which some observers had predicted a hasty demise, not only proved to be of lasting importance but was incorporated into many related idioms. There was a direct line, for example, from the bop of the 1950s to the hard-bop of **Art Blakey's** Jazz Messengers, formed in 1955 and prominent as the launching pad for **Horace Silver** (1928–), **Donald Byrd** (1932–), **Lee Morgan** (1938–72), **Benny Golson** (1929–) and many other major talents of the following decade.

Even while new movements proliferated and blossomed—the **Chico Hamilton** (1921–) Quintet with its unprecedented use of flute and classical cello, the revolutionary atonal ideas of **Ornette Coleman,** the free music of Sun Ra—during the incursion of all these developments, bop as an independent means of expression for jazz musicians continued to flourish. It had in fact become the lingua of jazz, the style in which almost all young musicians found themselves involved, just as the simpler improvisational and compositional qualities of the swing era had guided the adolescent jazzmen of the 1930s.

One major reason for this survival of bop was the continued presence and influence of some of the major figures who had taken part in its creation. It has often been said that bebop was held back by the tragic prevalence of drug addiction among the musicians associated with it. It is true that Charlie Parker died tragically young, as did **Fats Navarro** (1923–50), one of the brightest young trumpeters of the early bop years. But despite the various problems of racial bigotry, drug addiction and a hostile or apathetic public that either abhorred or misunderstood their music, many of the giants of bop not only overcame these difficulties but continued to maintain their level of accomplishment. Gillespie during the 1960s was involved with a number of important ventures with large orchestras, at festivals and on records, featuring himself as a centrepiece in extended compositions by

Lalo Schifrin, J.J. Johnson and others. **Sonny Stitt** became the first musician to make prominent use of the amplified saxophone. He has since given it up and continues to play in very much the same style that brought him to prominence three decades ago.

Thelonious Monk's achievement is even more remarkable. For many years he was a sort of grey eminence in bebop, talked about by musicians though all but unknown to the general public. Then in the 1950s he began recording regularly, was even seen on the cover of *Time,* and emerged from his role as obscure cult hero to achieve unprecedented recognition. Tunes he had written as far back as 1940 came into more and more general use as vehicles for improvisation and for orchestral arrangements. Monk himself appeared in occasional concerts surrounded by a big band.

The survival of bebop in general, and of Monk in particular, into the present generation is symbolized by the fact that a few years ago, in 1968, Monk entered a recording studio to produce new versions, with the help of big band arrangements by **Oliver Nelson** (1928–), of some of his old works. His regular saxophone soloist, **Charlie Rouse** (1924–), was featured on tenor, and together they revived numbers like *Brilliant Corners,* a typically jagged Monk line.

The world of jazz today is more fragmented than at any other time in its existence. Many musicians object even to the use of the word jazz, notably Miles Davis and other great black artists who feel it is a white man's word and demeaning. Many, of whom Davis is also typical, have crossed the boundaries into electronic music and rock. An increasing number of young musicians can be found dispensing entirely with the chord system and the straight four-four metre that was endemic to jazz in its bop stage of development.

Yet along with all these occurrences, a substantial body of brilliant men can still be found in whom some or all of bop's peculiarities may still be observed. Bird Lives! He lives in much of the alto saxophone work of **Phil Woods** (1931–), whose playing in the 1970s certainly shows many qualities that were beyond his conceptual scope when he came up as a young bebopper; yet the essence of Parker is still there in his sense of time, sometimes in his choice of material and certainly in the sound of his horn.

Bird lives too in the remarkable contributions of Supersax. At the core of this Hollywood-based group are five saxophonists playing arrangements of old Parker solos taken off the records and voiced in four or five part harmony. Perhaps because of the new dimension his music takes on in this guise, Parker today lives in this fashion more effectively for the young listener, than on the original recordings whose poor sound quality and ineffective rhythm section reproduction limits their appeal.

Bop lives too, of course, in the unflagging inspiration of Dizzy Gilles-pie. By now much of the negative publicity attached to him on the grounds of his emphasis on comedy has dissipated, because serious listeners are aware that when Gillespie really gets down to playing, he is as much a genius as ever. If he is imitating anyone, it is himself, and obviously nobody has a better right to reproduce what he himself wrought, so many years ago, against a barrage of opposition that seems in retrospect as foolish as it was ultimately ineffectual.

The greatest achievement of bop is that it opened up the floodgates of inspiration for a whole generation of musicians; it broke a sound barrier with its new scale of melodic, harmonic, rhythmic and tonal values; it showed the way at a time when very few listeners seemed to care to have a new way shown to them. Bop survived, and long after the men who fashioned it have gone, their records will be here to remind everyone of something that seemed so difficult to prove in the greatest days of Gillespie, Parker, Powell, Monk and the rest—that theirs was an idea whose time had come. And once arrived, that idea has proved to be beyond the onslaught of time, beyond the impact of change, and finally, beyond artistic mortality.

114

Ekkehard Jost

Free Jazz

Ekkehard Jost was born in 1938 in Breslau. From 1967 to 1972 he worked on the scientific side of the State Institute for Music Research in Berlin. In 1973 he was admitted to the Faculty of Music on the basis of a thesis on Free Jazz. In 1975 he became Professor of Systematic Musicology at the University of Giessen. Here he both conducts the seminars and courses on the history and theory of jazz and runs an improvisation group in which he plays piano and baritone sax.

At the end of the fifties **Ornette Coleman** (1930–) said: "Let's play music—and not its background". Coleman was one of the pioneers of the movement that became known as *Free Jazz*. With this sentence he announced a trend that probably represented the most decisive break so far in the history of jazz, which until then had run along rather straight lines. For by *background* he in fact meant the generally accepted frame of reference of jazz improvisation, which had become an incontrovertible norm right back in the embryonic phase of this music and which none of the stylistic switches to swing, bebop, cool jazz and so on had ever seriously called in question. Background meant a series of understandings which governed the development of the individual modes of expression of the improvizing musicians and regulated the way they played together in the group—the elementary structural principle of a jazz piece (theme, improvisations, theme); the harmonic and metric structure set by the theme; and the *beat* which, like a heartbeat, controlled the fundamental rhythm. Previous stylistic changes of direction in jazz had mainly, each in its different way, established a progressive change of techniques and modes of expression. They had, it is true, increasingly complicated the "background"; but in the years round 1960 this background gradually began to break up.

The rejection of the system of traditional rules and standards that Ornette Coleman proclaimed and countless young musicians practised created a situation that was full of contradiction. Inevitably liberation from the old norms gave rise to the question: "Freedom for what?" The path these musicians followed in the late fifties and the sixties was hedged round with overturned barriers. Yet it led them to an abundance and diversity of modes of expression and principles of construction unique in the history of jazz. It did not just lead them to the new and never-yet-heard but also led to material drawn from traditional jazz and blues forms, from third world music, from the Western avant-garde and from pop as well. This release from the standards of beat and layout and from a received ideal of the jazz sound did not mean that all those things *must* be pushed to one side, simply that they *could* be.

Thus Free Jazz only becomes tenable as a concept of style if the "freedom" it promises is taken as a freedom of choice between an almost infinite number of alternatives and not just as a revolt against tradition. Yet this also means that a Free Jazz style cannot exist as something clearly definable but only as an ancillary artefact which helps mutual understanding and is mainly distinguished by the diversity of phenomena it embraces.

This kaleidoscopic nature of Free Jazz makes it far from easy to discuss its associated transformations and innovations in a few pages. Maybe it will suffice to set out some of the main aspects briefly as a basis for discussion.

Free Jazz then means:
— questioning rules of every kind—which, as remarked above, is not the same thing as rejecting them;
— the increasing significance of spontaneous listening and reaction within the group;
— whence, to some extent at least, an ending of the distinction between soloist and accompanist and a mounting tendency to replace the solo with collective improvisation;
— elevation of tone colour to rank as a means of improvized construction in its own right, and thence the possibility of playing amelodically;
— emphasis on energy and intensity as elements of communication and triggers of collective ecstacy;
— recourse to third world musical cultures, and thence the blending into jazz of numerous non-European and non-American elements of style;
— increasing consciousness among the musicians of social, i.e. political and economic problems, and thence a changed view of themselves.

All these points represent tendencies; taken as a whole they could scarcely be related to any one musician or group. Let us now try to fit each of them into its place in the development of Free Jazz. The two central personalities in the initial phase of Free Jazz were undoubtedly the alto saxophonist **Ornette Coleman** and the pianist **Cecil Taylor** (1933–). It was not just that they became the focus of the attention of many younger musicians who were

Ornette Coleman at the Berlin **Jazztage** 1972

looking for a common denominator in the maze that faced them. They also became the target for a body of jazz critics whose aesthetic criteria were challenged by the new music. But these points, together with an unwillingness to tread the well-worn path of hard bop, are the only things these two very different men had in common.

Musically speaking Ornette Coleman had grown up with jazz or, to be more precise, with its roots. Brought up in the black ghettos of Fort Worth, Texas, he served his apprenticeship in the raw atmosphere of travelling tent shows, where blues and rhythm-and-blues were played in a very primitive way untouched by the glosses of jazz. When he turned to jazz in the mid-fifties he did indeed adapt himself to the established structural principles, but never completely and not for long. The first two recordings that Ornette Coleman was able to make after long years of hunger and frustration in Los Angeles show us a revolutionary, albeit a hesitant one, held down by the image of a company dedicated to West Coast jazz. His project of turning away from the traditional "background" could not be realized in this setting. The turning point came with a six months engagement in the New York jazz club *Five Spot;* it is documented by two LPs which Ornette Coleman taped in Autumn 1959 under the titles *The Shape of Jazz to Come* and *Change of the Century.* Raw though these may be, they showed what he had to offer. Meanwhile Coleman had gathered round him a group of musicians who not only understood his concept of free structuring but to a large extent supported it: the trumpeter **Don Cherry** (1936–), the bass player **Charles Haden** (1937–) and the drummer **Billy Higgins** (1936–). The jazz public of the day, together with critics and traditional style musicians, were by and large struck dumb both by the group's debut at the Five Spot and by their discs; those who could utter uttered unspoken protests. The main reason for this was the absence of some of the basic features engrained in the listening habits of the time—the predictability of the formal structure and the harmonic matching of theme and improvisations. What Coleman used to replace the rules he had slung out was

Archie Shepp at the **Donaueschingen Musiktage** 1967

Cecil Taylor

more subtle and only to be grasped by intensive listening. Coleman's themes no longer provide sequences of chords but act as triggers for the emotional content of his improvisations. In reality the unity of composition and improvisation goes much further here than the sharing of a laid-down plan of chords could of itself guarantee. Coleman's themes and improvisations both turn out to be an involved mixture of complexity and simplicity. Both have a blues character which is permanently distorted by angular phrasing without losing its essence. As in the Archaic Blues, Ornette Coleman ignores not just the layout of standardized shapes but the standards of the Western "tempered" system of pitch. For all this the improvisations are by no means as untidy as the jazz public of the early sixties continued to think them. On the contrary, released from the unifying framework of a predetermined harmonic sequence, his solos unfold with an inner logic which never loses its ability to surprise. One thought springs from another, is re-expressed, transformed and leads to yet another. But the details of this process often approach the simplicity of a folk song and only knit when brought together in a complex structure.

There were two main events in Ornette Coleman's further career which had a decisive influence on the development of Free Jazz. The first was the recording which gave its name to the whole trend. *Free Jazz* was a collective improvisation for eight players lasting about 36 minutes, in which the possibilities of free group playing were explored—a form of ensemble improvisation which took its shape exclusively from the interaction of the musicians, uninhibited by formal constraints. The second event was the way that, after a longish withdrawal from the jazz scene, Coleman re-entered it in 1965 with two new instruments—trumpet and violin. Both of these he used less as melody instruments than as producers of sounds and rhythms. And hand in hand with the sharpening of the conflict with the traditional jazz aesthetic new perspectives opened. Tone colour, up till then an important by-product of melodic development, took its place as a structural element in its own right.

Albert Ayler

The pianist **Cecil Taylor** was in many ways the musical antithesis of Ornette Coleman. Taylor grew up in middle-class New York society and graduated from the New England Conservatory at Boston. He came in from the outside just as much as Coleman did but from the opposite direction. He was familiar with the music of Bartók, Stravinsky and Schönberg, and right from the start he was concerned "to make the energies and techniques of the European composers useful, to blend them with the traditional music of the American Negro and thus create a new energy". Attempts at a blending of this kind had often been made before—from both sides be it noted—and each time they had failed. Taylor, too, had problems to begin with

in his efforts to incorporate elements of style from European New Music into jazz, particularly where rhythm was concerned. Many of his earlier recordings made at the end of the fifties show a peculiar cramping of the rhythm, which sometimes gave the impression of linking Stravinsky's music to a conventional jazz rhythm group.

Cecil Taylor overcame these initial difficulties by emphasizing as the central structural principle in the creation of rhythm quality a concept that came to be denoted among Free Jazz musicians by the not entirely happy term "energy". This concept, borrowed from physics and misused in the Free Jazz world as a meaningless catchword for anything that sounded like "force", needs closer

exploration. Energy is not simply volume, as many adherents of a misconceived freedom in jazz sometimes seem to think; it is first and foremost a function of time. Energy creates movement or is created by movement. The sound level is just *one* of the variables here and by no means a constant. The interrelation of time, intensity and pitch or melodic interval produces chains of dynamic impulses. These chains are of varying thickness and strength. It is true that their links are irregular, but the chains contain a certain dynamic coherence and thus evoke an impression of tempo.

It is perhaps easiest to see this coherence by thinking of the beat in traditional jazz as the steady pace of a long distance

122

runner. In these terms the rhythm that Cecil Taylor introduced into Free Jazz is more like the alternating strides and leaps of a hurdler whose hurdles have been set at rather irregular intervals. The key point is that these chains of impulses are not (as in traditional jazz) produced mainly by the actions of the rhythm section but arrive from an intensive interplay of rhythm between all musicians taking part. To this extent Cecil Taylor's music was *ab initio* more "group music" than Ornette Coleman's. It became clear very early on that the formula "theme, improvisations, theme" had no validity for him. Just as the transitions between solo and collective improvisations were blurred, it was by no means always clear where the composed parts stopped and the improvisation began.

Taylor's way of "collective composition" as he called it gave exceptional impulse to the development of Free Jazz, particularly in Europe. As the external constraints of bars and strophes, the allocation of solos and so on began to weaken, new internal shapes came increasingly to be formed by changes of register, dynamic gradations and instrumentation. A novel structuring of form in terms of *anacrusis, plane* and *area* of the kind Taylor introduced in his collective composition *Unit Structures* proved highly flexible. It created not so much bounds as directions, not so much predictable images as developments.

As a pianist Cecil Taylor was among the great virtuosi of his instrument. Yet his formidable technique was not an end in itself but for the most part used for a maximization of energy. Way back in the fifties one of the prominent features of his improvisations was a harmonic action in which functional, that is to say tonal, procedures were progressively weakened. The intensification of harmonic rhythm (i.e. the rate of harmonic change) which first fascinated Taylor in the music of the pianist **Dave Brubeck** (1920–) later led him to the use of cluster techniques and thus to a very pronounced percussive mode of execution. *Clusters* are groups of immediately adjacent notes, unaccountable in terms of tonal harmony but used earlier by such composers as Bartók, Henry Cowell etc, sometimes played on the piano with the fist or the elbow. The switch from chord to cluster marks—as does Ornette Coleman's violin playing—a decisive turning-point in the history of jazz—the suppression of melody and harmony in favour of tone colour and rhythm.

In the first half of the sixties a certain measure of stabilisation of structural principles became apparent in the music of both Ornette Coleman and Cecil Taylor. In contrast to this Free Jazz in general branched out around the middle of the decade in many different directions, some of them mutually divergent. Names like **Archie Shepp** (1937–), **Albert Ayler** (1936–1970), **Don Cherry**, **Pharoah Sanders** (1940–), **Marion Brown** (1935–) and others stand for numerous groups which formed, reformed and broke up because of financial problems only to form anew later on. Alongside these a number of outsiders appeared on the Free Jazz scene such as the groups led by the pianist and composer **Sun Ra** and the musicians' collective of the AACM (Association for the Advancement of Creative Musicians) in Chicago. There was the pianist **Paul Bley** (1932–) and the sax-player **Charles Lloyd** (1938–) who both leaned towards more polished forms of Free Jazz; or the jazz composers' orchestra under the joint leadership of pianist **Carla Bley** (1938–) and trumpeter **Mike Mantler** (1943–), which used various groupings to explore the possibilities of the new jazz for large orchestras. Finally there resulted a European jazz scene that was awakening to a new life, that under the influence of Free Jazz for the first time made a serious effort to develop its own musical usages and turn away from the American models.

The central figure to emerge in the developments that took place around 1965 was the tenor sax-player **John Coltrane** (1926–1967). Years earlier Coltrane had had a decisive influence on the musical mode of expression of numerous Free Jazz players without ever completely freeing himself from the tone and rhythm-based forms of late bop. Admittedly in the form of modal improvisation (i.e. improvisation based on scales instead of chords) that he developed together with Miles Davis Coltrane had moved away from the traditional layouts; and in conjunction

123

John Coltrane

with his drummer Elvin Jones he had broken up the rhythmic basis of the beat as far as he could without completely destroying it. Yet in comparison with the way-out attitude of Coleman and Taylor he had up to this time stayed sitting on the fence between the styles. New events served to narrow at a stroke the gap between Coltrane and the young musicians of the New York scene. In March 1965, he took part in a benefit concert, arranged on the initiative of the author and jazz critic Leroi Jones, and called "New Black Music", largely as a demonstration of a new black self-realisation. The fact that Coltrane, successful musician that he was, took his place among his socially underprivileged colleagues of the New York circle and at

Carla Bley, composer and pianist

the same time played music which in no way lagged behind that of these young musicians in force and power of expression but surpassed it in achievement and maturity, was seen as a signal. As the large number of titles by musicians like Archie Shepp, Marion Brown and Albert Ayler bear witness, the movement received a new guiding light. The social and psychological results of all this had their musical consequences too. Three months after this concert a collective improvisation under Coltrane's direction and lasting three quarters of an hour was performed for the Impulse record company. For this Coltrane enlarged his quartet with some of the most important avant-garde musicians—trumpeters **Dewey Johnson**

Don Cherry with a Balinese instrument at the rehearsals for *Eternal rhythm*, the first link between jazz and Balinese music, in 1967 (left Cherry's son Eagle Eye)

(1936–) and **Freddie Hubbard** (1938–); and sax-players **Marion Brown**, **Archie Shepp**, **John Tchicai** (1936–) and **Pharoah Sanders**.

This piece, entitled *Ascension*, resembles Ornette Coleman's *Free Jazz* in its dimensions and its underlying concept; and it occupies an equally prominent place in the history of jazz. In many ways it is symptomatic not only of Coltrane's further creative development but of the Free Jazz of this period as a whole. The parts of the individual musicians blend into sound fields, moved forward by the driving force of an uninhibited rhythm section, and with an intensity that seems to reach bursting point, the whole thing seems like a collective, euphoric cry. Along this path opened up by *Ascension*

followed further Coltrane LPs with titles like *Meditation, Love, Compassion, Serenity* and so on. They all bore witness to a new spirituality translated into musical terms, one whose dynamic character scarcely allowed it to be suspected of escapism. When John Coltrane died in 1967 at the age of 40, the New Jazz lost not just one of its most brilliant improvisers but its principal father-figure.

Three saxophone players who each in his own way spread Coltrane's message deserve mention—Pharoah Sanders, Albert Ayler and Archie Shepp. Sanders, who played with Coltrane from 1965 to 1967, stayed closest to the modes of expression Coltrane had developed. His far-reaching manner of phrasing, ending again and again in overblown

harmonies, had a power like that of Coltrane's, a power sometimes described as "hymnic".

Right at the beginning of the sixties Albert Ayler had shocked the world of jazz with his improvisations which combined folklore and a kind of chaotic appeal. Up to his death in 1970 he remained one of the most controversial personalities of Free Jazz, and for reasons suggested by what the French jazz critic Alain Gerber wrote on first hearing Ayler's *Ghosts:* "I was torn to pieces, washed out. It was terrible . . . I wanted to grind my teeth. But at the same time I was overcome by an overwhelming joy". This polarisation of horror and euphoria was not merely just the subjective response of a shaken

Sun Ra, leader and master of ceremonies of
his Intergalactic Research Orchestra.

listener, but was imminent in Ayler's
music as a principle. From the musical
point of view it is the contradiction
between a brutal harshness of splintered
sounds and shrieks on the one hand, and
on the other a melodic bliss, a strange
union of the gaiety of folk song and the
might of pathos.

Equally contradictory at root is the music
of **Archie Shepp**, who more and more as
time went on infused the Free Jazz idiom
with elements of traditional Afro-
American music. He worked both with
blues musicians and with the avant-
garde members of the New York circle,
and in this way arrived at a style of
performance which embraced both the
extrovert manner of sax-players like
Coleman Hawkins and Ben Webster and

the "torn up" phrasing of Albert Ayler. It was a political motive that inspired Shepp's efforts to put the blues, gospel music and the work song—as the Afro-Americans' most characteristic and fundamental means of expression—into a new setting. He sought to make the black population of the big city ghettos aware of their own cultural values, to give them a music which they could identify with and understand without its being banal.

In the second half of the sixties a movement towards broadening the base is also to be found in the music of the trumpeter **Don Cherry**, who had taken part in the first tentative experiments of the Free Jazz trend as a member of the Ornette Coleman quartet. Cherry, who moved to Europe in 1964, made the "freedom of choice" implicit in Free Jazz the overriding principle of his creative work. By drawing on the music of the third world, of Arabia, India and Indonesia, as few jazz musicians had done before, he came to a new style, the divergent elements of which are only held together by the integrating power of his personality. Don Cherry's music has given rise to many misunderstandings. It has been deprecated as an escape to exoticism and praised as a new kind of world music.

Both arguments fall down when one understands the social and psychological control mechanisms that underlie Cherry's music. The fact that he reaches out beyond the scope of his own Afro-American culture should evoke no more surprise than the way in which central European musicians have turned to New Orleans jazz. Further it must be realized that Don Cherry, who can stand here for many Free Jazz men, far from choosing his material at random, selected it so that it could be smoothly integrated into the constellation of his own psychic and cultural needs and experiences.

Certain parallels to Don Cherry's approach—the seeking after new sounds and modes of expression for multi-instrumentalists—are to be found in the music of two groups which geographically lay on the periphery of Free Jazz, in Chicago—the Art Ensemble of Chicago and the orchestra led by the composter, pianist, organist and performer on the synthesizer, Sun Ra. The Art Ensemble represents the hard core of a larger musicians' co-operative which formed in the early sixties around the pianist Richard Abrams. Taken as a whole the music of this group is probably at once the most colourful and the freest from stylistic bonds in Free Jazz. In it sensitive collective improvisation on dozens of unconventional means of producing sound are combined with a deliberately arranged uproar; traditional examples of blues, Swing and bebop are mixed with way-out sound compositions. All this is transformed by the theatrical way in which it is presented, using amongst other things poetry and music, dramatic action and musicians dressed up in colourful costumes.

Equally theatrical are the performances of the **Sun Ra Orchestra** which stages a truly monumental show, using as its slogan the "intergalactic" or space-oriented message. What struck his rational contemporaries as the absurd philosophy of Sun Ra, together with his spectacular appearances, brought a shower of accusations of charlatanry, which completely ignored his orchestra's musical achievements. In the event Sun Ra's *Super-Show* seems to be the legitimate offspring of the old tradition of the black vaudeville theatre, which cannot really be evaluated in terms of *kitsch,* art and so on. Musically speaking, Sun Ra's role as the "prophet" of Free Jazz as a whole is sometimes overestimated, for his recordings of the fifties show a quite conventional character tending towards hard bop with a few daubs of Ellington and of exoticism. Yet Sun Ra was clearly the first to tackle in any convincing way the problem of bringing the structural principles of Free Jazz to bear on a large orchestra. Despite a tendency towards vitalism or even chaos which is never far from the surface, the formidable discipline of his orchestra always breaks through to a synthesis that never ceases to surprise. In the United States a further impulse towards the solution of the contradiction between the rigid musical organisations of a big band, hitherto regarded as indispensable, and free improvisation came from a group of musicians who came together sporadically under the name of the Jazz Composers' Orchestra Association (*JCOA*). Their first album, which attracted a great deal of attention,

Albert Mangelsdorff

came out in 1968. The Mike Mantler
compositions used for this drew heavily
in many ways on the usages of European
avant-garde, particularly Penderecki's
free time and cluster techniques, without
losing their jazz character. Over an
orchestral background sound achieved
by free notation the leading improvisers
of the New York circle struck forth,
among them Cecil Taylor, Don Cherry,
Pharoah Sanders, the trombone player
Roswell Rudd (1935–) and the tenor
sax player **Gato Barbieri** (1933–).
This JCOA production hardly succeeded in bridging the traditional gap
between the members of the orchestra
who simply played written parts and the
soloist who improvised freely. But two
years earlier in Europe, on the occasion

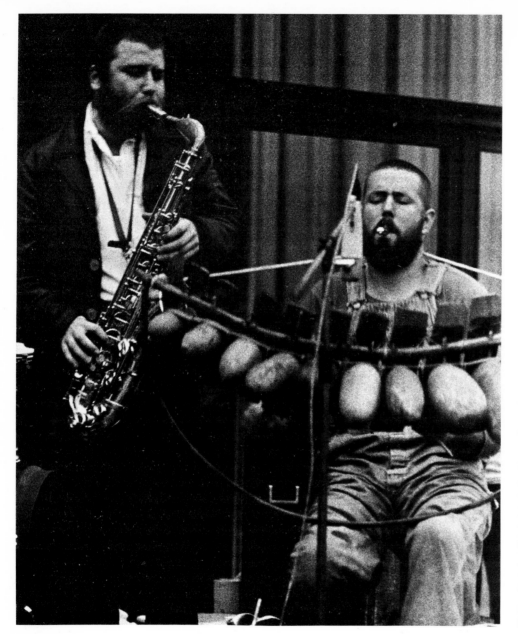

Peter Brötzmann and Han Bennink

Gunter Hampel

of the 1966 Berlin *Jazztage*, an orchestra had formed in which the traditional division of roles into accompanist and accompanied was radically broken down. This group went by the implication-packed name of Globe Unity Orchestra. Under its leader, the composer and pianist **Alexander von Schlippenbach** (1938–) it included the cream of a new generation of European musicians—among them the trumpeter **Manfred Schoof** (1936–), the sax-players **Peter Brötzmann** (1941–), **Gerd Dudek** (1938–) and **Willem Breuker,** the vibraharpists **Gunter Hampel** (1937–) and **Karl Berger,** and the bass players **Buschi Niebergall** (1938–) and **Peter Kowald.**
Globe Unity was at first laughed out of

130

improvisations of Free Jazz and the vitality of a rhythm and blues band. In *Ode for Jazz Orchestra* bass player **Barry Guy's** London Jazz Composers' Orchestra produced one of the most convincing compositions in the history of Free Jazz. Notable among British soloists whose influence generally made itself felt on the Continent were the sax-players **John Surmann**, **Alan Skidmore** and **Evan Parker** and the trombonists **Paul Rutherford** and **Malcolm Griffith**.

The France of the sixties became the temporary home of many Afro-American musicians. The Art Ensemble of Chicago, drummer **Sunny Murray** (1937–) and the sax-player **Frank Wright's** (1937–) quartet heavily influenced the French scene. At the same time they made life difficult for French Free Jazz players whose main vehicles for creative development were the groups led by bass clarinettist **Michel Portal** and pianist **François Tusques**.

To begin with the West German Free Jazz scene received major impetus from Manfred Schoof and Alexander von Schlippenbach. Around 1968 Peter Brötzmann caused a stir. His extrovert *powerplay*, which went beyond every traditional notion of aesthetics, was seen as an affront to the need for beauty—whatever that was understood to be. Since then the stormy sea has got smoother. Financial problems apart, Brötzmann's Trio with the Belgian pianist **Fred van Hove** and the Dutch percussion player **Han Bennink** is among the most successful combos of

court as a grown-up schoolboy prank but later accepted as one of the most important driving forces in European jazz. It was indeed a turning point in the development of European jazz. Right up to the hard bop phase European musicians were usually content with more or less accomplished adaptations of what their "great American models" provided in the way of samples. In Europe, the liberation from traditional standard forms, sparked off by the Free Jazz movement, also led to an ongoing liberation from the standardizing role of structural principles first formulated in the USA.

Shouted from the rooftops as it was, there was *one* bond this emancipation of European musicians did not

change—the essence of their music remained for the most part rooted in the Afro-American idiom.

Even though this fact may have made the European rejection of its American heritage seem rather like a psychological parricide that never quite came off, the large number of independent individual and group styles that crystallized in Europe fully sufficed to justify the phrase "European Free Jazz".

In Britain, which had previously focused its attention primarily on very old jazz, two big bands widely different in conception made their appearance. The Brotherhood of Breath, under the leadership of the pianist **Chris McGregor**, combined elements of South African kwela music with the collective

European Free Jazz; and it has achieved this without softening the uncompromising character of its approach. The music of two German pianists shows an extremely wide range of means of expression. At one time or another **Joachim Kühn** (1943–) and **Wolfgang Dauner** (1935–) absorbed not only elements of rock but structural principles of the European avant-garde, of romanticism (Kühn) and electronics (Dauner). In the late sixties the trombone player **Albert Mangelsdorff** (1928–), one of the central personalities of jazz in Germany, turned to Free Jazz. In his work with Brötzmann and the Globe Unity Orchestra as well as with his own group, Mangelsdorff showed how smoothly experience gained in the traditional styles could be integrated with a new concept, given boldness and creative power. His technique of circular breathing enabled Mangelsdorff to produce multiple sounds, even chordal improvisation that broadened the instrumental and technical vocabulary of the trombone to a degree that would have been unthinkable a few years earlier.

Like all other jazz styles, Free Jazz is not the work of a single brilliant creative musician working away in isolation at the "invention" of a new music. It represents the collective efforts of many, all of whom started off from the same point—the desire to get away from the rigidity of the hard bop era, to bring new life to the creative capacities of jazz and to create a music that would allow the development of new ideas beyond the cliché-rhythm and commercialized forms of soul jazz and the bossa nova. The musical forces that inspired these men were thus closely interwoven with the social upheavals that characterized the late fifties. The gathering momentum of the emancipation of the coloured population of the United States; the vanishing illusions of the "American dream" and the psychological effect of wars whose idiocy could no longer be hidden behind patriotic flourishes—all these things created a climate that left its mark even on those hitherto socially uncommitted beings, the jazz musicians. The deep-lying changes in the self-realisation of many musicians shown in interviews and discussions in the early sixties first showed themselves in their rejection of their traditional role of entertainer.

In previous decades interviews with musicians had tended to match their role as "moodmakers" and consist mainly of anecdotes and reminiscences of musical life. Now they began to ponder on this role and at the same time to stand back from it. The most conspicuous symptom of this new self-realisation was the numerous musicians' co-operatives. In the United States these included, as already mentioned, the AACM in Chicago and the JCOA in New York. Then there is the London Jazz Centre Society in England, Free Music Production in Germany, the Instant Composers' Pool in Holland and so on. The aim of the musicians in combining in this way was to gain control over their product, jazz, and not to leave it any longer entirely in the hands of a profit-oriented entertainment industry.

On the musical side the first consequences of the musicians' changed view of themselves was a group of recordings with the problem of racial discrimination as their theme. To begin with this political commitment on the part of musicians who had always been regarded as essentially apolitical was apparent only in the titles of their compositions. Nevertheless it let loose a wave of indignation among the predominantly white body of jazz critics and was to some extent acknowledged by the record industry with open repression. A striking example of this was provided by a **Sonny Rollins** (1929–) LP cut as early as 1958 under the comparatively innocuous title of *Freedom Suite*. The protests from the American jazz press, giving vent to their fears that jazz was becoming political, were so strong that the record company hastily withdrew the disc to market it again later under the toothless title of *Shadow Waltz*. At the end of the fifties works like this were still few and far between, but the tendency towards the musical propagation of political messages grew sharply in pace and scope with the coming of Free Jazz. Among the important exponents of this trend were: **Archie Shepp** (*Attica Blues, Poem for Malcolm, Things have got to Change,* etc.); **Grachan Moncur III** (*New Africa*); **Sunny Murray** (*Homage to Africa*); the Art Ensemble of Chicago

(Certain Blacks, Message to our Folks); **Clifford Thornton** *(The Panther and the Lash);* **Eddie Gale** *(Ghetto Music);* **François Tusques** *(Intercommunal Music).* One of the best known instances of the translation of political messages into the Free Jazz idiom is bass player **Charles Haden's** *Liberation Music* published in 1970. This is built round Republic battle songs from the Spanish Civil War plus Hans Eisher's *Song of the United Front* and Haden's own *Song for Che.*

It is clear enough that the openly expressed social commitment of Free Jazz and those who made it found musical expression in texts, titles and politically-loaded material to a degree that would previously have been unthinkable. Yet it would be naive to conclude that Free Jazz invariably showed such commitment or that effects aimed at social change were an inevitable part of it. There is little ground for generalized conclusions on the presence or absence of political consciousness among Free Jazz men; and there is equally little in the structural character of the music to justify the assumption of an unambiguously goal-oriented message. To say, as the jazz promotion men are sometimes apt to do, that breaking up accepted forms and emancipation from set scales stem from social concepts like "liberation from constraints" or "destruction of hierarchies", does no more than state an analogy. It is no more meaningful than equating the principles of composition of Bach fugues with the power structures of absolute monarchy.

The modes of expression and structuring of Free Jazz are revolutionary or rebellious simply to the extent that they call into question and modify our listening habits and our musical consciousness. It seems hardly likely that Free Jazz will ever turn a political reactionary into a liberal or left winger. The Free Jazz musicians threw overboard a large number of time-honoured basic rules and thus provoked a crop of misunderstandings which persisted well into the sixties. Their enemies abused them as charlatans; and even "recognized" jazz experts, who fifteen years earlier had been young and open-minded enough to defend Charlie Parker against his enemies, dismissed their music as "anti-jazz". The new musicians' fans on the other hand greeted them as the heralds of a boundless freedom in which the principle of everyone doing his own thing promised success even to those who knew a scale only by hearsay.

In the meantime it has become clear to all that Free Jazz does not mean either musical arbitrariness or a break with jazz tradition. The aesthetic standards of tonality and form which it broke away from were not principles inherent in natural law but conventions agreed between men. They were not physical formulae but culture-linked historical phenomena.

Once this is understood, Free Jazz ceases to be an impenetrable enigma and becomes a source of revelation—revelation about aggression and bitterness, but no less about joy, communication and humour. This emotional power establishes it in the jazz tradition more surely than any convention of style—no matter whether we think of King Oliver, of Ben Webster or of Charlie Parker.

Manfred Miller

Blues Today

Biographical note on author—see chapter "Blues".

"It would be a mistake to deprecate the blues and simply dismiss **B.B. King** and the rest. For that would split us off socially from the mass of the people. We must play the people's music; and when we do that we must believe in it too. If we don't do that we're nothing but bourgeois snobs".

'Blues as music of the people'—this assessment comes, perhaps surprisingly, from one of the most reviled yet also most highly rated avant-garde jazzmen, **Archie Shepp**. And in saying it this man, who had only a few years earlier been blamed for the radical break with jazz tradition ("nerve-shattering Free Jazz excesses") was not just paying lip service to the taproot of jazz but showing his views in his music. He plays political pieces like *Money Blues* ("I worked all day, I got no pay. I want my money!"—a summary of 350 years of Afro-American experience), the *Blues for Brother George Jackson* (dedicated to the Black Panther spokesman shot during an alleged attempt to escape from prison) and *Attica Blues* (for the victims of the brutally suppressed prisoners' revolt in the New York State Prison). Or he writes compositions that bring the blues tradition up-to-date both musically and in their idiomatic titles—*Pitchin' Can* for instance (*Southern Can* was a remarkable joyfully obscene blues disc cut by Willie McTell in the thirties) and *Slow Drag* (the sensuous blues dance of the black proletariat around the turn of the century—"after midnight, when the coats come off and the braces are unbuttoned"). And these allusions to the blues, consciously turned inside out and musically streamlined as they may have been, were by no means new in Shepp's work; in his early compositions they were already there as an undercurrent. Even at that time this bringing in of the blues had already come to stand for Afro-American historical experience captured in music.

Archie Shepp is not the only free jazz musician to discover, over the last few years, the turns of phrase of Afro-American folk music as a source of energy for his own playing. **Albert Ayler**, in the final, incomplete development of his style just before his mysterious death, was deeply influenced in his playing by Rhythm and Blues. Likewise **Ornette Coleman** on his LP *Friends and Neighbors.* The circle of the Association for the Advancement of Creative Musicians (AACM), which also numbered among its aims the "preservation and passing on of the Great Black Music" and had set up its own free music school to that end, now carried over the exposition of the black musical tradition into its music too and added blues to its repertoire. The "reunification of the 'spiritual' and 'physical' lines of development of black music", which Leroi Jones had thought to promote some ten years back in his influential book *Blues People* and which is today being brought about by the young generation of black avant-garde jazzmen, is unthinkable without Rhythm and Blues as its basis. Even **Karl Berger**—the vibraharp player and pianist of German origin and one of the very few non-American musicians to be associated with the New York avant-garde—created the basis for his concept of a "world music" by taking into it the folk music forms of all peoples when he thought he could recognize the "blues cry" in these forms. His hypothesis may or may not be theoretically tenable but is certainly musically feasible. In the suite *Eternal Rhythm* Berger, playing with **Don Cherry's** Ensemble at the 1968 Berlin *Jazztage,* produced a spellbinding blues-based section, entitled *Screaming J* and patently influenced by the blues piano of **Otis Spann** who, together with the **Muddy Waters Band,** had starred at the *Jazztage* the evening before this recording was made.

In very broad terms the development of jazz from the turn of the century up to around 1940 can be described as a process in which Afro-American modes of musical expression were increasingly aligned to the standards of entertainment music derived from European middle-class light music. With swing, jazz and entertainment music had become virtually identical. From then on this trend was reversed—jazz was once again in an increasing measure "blackened"—mainly by taking over elements of the blues. Bebop thus has to be seen as representing not just a refinement of the means of expression offered by harmony, melody and rhythm, but at the same time an intensification of them. And this too can be attributed to blues influences in bop. (For Charlie Parker blues was a central formative element of his playing). After the cool entr'acte, it was no coincidence that the first hard bop recording which took the reference back to the black musical tradition one stage further was a blues, **Miles Davis's** *Walkin'*. It is illustrative of the initially ambivalent attitude of the Afro-American intelligentsia to the proletarian "nigger" blues that a little earlier Miles used to talk of the blues as "a sequence of chords like any other", deliberately denying the link with the musical tradition of his people. In 1954, the same year as *Walkin'* was cut, the black civil rights movement had its first great success. The "separate but equal" doctrine established as a legal principle by Plessy *vs.* Ferguson in 1896 was upset as unconstitutional by the United States Supreme Court. Even if only a paper one, this first success of the civil rights movement took the struggle for political equal rights into a patently more militant phase. It was only natural that the black musicians should follow this trend by showing a more highly developed consciousness of what the roots of their music, stunted in the process of adaptation, were about. The civil rights movement increasingly based its struggle on the historical and cultural identity of the Afro-American, which that same struggle had just won back. Likewise the black musicians found their identity by assimilating the Afro-American folk music tradition into the music they played.

John Lee Hooker

Quite a number of the important moves towards Free Jazz in the early sixties were directly or indirectly based on the blues. **Charles Mingus** (1922–) called one of his influential LPs *Blues and Roots* and entitled one of the first really "free" pieces in the history of jazz, a dialogue with **Eric Dolphy** (1928–1964), *Folk Forms.* For his part Dolphy, following the Parker tradition, developed an extraordinarily speech-like instrumental declamation, thus giving reality, at a new stage in the development of jazz, to the ideal of a "black", blues-like execution. And it was in a blues, *Chasin' the Trane* that **John Coltrane** first demonstrated the change of emphasis of his improvizations from harmonic density to motivic development on both melodic and rhythmic planes.

137

Sonny Boy Williamson (mouth organ) and Muddy Waters at at German South West Radio television production of the "American Blues Festival"

Charlie Mingus, avant-garde musician of the fifties and sixties with a leaning towards blues and gospel.

The jazz rock development of recent years is completely unthinkable without blues as a basis. **Larry Coryell** who with his *Free Spirits* was one of the first to venture to ignore the borderline between jazz and rock, that (in 1967) was still stoutly upheld by the purists, started off as a top rate blues guitarist. Another innovation of his was to use electronic amplification in jazz to make the instrument's intonation more flexible and to give the melodic lines more strength. This was a device he took not from the jazz guitarist but from blues men like **T-Bone Walker** (1913–) and **B.B. King** (1925–). Like Larry Coryell, all the bold pioneers of the early days of jazz rock took blues as the common musical basis of the two idioms and thus

as the key to success in fusing them. It is interesting to note that the heavily promoted union of jazz and "serious" music known as the Third Stream, has now shrunk to a trickle that permeates the refined entertainment music of radio's midday and promenade concerts. By contrast, despite opposition from some of the critics, the fusion of jazz and rock, with the blues as a common denominator, has now become a mainstream of jazz development.

No less worthy of note is the fact that it is primarily those jazz musicians who shape their music mainly to its social function who turned, and are still turning, to blues as the model of musical expression—notable among them **Mingus** (cf. his *Fables of Faubus*, a biting satire

on a bedrock reactionary Southern senator) or the group of "black nationalist" musicians inspired by **Leroi Jones. Gary Bartz** for instance turned expressly to the social aspect of African music in trying to formulate rules for his pieces derived from Rhythm and Blues models—"To hell with it, I won't fight any more in your dirty wars. I've got my own battles to fight". Conversely those jazz musicians whose view was best expressed in an LP titled *Blues: The Common Ground* are tending more and more to link their music to social experience. In *The Price You Gotta Pay to be Free*, **Cannonball Adderley** has this to say about the murder of Martin Luther King:

"When Massa Lincoln was the President way back when

Talkin' 'bout emancipation
He didn't want to give me my freedom then
So he put me on probation
And there it is a century later
Just shot down a great emancipator
You wonder why I give my life
To get together this bullshit nation
How much longer will it be
Oh, the price you gotta pay to be free".

The organist **Jimmy Smith** sang of *Recession or Depression* and how it all came to the same thing:

"The rich folk keep gettin' richer
And the poor folks keep gettin' poorer/By the day".

And drummer **Jack DeJohnette,** stretching his legs in the jazz rock idiom, gave voice to the *Inflation Blues:*

"A dollar's worth/About thirty cents
You're workin' your behind off/And you still can't pay the rent".

Another key reason for the powerful impact the blues is having on today's scene—an impact so widespread that it is not always easily seen for what it is—is the way that from 1954 onwards the blues have been the basis and reference frame for the pop music produced for the youth market. (Even the West German music industry's arrangers have reached a point where they can no longer do without the pull of a boogie bass or a blue guitar riff for their smoochy accompaniments).

Rock star **Eric Clapton** (1945–) reduced the relationship of rock to blues to a terse formula when he said in an interview: "Rock is like a battery. From time to time you have to go back to the blues to recharge your batteries".

In fact many switches and new stylistic trends in the history of rock can be explained as this periodical "recharging of batteries from the blues". It started back with *rock 'n' roll*, whose origin is still quite wrongly defined in the latest reference books by the formula "(black) blues plus (white) country music". Broadly speaking we can distinguish five rock 'n roll styles in the foundation years (up to around 1958), and three of these showed no trace of country music whatever. These are the rock 'n rollers of the Chicago school (Chuck Berry, Bo Diddley etc), the New Orleans trend (Fats Domino, Lloyd Price, Professor Longhair etc) which are completely based on their respective local blues traditions, and the rock 'n roll style of the vocal groups (The Drifters, The Coasters, The Dominoes etc). Their inspiration was the vocal style of the Ink Spots and the Mills Brothers, popular in the thirties and forties, plus jump blues and gospel. The groups of the Northern band rock 'n roll (Bill Haley & The Comets, Freddie Bell and the Bellboys etc) derived the basis of their music from jump blues; the "white" influences in their rock 'n roll came much less from country music (in as far as this is taken to mean the country folk music of the whites) than from "Western Swing", which, as its name suggests, was a commercialized, heavily swing-orientated style of white string bands. Finally, the fifth style, the early "rocka-billy" records of people like **Elvis Presley** and **Carl Perkins** showed not a mixture of blues and country music so much as a coupling in the exact meaning bestowed on that word by the record industry. Each of their early singles has a blues on one side and a country piece on the other. Incidentally this was nothing new; this "coupling", with the two sides contrasting in just the same way, can be found back in the twenties, in the earliest stage of the record industry's exploitation of primitive folk music—notably in the case of Jimmie Rodgers.

It was the British beat that gave pop music its next injection of blues. As **Eric Burdon** (1941–) put it in 1966: "The reason why the Beatles arrived at their sound was that just like me and many of my friends, they followed the American music scene absolutely fanatically. For young English people **Chuck Berry, Bo Diddley, Ray Charles, Etta James, Screaming Jay Hawkins** and countless others are gods".

Copying these "gods", a few of the beat musicians themselves became popular idols. One example is the way the **Rolling Stones** first hit the charts at the end of 1964 with *Little Red Rooster,* which was "taken over" almost unchanged from a record by the Chicago blues man **Howlin' Wolf** (Chester Burnett, 1910–).

Likewise America's answer to the British beat invasion—the *folk rockers* was linked to the blues. They had two main points of departure. One was the music of the country bluesmen, which had just been rediscovered by young blues enthusiasts particularly **Bob Dylan** (1941–). There are even records from his salad days in which he tried to accompany **Big Joe Williams** (1903–) on the mouth organ. The second was the musicians of the West Coast hippy sub-culture, many of whom had started their career in folk blues combos. (In **Jefferson Airplane's** first album, for instance, there was a 1941 blues of Memphis Minnie. This suggests a more than fortuitous and superficial preoccupation with the blues tradition.)

It is reasonably true to say that the superstars of the heyday of rock were all "bluesniks", **Eric Clapton, Jim Morrison, Van Morrison** and **Janis Joplin** (1943–1970). Janis Joplin's admiration for Bessie Smith was so great that she collected for and herself subscribed to a gravestone for the "Empress of the blues", but stayed away from its unveiling to stop her action being misinterpreted as a publicity gimmick. Then again there were **Joe Cocker, Eric Burdon, Mike Bloomfield** and **Paul Butterfield**, and finally **Jimi Hendrix** (1942–1970), who had started as a Rhythm and Blues player, but used to play more "pure" blues in the last years of his life, and is said, just before he died, to have been toying with the idea of starting a proper blues band. True enough, few of these people often or always played "real" blues (apart from anything else, their record companies took care of that!) or even just blues-based pieces. But their means of

Eric Clapton, star rock guitarist

expression were derived in unbroken line from the blues tradition.

The situation at that time is shown by the fact that early in 1969 the record subsidiary of the American media group CBS paid the highest advance in the corporation's history to get under contract **Johnny Winter** (1944–), a guitarist who was then not even nationally known, and built him up into a rock star. He was a musician who up to that point had had an up and down time on the (mainly black) regional blues market of the Midwest and Texas, with engagements in blues joints and small clubs and recordings for small companies which concentrated mainly on the local Rhythm and Blues market. "A new generation has taken over the pop scene'', the American magazine *Newsweek* affirmed a year later, "it is singing the blues".

And they didn't just sing it. They tried in their whole life style to imitate the behaviour of the blues people, from social attitudes and speech idiom to habits of movement—and not just on the dance floor. Doubtless the prerequisite for this change of life style, which completely transformed the attitude of youth in the industrial nations, lay in fundamental social changes. But it expressed itself, indirectly, in the blues.

The *Newsweek* story "Rebirth of the Blues" was exaggerated. But there is an inevitable and widespread view that a form of music has only arrived when the big entertainment groups have made it into a profitable business. Conversely and just as vigorously, both the right of white musicians to play the blues and their ability to do so were denied. The vicious cry of "blue-eyed soulthieves" went the rounds. Leroi Jones bitterly noted: "They always make it with their comic hats and their comic names—these young whites who capitalize on original, genuine passion ... they live as entertainers by giving out surrogates of reality. Stealing music, stealing energy. They swipe everything and turn it into showbiz, a showbiz that sticks in your throat with types like the Beatles and the Stones, who say: 'Yeah, I owe it all to Chuck Berry', but never mention the punchline, the triumphant: 'but it's me that pulls in the bread'".

In his book *Listen to the Lambs,* **Johnny Otis** (1922–) writes about the white rock blues bands and the reaction of Afro-Americans to their music: "The young whites often use the words 'soul' and 'groovy' these days, but very few of them have any idea what these expressions really mean. And because of the strong national feeling that is developing among Negros, we hear this music, which has been taken over from us and distorted, as the sound of the enemy". Ironically Otis is a white; his parents being Greek immigrants. But this important Rhythm and Blues musician grew up in a predominantly black quarter. "When society faced me with the decision whether to be 'black' or whether to be 'white'", he decided "to be black". Under the California race laws his son is a Negro; and Johnny Otis himself is "black" as far as his social position and way of life are concerned. What he is fighting is the unscrupulous and unthinking appropriation and exploitation of a music that is his too. As he sees it, the commercial success of the young whites blues adepts goes back to the way that racial prejudice penetrates even to the world of music and the myth of white superiority—"white is right"—is upheld and confirmed. There is no doubt he is right. The example of *Little Red Rooster* already quoted is only one in a long list of numbers of which the white version has sold much better than the black original. One of Presley's first hits *That's Alright* was a blues by **Arthur "Big Boy" Crudup** (d. 1974), and *Hound*

Dog was first recorded by the blues singer **Willie Mae "Big Mama" Thornton**.

But let us get this quite clear. Leroi Jones and Johnny Otis are talking about a musical culture which is being exploited—the culture of the Afro-American proletariat. They are not for one moment suggesting that "culture" is spelt with a ch like "chromosomes". As Jones has it: "Even the *black* bourgeoisie doesn't want to know about blues", or again "Even the most washed out rock 'n roll preserves something of the momentum of upsurge against middle-class America that the blues have". So it in no way conflicted with their views when, in an interview, **Muddy Waters** (1915–) described as the best recordings he had

Fats Domino from New Orleans whose piano and vocal style had a marked influence on rock

Howlin' Wolf (Chester Burnett)

made for a long time those with (white) guitarist **Mike Bloomfield** (1943–) and (white) harmonica player **Paul Butterfield** (1941–) for the 1969 *Fathers and Sons Album,* which has since become legendary and very rightly so. "The music has the same feeling as it used to have with Otis (Spann), Jimmy Rogers and Little Walter. And that was the best band I ever played with". Muddy brushes aside with unusual briskness the question of the authenticity of Bloomfield's and Butterfield's execution: "Anyone who comes at me again with this black-white rubbish will get it shoved back down his own throat. Anyway Mike and Paul lived and played with us for years when a blues boom in pop music seemed absolutely unthinka-

ble". So be it. Blues is an expression of the culture of the Afro-American proletariat, not of the colour of their skin. Or more precisely, blues is only indirectly connected with skin colour, to the extent that in the United States skin colour remains the signal that triggers off discrimination and suppression. In much the same way the moment chosen for massive promotion of a "rebirth" of the (black) blues was the one where it became firmly geared into the exploitation machinery of the white music industry.

The fact is that it was the blues' unbroken vitality that made it a reference point for jazz and rock development. If the blues is now to be found everywhere from rock 'n roll to

Free Jazz, this is not because of any "rebirth" but because it had always remained alive as a folk music style regardless of whether or not the record industry acknowledged its existence. At the beginning of the time under discussion here, the mid-forties, the picture on the blues record market was anything but rosy. Around 1940 the concentration of the blues business into the two groups RCA-Victor (with their race label "Bluebird") and CBS-Columbia (with several blues labels like Vocalion, Okeh, ARC, Conqueror), with a subsidiary of the English firm Decca as their only competition, had led to a far-reaching standardization of record production. Both the consortia left the recording of most of their discs aimed at

143

Janis Joplin

the black music market to Lester Melrose, a white music publisher. "From March 1934 to February 1951 I recorded at least 90 per cent of all blues artists on RCA-Victor and Columbia labels", Melrose boasted. And even if this self-assessment is perhaps exaggerated, he certainly had under contract at that time by far the most commercially successful blues people—**Big Bill Broonzy,** (1893–1958), **Walter Davis** (1912–1964), **Jazz Gillum** (1904–1966), **Lonnie Johnson** (1889–1970), **Memphis Minnie** (1900–), **Roosevelt Sykes** (1906–), **Tampa Red** (1900–), **Johnny Temple, Washboard Sam** (1906–1966), **Big Joe Williams** (1903–) and **John Lee 'Sonnyboy' Williamson** (1921–1948). And these are only the most famous

144

names from Mr Melrose's blues factory. For factory it was—Melrose took production rationalization to the furthest imaginable extent. He had his contract artists take it in turns to play as accompanists for each others' recordings. The blues researcher Mike Rowe has an ironic comment on the results: "True, it was no holds barred for the big firms in their efforts to record musicians who sounded as much like one another as possible; but Melrose supplied them with musicians who were exactly the same as one another. The final stage of this musical incest was reached when these musicians began to swap songs with one another too".

The strange movements of production figures for blues records after the Depression are little wonder when all this was going on. In the throes of economic recovery between 1935 and 1937 they quickly rose again to 580 published titles per year, yet although the general economic situation by no means worsened, the figures fell back to an average of 444 for the years 1939–41. This was certainly no dramatic collapse, but the cutback of 25 per cent in published titles—behind which a corresponding fall of absolute sales figures can reasonably be assumed to lie—meant that it was the production of blues records that was the first to be cut right back when shellac was rationed as a result of the USA's entry into the war in December 1941. (Shellac, at that time the basic material for record manufacture, was made up of materials that were more urgently needed for the armaments industry).

However the 50 per cent cut in blues record production was not left long to take effect. The American Federation of Musicians saw their members' existence threatened by the increasing popularity of the juke box, and in July 1942 their president J.C. Petrillo called a strike against commercial record production. The recording studios closed for two years. After this enforced pause the big companies did start recording blues again, but there no longer seemed to be any money in it. In April 1950 CBS-Columbia terminated their "30,000" blues series, and in the same year Victor stopped production under the Bluebird label.

And this was at a time of which musicians who had certainly not made a start by playing only blues came to say: "Man, if you hadn't got blues you could just starve to death". Clearly however it was not going to be blues from the Melrose factory that would satisfy this demand.

In the decade 1940–50 the war boom and the associated labour requirements had sharply intensified the established tradition of migration of Afro-Americans from the Southern states. In normal times the ghastly living conditions in the rural areas of the South and the more blatant race discrimination there provided reason enough for this migration; and periods of rapid economic growth naturally increased the attraction of the industrial centres of the North and the Northwest—and in the forties to the West with its armaments industry too. In 1949 a black worker's wages in Mississippi averaged 449 dollars a year; his colleagues in Detroit or Chicago were earning about five times that amount. Between 1940 and 1950 roughly a quarter of its black population had left Mississippi, mainly headed north for Chicago, and the total figure for migration from the South in that decade approached 1.6 million. Between 1950 and 1960 a further 1¼ million followed. But to understand the changes in the blues scene one has to take account not only of this striking migration but also of urbanization. Even in the Southern states of today, far more coloured people are living in towns than in rural areas.

Along with the coloured workers country blues people came to town. They too were mostly workers and they usually came to earn their living on the assembly line and not as professional musicians. As had happened in the past, they shared the life, changed as it was, of those for whom they made music in their spare time. Only the very few whose records made them a name beyond their own region succeeded in setting up as professional musicians. It is doubly important to realize this. Professional musicians see themselves as more exposed than amateurs to the pressures of commercial adaptation; and on top of this their way of life and working conditions undergo considerable change. Thus both their interests and their needs tend to move away from

Ray Charles

The Norwood Singers at the German South West Radio "American Spiritual and Gospel Festival", 1966.

those of their public. The reason the blues has always been able to tell of the interests, wishes, anxieties and hopes of its public the way they are—and their social experiences too—is largely the fact that the blues has never been exclusively the music of professionals and has thus never been exclusively the affair of the music industry.

The changes which the country blues underwent in the cities were less the result of commercial influences—although they doubtless picked up some tricks from the Melrose factory, notably on the subject of playing together in a group—as the result of the new conditions under which music was made and listened to. To make themselves heard in a busy city street or in a packed city joint the musicians needed electrical amplification whenever they could get it. In their turn amplifiers meant that the complex playing techniques of the acoustic instruments had to be abandoned. The country guitarists had been used to combining the melody line in the treble, the accompanying chords and the bass lines on one solo instrument. Now they divided these functions among two and later among three or more guitars. The loss of internal tension that this "disentangling" resulted in was made up for by a heavily stressed ground beat. As early as 1946 this "translation" of the country blues style from the Mississippi delta into the city idiom of the Chicago blues had brought to fruition a new style, as evinced by the records made by the pianist **Sunnyland Slim** (1907–) with the guitarists and singers **Muddy Waters** (1915–), **Homer Harris** and **James "Beale Street" Clark.**

These records straightened out a piece of blues history. Until then the discs Muddy Waters cut in 1948, accompanied only by the bass player Big Crawford, had been taken as characteristic of the early Chicago blues. These recordings differed only from the country blues of the Delta musicians in the use of amplification and the bass (mainly used as the foundation of the rhythm). Thus Muddy's first big hit *I Can't Be Satisfied* was simply an electrified variation of his *I Be's Troubled,* which he made for the Library of Congress in 1941, when he was still in Mississippi and completely

146

faithful to the country blues tradition. Muddy has often stressed that these records were wholly unrepresentative of the actual state of development of his own combo, and that they suppressed a large part of the adaptation to urban conditions; and we can hear this from his 1946 records. Nonetheless these too were made for an audience which had not yet fully adapted itself to the ways of life of the big city ghetto. *Jitterbug Blues* expresses the deep mistrust of the cool cat, who follows every new turn of fashion, of the hustler who wears way-out gear, who knows every latest twist and turn of jazz and dance and who—as the lyric stresses—is kept by his women. In this record Waters opens up a theme that, not surprisingly in view of the migration rate, comes up again and again in the Chicago blues—the conflict between country and town that has itself migrated into the urban ghetto. The record company for which he recorded this title probably also found this blues too primitive—meaning far too crude and aggressive by the standards of the Melrose production line. Columbia did not press a single one of its recordings of these first Chicago blues.

It was not the big record companies that went into business with the city adaptations of country blues styles. They all had their stars under contract and thought they could control the market, which was limited anyway, without further expense. The first recordings of these urbanized country blues were made by small independent firms—"indies" as the jargon has it. Founded in the prosperous times after World War II, these firms recorded a special kind of local music for a special kind of local market. Literally hundreds of these tiny concerns sprang up from 1946 onwards. Most of them started by trying to copy as exactly as possible the production of the "bigs"—but with little success, since the specialists in this kind of blues were tied by their contracts with Melrose. It was really by coincidence that the "indies" found that there was also a demand for the music of those people whom they *could* record—the electrified country blues of people who had moved up from the South. Leonard Chess, co-founder of Chess Records, one of the most successful of the independents, on first hearing the tape of Muddy Water's *I Can't Be Satisfied,* is supposed to have grumbled: "What's he singing there, I don't understand what he's singing!" Nevertheless his partner persuaded him to bring the record out. Legend has it that the first edition, which Chess had delivered by truck to his 180 dealers on the South Side (the largest of Chicago's coloured ghettos) was sold out within the hour. As a result Chess, as already mentioned, prevailed upon Muddy to stick to this idiom for his next record too, uncharacteristic as it was of the state of development of his combo. It is thus quite untrue that the independents had no influence on the music they marketed, although they did not *produce* it like the bigs did. Since however the "indies" started by making records for

local markets with clearly defined interests and musical tastes, their influence did not lead to any general standardization. That only started to happen when the Chicago blues became an interesting property on the national Rhythm and Blues market.

In 1951 Muddy Waters had four titles in the charts at the same time, and with his first published recording *How Many More Years,* Howlin' Wolf put himself in the Top Ten of Rhythm and Blues. (The term "Rhythm and Blues" was introduced in the trade press around 1950 as a "neutral" name for what had previously been called "race records", implying discrimination). Muddy and Wolf, and with them **Elmore James**, **Little Walter (Jacobs)**, **Eddy Boyd**, **Willie Mabon**, **Jimmy Reed** and with isolated hits **J.B. Lenoir**, **Otis Rush** and **Sonnyboy Williamson** ("Rice" Miller, c. 1893–1965)—those were the Chicago musicians who made coast-to-coast hits with the local blues style in the years up to 1959. Understandably enough their various styles became models for other Chicago blues people. Since, in addition, the bass player **Willie Dixon** (1915–   ) was gradually setting up for himself in Chicago a key position as a blues producer, not unlike Lester Melrose's in the prewar years, there was an increasing measure of standardization from the mid-fifties onwards. Dixon only contributed directly to this in as much as he himself wrote a large proportion of the songs for the artists he produced and in doing so usually tended to choose very

similar rhythmic shapes. It would however be less than fair to Dixon to describe his influence as wholly negative. For along with a whole string of deplorable little songs like Wolf's *Hidden Charms,* many Chicago blues classics came from him too—Muddy's aggressive *I'm Ready* and his proud, bouncy *Hoochie Coochie Man,* Sonnyboy Williamson's *Close to You,* and Wolf's *I Ain't Superstitious, Tail Dragger* and *Back Door Man.* In addition, with his cunning adaptations of traditional material, Dixon did a certain amount to enrich the repertoire of form and text—notably in the way he made *My Babe* for Little Walter out of the gospel song *This Train* or the fabulous *Wang Dang Doodle* from the *The Bulldykers' Ball,* a song about lesbian love. (Though admittedly in doing so he bowdlerized "Fast Fuckin' Fannie" to "Fast Talkin' Fannie"). True, the way Dixon aimed to get the ensemble playing in his productions as homogeneous as possible, and thus imposed a discipline on his musicians, did deprive the Chicago blues of much of its spontaneity and freshness. On the other hand it was the only way of retaining the perfection of balance exemplified in combinations such as the pianist **Otis Spann** (1930–1970) and the guitarist **Robert Lockwood Jr**. In *The Hard Way* Spann sings:

"I came up the hard way/I just about raised myself
I been in and out of trouble/But I never begged no one for help".

That is characteristic of the blues.

B.B. King

Unpleasant experiences—experiences typical of the social group, so that the singer always shares them with his audience—are not pushed aside but told the way they are. And in contrast with these experiences the blues give those who hear them the strength to insist on their right to a reality that offers a happy, fulfilled life. This they may do by a self-affirming turn of the lyric, by irony, by the way they are put together musically or by a jaunty blues such as *Hoochie Coochie Man.* The Afro-American culture, described by Lerone Bennett jr. as the "unpuritanical, untechnocratic, unexploiting tradition", defines human life as satisfying, happy living, or in psychological terms as the achievement of a balance between the pleasure principle and the reality principle. The right to a life like this is not an individual but a collective one. Everyone has the inalienable right to make active use of the strength and talents within him. If the organisation of social life prevents this—as is invariably the case for the underprivileged in a racist, capitalist society—danger arises that occasions of failure are experienced and intensified as individual failures. In the end this actually leads to failure and to inability to act. In this situation of a distorted relationship between the right to "happiness" and a social reality which basically denies "happiness" the blues broadly speaking has a threefold function.

First, it describes this contradiction realistically in terms of its effects—that is it depicts reality as in need of change, thus stopping the conflict being suppressed and bottled up. Second, it describes the contradiction in ways suggesting that the conflict is not incapable of resolution—that is, it presents the frustrating reality of the here-and-now not as an eternal, unalterable condition but as something that can be changed; in this way it keeps the possibility of action to change things in view. Third, the blues describes the contradiction in a manner that announces superiority over frustrating reality—that is, it depicts the inherent ability to solve by active means the conflicts of which it tells and thus serves to restore or reinforce the ability to act. The sociologist Charles Keil has used the term "naming and curing" to describe the process that players and public alike undergo through the blues in concerts by **B.B. King, Little Milton, Bobby Bland, Junior Parker, Alfred King** or **Freddie King.** In this school, the most important modern blues school after the Chicago blues, the therapeutic function of the blues is elevated to a collective enabling ritual.

Although the common characteristics of this school were developed in Memphis around 1950, it would be wrong to speak of it as the Memphis Blues by analogy with the Chicago Blues. The Chicago blues people who, like most migrants headed for the Windy City came from Mississippi, brought with them a regional musical tradition and carried on under new conditions the development of a blues language that to begin with was also regional. In Memphis on the other hand the point of departure was not country styles. An important contribution came from the swing-oriented supraregional *jump blues* of the city bands with their wind sections as an answering "chorus" for their vocalists. The ecstasy-arousing techniques of the gospel preachers and singers were introduced to add punch to the effect of stimulation, and on top of this came a further development of the interplay between voice and guitar to be found in all country blues styles. The lead guitar becomes the most important solo instrument. Electrically amplified and used solely as a melodic instrument, it becomes another "singing part".

B.B. King is the master of this Blues school and without any doubt by far the most influential bluesman of the last fifteen years—"without him a whole generation of rock guitarists just wouldn't know what to play". In his music he dramatizes in a way never heard before a basic theme of the blues—the unusual sharpening of the conflict between the sexes as a result of the working and living conditions of the Afro-American proletariat. (For instance by the much higher unemployment rate among the men, reaching as much as 40 per cent among young people!). He does more than "name" this conflict with his blues, more even than "cure" it. He plays it out loud and clear in the tension between the vocal and the instrumental "singing" parts. B.B.'s voice stands unmistakably for the male part. The use of the ecstatic gospel techniques gains added significance in this context, for in African and Afro-American traditions alike, the expressive switch of the voice into the falsetto register is taken to signify the height of virility. B.B. King's guitar lines represent the "female" part—for instance he plays pitch inflections, glissandi and rhythmic "blocks" as unmistakable erotic stimuli. It is also significant and by no means just a publicity stunt that he has given his guitar a woman's name—Lucille. Or that his audience uses this name of his instrument in the responses of the blues ritual—"Sing it, Lucille, tell it like it is!" By their musical treatment alone King's blues transform the battle of the sexes into a *productive* tension—surely one of the main reasons why B.B. is today the undisputed king of the blues. In *Eyesight to the Blind* B.B. King quotes a relatively old blues of Sonnyboy Williamson ("Rice" Miller):

"Oh, I remember one Friday morning, we was/Layin' down across the bed A man was in the next room cryin', stopped cryin' and/Raised up his head And said: Lawd, ain't she pretty/The whole state knows she's fine

When she starts walking/She brings eyesight to the blind".

On the surface it sounds like nothing more or less than a fantasized and enthusiastic description of a remarkable woman. The real meaning and function of this blues was explained by a Negro from the Delta in discussion with the ethnologist and blues researcher William Ferris. Without prompting or being asked he started talking about Sonnyboy Williamson's *Eyesight to the Blind* after depicting the suppression to which he and all other black agricultural workers were subjected: "Tell the whole world how the whole state apparatus treats us here. And then there was Sonnyboy Williamson, he said: 'Now look here! *I* say you're beautiful and the whole State knows how fine your are'". Then this farmworker added: "Do you know what he's really saying there? He's saying that we blacks must defend ourselves against the whites".

If a black man sings: "I say you're beautiful and the whole State know how fine you are", what that means to the

Afro-American is—that goes for all of us. "And do you know what happened when Sonnyboy sang that? It brought eyesight to the blind!"

The soul singers were not the first to spell out the proud self-affirmation of the slogan "black is beautiful". For Afro-Americans at least, it was already there in blues like *Eyesight to the Blind.* When the journalists play their favourite game of "the blues is dead, long live soul!", they are playing with mixed-up marks on their cards. True, some "soul" trends, most recently the Philadelphia Sound that was being plugged all over the place—were and are produced exclusively with the world entertainment music market in view; the only thing they have to do with the black musical tradition is that they stir a few elements of it into the entertainment sauce like exotic and erotic spices. But it is also true that **Aretha Franklin** and **James Brown, Etta James** and **Otis Redding, Esther Phillips** and **Curtis Mayfield** are legitimate heirs to the Rhythm and Blues tradition. They are soul musicians in the original sense of the term "soul"—a metaphor for the ethnic and cultural identity of the Afro-Americans which justifies even an advertising slogan like "B.B. King is Soul".

But this is not the only reason why the prophets are wrong when they see the success of soul as the death of the blues. The first of these forecasts from the critics are now more than one blues boom old. And even in those days, fifteen years ago, they failed to see that the vitality of blues as *folk music* was not reflected in the charts for the Rhythm and Blues product. What is more, the pointers to the health of the blues are not so much the hits of B.B., Little Milton, Bland and other stars as the host of records which are still being produced by tiny firms for the local market. These recordings are often made by young musicians—further evidence that blues is no "aged" music—musicians like **Jimmy Dawkins**, **Lefty Diaz**, **Son Seals** in Chicago, **Hi Tide Harris**, **Luther Allison**, **Bee Houston**, **Shuggie Otis** on the West Coast, **Frank Frost**, **Clarence Edwards** and **George "Wild Child" Butler** in the South. But the key reason why blues is not about to pass into history for lack of demand is the adaptability of both its music and lyrics. When these young musicians translate the influences thrown back from soul and rock into a more aggressive musical language, their lyrics more and more closely reflect the Afro-American self-realisation gained in the political struggle for equal rights. This is well illustrated in **Otis Spann's** *Moon Blues,* with its ironic contrast of the space programme with the economic situation of the ghetto-dwellers:

"It is a brand new moon/Since two men walked up there
But it's the same old world for us/Baby, you know, we ain't goin' nowhere.
Oh, ooh, ooh, ooh/You know, I just got the moon blues
For all we got down here on earth Baby, I said, we might as well go to the moon".

In *Funny Money,* **Weldon "Juke Boy" Bonner** attacks the cutback of government support for the poor:

"Doctor took me off penicillin/Because it gave me a rash
Now the President took me/Off the cash
Now my money got funny..."

In the fifties and early sixties **J.B. Lenoir** seemed to be an exception among the blues people with his blues attacks against the American tax system (in *Eisenhower Blues,* a record which was withdrawn possibly under government pressure) and his racial agitation in the Southern States. Since then however the new note in the blues is clear for all to hear. And that goes not just for the younger musicians but for blues people of the older generation too. People like **John Lee Hooker** (1917–), **T-Bone Walker**, **Champion Jack Dupree** (1910–), **Robert Pete Williams** and **Guitar Slim Green** used blues to attack the United States government's Vietnam policy—Guitar Slim for instance with the striking lines:

"Ah, I've gotta go kill a brown man for the White Man
Listen! I know this war ain't right".

The more conscious self-understanding of the blues musicians is characterized by the West Coast guitarist **Bee Houston** in *Be Proud To Be a Black Man:*

"Take the blues/Can't take it away
Just like the black skin/There's no wrong to pay
This part of you/You'll never deny (...)
Always be proud/That you're a black man".

Again *Warning Blues,* a number by the **Mandrill** group, sums up 350 years of Afro-American history:

"Well, I built you a house to live in/And you threw me out the door
You know, I helped to make your riches/And you left me oh so poor.
And I made you boots to walk with/And you walked all over me
You had the nerve to scratch my name/Out of the books of history.
You gotta stop/Put your ears down to the ground
There's a brand new generation/They ain't gon' stand your doggin' 'round".

In reality the "new generation" no longer lets itself be "treated like a dog". And you don't need to put your ear to the ground to hear this. People like **Johnny Otis** with his at once vicious and coolly ironic talking blues *It's Good to be Free* are making "people's music" in a very precise and unmistakable way:

"Y'know, I read the paper the other day
About all the progress we done made
Said, opportunity was really there/After all the dues we done paid
Said, a good education is all you need
And you can get that in our schools
'f course y'have to act responsible and don't socialize
With them crazy militant fools
And I said: Oooh-oh-oooh, it sure is good to be free
But I'm just sittin' here thinkin':/Who they think they're kiddin'
With their jive.

Y'know, my pastor told me the other day/Said, practise the golden rule
Said, son, you free now, so love ev'rybody
'n' don't mess around 'n' lose your cool
That night I was walkin' home, feelin' good/Prayin' like a sonovagun
When a cop yelled: Hey nigger, you look guilty, come here
What the hell has you done done?
I say: Ooh, oh, oooh, obviously you must not have heard: I'm free
Listen: I'm just thinkin'/Who the hell they're shuckin'/With their jive?
Well, they're really workin' on some new stuff now
We gon' have a cooperation here next
That's where a brother will own a big factory, see
And then we'll all be real fit
Now I know it's hard to figure how it helps me and you/But, hell, try
'Cause it gotta be so, 'cause the Man told me so
And, baby, you know he don't lie
I say, Oooh-oh-oooh, it sure is good to be free
But you know somethin'?/Who they think they're foolin'/With their jive.
Hey, looka here, you know somethin'?:
All them politicians downtown, they got a committee
And they tell me the ribbon is blue
They gonna figure how to stop all those burnin' and lootin'
And the Army is workin' on the problem, too

Say, come here, boy, grab that rifle here, we're goin'
But we won't be gone long
All those free Americans gonna save them good guys' From them damn Vietcong
I say, oooh-oh-oooh, it sure is good to be free
But wait a minute:
Who the hell they think they're jivin' With their jive?"

Karl Lippegaus

Rock Jazz

Karl Lippegaus, born in Cologne in 1954, wrote his first jazz programme for South West German Radio at the early age of 17. Since then he has been writing regularly on jazz and rock for the magazine *Sounds* and South West German Radio. Lippegaus is reading musicology, German language and literature and philosophy at the University of Cologne.

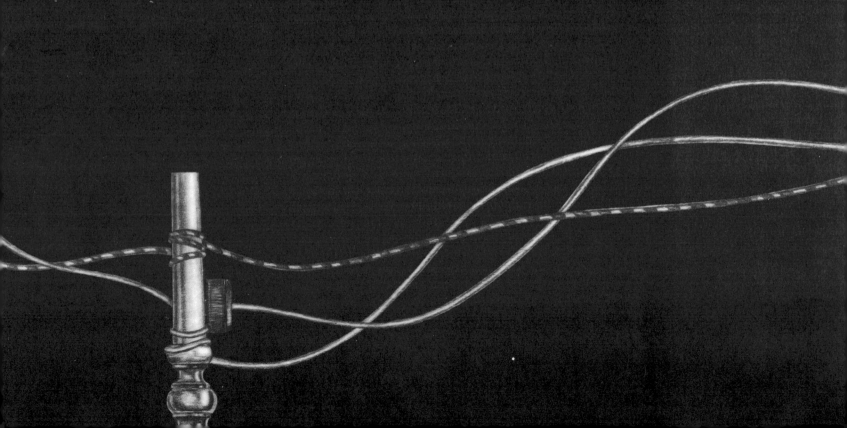

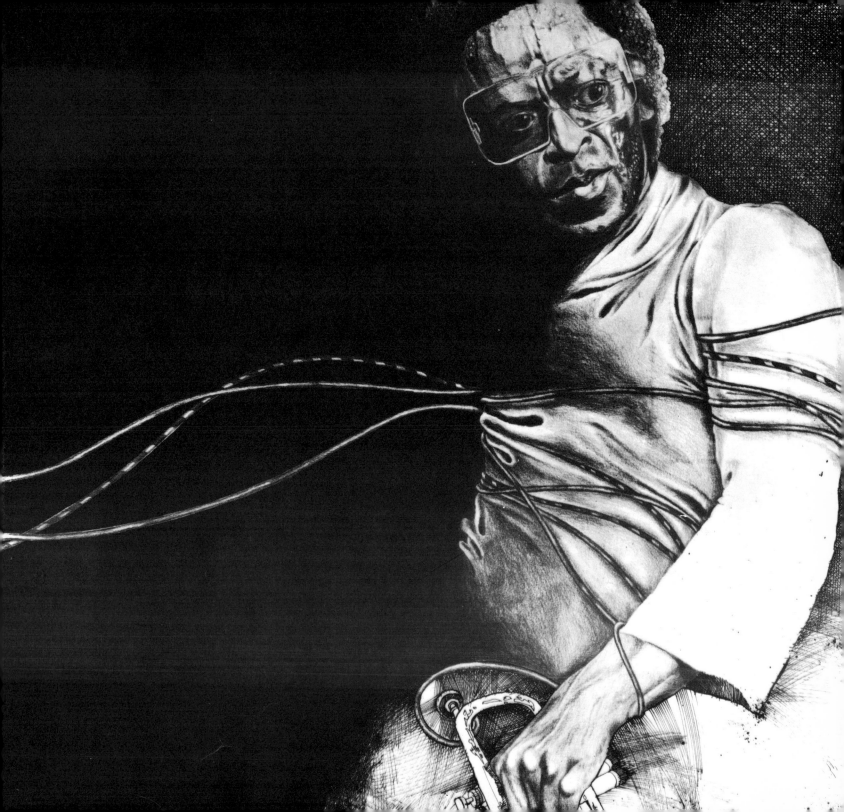

In 1970, when trumpeter **Miles Davis** brought out a double LP album under the title *Bitches' Brew,* the jazz world saw in a flash that this music marked a turning point in the history of jazz. *Bitches' Brew* became the starting point for a new phase of development. With this recording the period after Free Jazz had begun—or rather, Free Jazz had been joined by a new trend in style which was indeed fundamentally different yet could only have been created in the context of the music of the sixties.

Bitches' Brew had raised the attempts to combine jazz and rock music to a new level. The music that Miles Davis was playing in 1970 succeeded in introducing new trends—with a whole generation of young musicians. The idea of a synthesis of jazz and rock was of course older than these Miles Davis recordings. It had long been one of the most controversial topics among players, critics and public alike. And yet up to this point no-one had succeeded in achieving the much-talked-about synthesis. For years this subject was surrounded by an atmosphere of tension. One new band after another claimed that it played jazz-rock, rock jazz, pop-jazz or whatever they called it—and yet it was all no more than a compromise. Then came *Bitches' Brew,* heralded in 1969 by the Miles Davis Group disc *In a Silent Way.* Today it is difficult to recapture the impressions this music produced. One gets some idea of it from the speed with which it has since been developed along individual lines by a rapidly growing number of musicians. One could almost say that never before in the history of jazz had a new trend in style established itself and its identity so comprehensively; never before have so many newcomers gained fame as in the short time between 1970 and the present. Up to 1970 all these different descriptions had been invented to boost the sales of the music that groups like Blood, Sweat & Tears or Chicago were playing. But that music failed to live up to them; in fact it was packed with compromises and artistically unsatisfying—certainly it lacked the power to open up new perspectives. These bands, the first two to succeed in plugging the market gap in the pop sector, exemplify the grotesque overrating of their own qualities. The two groups and their fans used to quarrel in public over who had first thought of "jazz-rock".

Their concept of this thing they called "jazz-rock" was at once simple, and thus easy to reproduce, and of great commercial promise. Second and third grade jazz musicians—or even cunning studio musicians—improvized conventional jazz phrases on straightforward pop songs. Wind arrangements were used, similar to but far less complex and demanding than those that had already been played in the big bands of Stan Kenton, Woody Herman and Don Ellis. The wind ensemble was "underlaid" by an equally conventional rhythm section made up from rock musicians. Bands like this mushroomed. Miles Davis' music was "different" and thus needs to be set apart from that of his forerunners. In the rock music of the second half of the sixties, the "progressive rock era" as it is known, there were other bands who gave the impression of having integrated modern jazz into their playing. There were the numerous groups of the San Francisco scene, outstanding among them Jefferson Airplane, Grateful Dead and Quicksilver Messenger Service; in Los Angeles Frank Zappa and The Mothers of Invention and the group Spirit; then of course **Jimi Hendrix** and, in England, Soft Machine, The Cream and Traffic. The dominance of Jimi Hendrix in this, the most creative phase of his career, makes him a key figure from the realms of pop in this new jazz of the seventies.

What makes the transitory closeness to modern jazz of so many advanced rock bands of those days so particularly interesting and important is the number of different ways and levels in which it relates to **John Coltrane**—also to **Cecil Taylor** and the greats of bebop, but above all to Coltrane. The American critic Frank Kofsky has set out in depth the extent to which Coltrane's music and his whole philosophy influenced the rock scene and how far-reaching this influence proved to be.

Kofsky writes: "For many of my rock friends John Coltrane was identical with jazz and, although they said they 'hated' jazz, they hastened to add they loved Coltrane". For many of them John Coltrane represented a close relationship between music and personal

Miles Davis in the seventies (with electric trumpet)

philosophy and most of all an open door leading to other musical cultures and trends and their associated modes of thought. More and more people turned to Indian and African music, interested themselves in jazz, blues and folk music, and discovered classical and avant-garde European music. The seriousness with which all this was undertaken can largely be attributed to Coltrane's outstanding personality. In almost every case these searchings were more intensive and musically more successful than the "magical mystery tours" that became popular in the days of the Beatles.

For their increasingly extensive improvisations the rock musicians took over the principles of jazz playing as represented by Miles Davis, Coltrane and to some

157

Frank Zappa blends rock, jazz and avant-garde European music

Aretha Franklin

extent Thelonious Monk too. Davis and Coltrane in particular became more and more concerned with building as much freedom of expression as possible into the composition and arrangement of their pieces—not so much in the Free Jazz sense of total freedom, but more a controlled and directed freedom. Miles Davis likes to lay great emphasis on this factual concept of "controlled freedom". What was known as "modal playing" developed in various forms. This ensured maximum musical freedom of expression by imposing a minimum of constraints on form. The players were simply given some broad common basis—generally in the form of a single chord, a scale or a "big" note known simply as a "tonal centre". Up to

the time of Free Jazz almost everyone
except the Miles Davis Quintet improvized on chord combinations that
became more and more complicated.
Modal playing on the other hand is less
an innovation in jazz than a throwback to
its blues roots. There innumerable
examples of "modality" are to be found
all over the place. Even the most popular
form of the blues with three harmonies
repeated in a definite sequence can be
seen as an extended form of modal
playing; for here the form is not a
constraint but an open space, a basis for
free development that specifically over-
comes constraints on form.

Even the soul music of **James Brown**, **Sly
Stone**, **Marvin Gaye** or **Stevie Wonder**
tends here to link back to the blues roots.
The extent to which Miles Davis' new
music is orientated towards soul has long
been recognized. In this way Miles, as
later became clear in the case of his
fellow musicians and their own bands
too, achieved a synthesis of jazz and rock
by a much more direct route than the
jazz-rock bands. When Miles Davis
points to **James Brown**, **Aretha Franklin**
and **Sly Stone** as important influences on
the way he now plays, he is in effect
articulating a common tradition of all
forms of black music. Miles hates all this
categorizing—jazz, soul, blues: "I don't
know what you want with these names.
They're names the white man gave this
music. For me it is black music".

After *Bitches' Brew* there was a virtual
explosion of important new groups. To
begin with they all centred round

musicians that had either been playing with Miles until recently or appeared later in the various Miles Davis groups. Davis had done more than make one of the greatest recordings in the history of jazz. The "Miles Davis clique" has maintained over and over again that they only found their own identity in the new music through Miles and that he gave them strength to follow their own trends. Miles has been described as a catalyst, and the music that all these groups were playing from 1970 onwards confirms this.

First it was Lifetime, the group led by the drummer **Tony Williams** (1945–) who had played for years in the famous Miles Davis Quintet and formed his own band after *In A Silent Way*. Among its members were the organist **Khalid Yasin (Larry Young)**, the guitarist **John McLaughlin** (1942–) and **Jack Bruce** (1943–), formerly the bassist of the British group *Cream*.

Lifetime was marked by powerful musical and personal tensions, which discharged themselves in long exciting collective improvisations but were not exactly calculated to ensure a long life for the group. It was a "jam band", only made important by its outstanding make-up. Tony Williams' psychological problems showed through again and again in Lifetime's music. In the long term it proved to be beyond Williams to impose a decisive shape on the enormous potential that lay within this group.

The group Weather Report developed through a long process of internal consolidation. It was formed in 1970 by the pianist **Joe Zawinul** (1932–) and the sax-player **Wayne Shorter** (1933–), joined initially by the drummer **Alphonze Mouzon**, the percussionist Airto Moreira and the bass man **Mirouslav Vitous** (1947–). Zawinul and Shorter had a large hand in the creation of *In A Silent Way* and *Bitches' Brew;* and from 1970 onwards, after he had made his records with Miles Davis, the South American Airto Moreira was largely responsible for the important influence of Brazilian music on jazz. Joe Zawinul, who comes from Austria, is one of the representatives of contemporary Electric Jazz, which set trends for this whole development and has given it many new accents. This shows through in all his recordings with Wayne Shorter and Miles Davis, where he constantly creates structures in and around the flowing improvizations. His music is never without aim or shape unless the theme requires it to be.

For a long time **Herbie Hancock** was the pianist in the Miles Davis Quintet with Wayne Shorter, Tony Williams and **Ron Carter**. With the saxophone and bass clarinet player **Bennie Maupin**, Hancock formed a quintet that was distinguished from the start by the exceptionally creative and inspired way it played together. In 1973 Hancock enlarged his group to a sextet by taking in the synthesizer player **Patrick Gleeson**; in the same year however financial problems forced him to break this up. He once again reduced his ensemble to a quintet; but this time—to his great surprise, as he freely admits,—it achieved commercial successes hitherto unknown in the jazz world.

Back in the sixties **Charles Lloyd** and **Miles Davis** had broken through the barrier with spectacular appearances at the New York "rock temple" Fillmore East. In the years that followed there was a need for more bands to bring jazz out of its long years of—as we see it today—ever more stifling isolation and take it to a broader public. The first two groups to achieve this with consistently increasing success were the guitarist **John McLaughlin's** Mahavishnu Orchestra and **Chick Corea's** (1941–) *Return to Forever*. **Lenny White**, *Return to Forever's* drummer, calls this music "sophistifunk" because it is at once sophisticated and funky. And this is how it struck the steadily increasing proportion of rock fans who took to it—as skilfully fashioned, cunning, the tops musically and technically; and at the same time funky, with much of the expressiveness of the blues and the feeling of carrying you with it. In 1972 the Mahavishnu Orchestra was hailed as the most sensational new band on the rock scene.

Their first disc, *Inner Mounting Flame,* is regarded as the second decisive step, after *Bitches' Brew,* in the development of the jazz of the seventies. The music had now become more compact, still more powerfully compressed in rhythm and melody. With the Mahavishnu Orchestra the much-talked-of grey zone between

Wayne Shorter, co-leader of the group
Weather Report

jazz and rock was filled even more
convincingly than before. McLaughlin
and the other four in his team
improvized with an extraordinarily
close-woven ensemble style and with unequalled intensity and dedication.
McLaughlin's group was made up of
pianist **Jan Hammer** (1948–   ), violinist
Jerry Goodman (1943–   ) from the rock
band The Flock, bass player **Rick Laird**
and drummer **Billy Cobham**. Unfortu-
nately its life was to be a short one.
Personality clashes, the demands of
leadership and McLaughlin's personal
problems, to mention only a few of the
factors, led to the break-up of the
Mahavishnu Orchestra at the end of
1973. For a short time this ensemble had
dominated the scene, until non-musical

161

Herbie Hancock

circumstances, which had given rise to mounting criticism, began to affect and call in question the music itself. Largely as a result of these problems, John McLaughlin has not so far succeeded in following up this brief and deeply impressive phase with anything to match it.

In the Mahavishnu Orchestra the philosophic and religious background of the new jazz comes through particularly clearly. Simultaneously and in mounting degree they preoccupied themselves with the widest variety of doctrines, religions and philosophies, almost all of them of oriental origin. McLaughlin has an Indian guru, Sri Chimnoy, who—as he always likes to emphasize—gives him the strength and motivation to play this

162

music "for the honour of God". This guru is shared by **Carlos Santana** (1947–) whose conversion appeared to run parallel with his turning to the music of John Coltrane—yet another example of the overwhelming influence of John Coltrane in all these efforts. **Chick Corea**, like **Dave Holland**, the bass man of *Bitches' Brew* and other recent Miles Davis discs, is an adherent of Scientology. **Herbie Hancock** and **Wayne Shorter** call themselves Nichiren-Shoshu Buddhists. It is only Miles himself who doesn't want to know about all that: "I don't believe in God or the devil ..."
The British critic Michael Watts differentiates here between the coloured and white followers of religion. The blacks, he writes, were mainly in search of a cultural identity, as indeed their century-old relationship with Christianity has always confirmed. This search is clearly expressed in sayings like "Back to Africa!—Back to the roots!" The whites on the other hand, as Watts has it, were looking for freedom of the individual and seeking inner peace and balance. Devastating experiences with drugs gave them a longing for old and new doctrines and rules of life—even if admittedly this sometimes led to the thoughtless substitution of one drug for another.
The pianist **Chick Corea** went through a particularly interesting musical development. After he had made his name thanks to Miles Davis—in that remarkable combination of two pianists, Herbie Hancock and Chic Corea on two electric pianos—he took part in every imagina-

ble kind of production of the jazz avant-garde. In this process Corea's music became steadily more complex and difficult until finally a reaction set in. All at once his unaccompanied solo concerts began to show a drive for simplicity and for originality with a philosophical basis. With his group Return to Forever he then came under the influences of Brazilian music, this being mainly attributable to the percussion player and drummer **Airto Moreira**, already mentioned in the context of Miles Davis and Weather Report, and Airto's wife, the singer **Flora Purim**. At the same time Corea showed a rather marked leaning towards the music of the Mahavishnu Orchestra. When Return to Forever, in its first form, starred for a fortnight at Ronnie Scott's London jazz club, the pop stars flocked to hear them and raved about them.
A long time before this others had joined the members of the "Miles clique" in making personal contributions to the new jazz in a number of bands. Other jazz musicians before Miles Davis had tried to meld jazz and rock into a real artistic entity. There was guitarist **Larry Coryell's** (1943–) group Free Spirit, Jeremy & The Satyrs with the flautist **Jeremy Steig** (1942–), and from San Francisco the Jerry Hahn Brotherhood or The Fourth Way with pianist **Mike Nock** and violinist **Michael White**. Thus in San Francisco it was not just the rock bands based there which were striving for an integration of jazz and rock; its jazz musicians too were moving in the

same direction. But the time was not yet right; the musicians fell between two stools, meeting with lack of understanding, rejection and ignorance in the jazz and pop scenes alike. Probably the only exception to this was the Gary Burton Quartet (Burton, 1943–) with **Larry Coryell**, bass player **Steve Swallow** (1940–) and drummer **Bobby Moses**. In a short time this group became the best known and probably also the most successful among the forerunners of today's jazz rock. After the 1970 turning point many emerged from a state of near-resignation with new commitment and played better than ever.
Carlos Santana's band Santana became popular with a style called "Latin rock", a particularly accomplished and pleasing combination of rock and blues with Latin American motifs and rhythms. Their fourth disc, *Caravanserai*, appeared in 1972 and still remains one of the most beautiful and richest tone poems to be found in the popular music of recent years. Since that time Santana has shown signs of being heavily influenced by Coltrane; this influence has permeated into Santana's human and religious development too and had the effect of widening the spectrum of his musical expression.
The new jazz trends have left their mark on Europe too, and there is now too long a list to name of bands for whom the "jazz" and "rock" categories have become empty formulas over which one plays onwards and outwards. To spell out all their names and details would be

John McLaughlin at the Olympia Jazz Festival, Munich 1972

Chick Corea

impossible, so let us mention just two, the first and—at the time of writing—the latest, both of them rooted in this tradition and worthy of special attention. The oldest is the English Soft Machine and the youngest Pork Pie with the Dutchman **Jasper van't Hof**. Soft Machine has gone its own way since it was formed in 1966. Even at that time its members were not committed to any particular musical trend. They created work of extreme individuality which led British jazz critics to call them "the Beatles of the year 2000". The roads this band and its splinter groups followed are so many and devious that the "Soft Machine Story" would fill a book on its own.

Pork Pie is the group formed by the

keyboards player Jasper van't Hof after his parting of the ways with the German-Dutch Association P.C. After Soft Machine, Association was one of the first European ensembles to play "Electric Jazz" independently of Miles Davis. Pork Pie is now regarded as the most interesting new band in this trend. In American terms its make-up would earn it the name of "supergroup". Alongside **Jasper van't Hof** there are the Belgian guitarist **Philip Catherine**, the French bassist **Jean-Francois Jenny Clark** and the Italian drummer **Aldo Romano**—all of them in the top rank of European musicians. In addition they have been joined by **Charlie Mariano** (1923–), who since the fifties has been one of the richest of American sax-players in fantasy and ideas. Admittedly he may sooner or later be replaced by another wind instrumentalist, as he himself is keen to resume teaching in his home town of Boston. Pork Pie plays the jazz of the seventies with new logic and conviction. At its best, this music has more dimensions and facets than most of the American bands.

The adjective "electric" crops up again and again in connection with the new jazz. All the bands in this trend play "electric"; there are of course exceptions, but they only prove the rule. "Electric playing" means two things—on the one hand conventional acoustic instruments have their own sounds electrically amplified, and on the other there is a range of instruments and apparatus which function completely

electronically. In many cases these were developed decades ago in the studios of experimental avant-garde music; but only in recent years have they been used by jazz musicians.

So far we have only scratched at the surface of these vast realms of sound; indeed we can hardly conceive of them. But people all over the place have made a start and shown that it is possible to work creatively with this medium. The pop musicians have made electronic music into a mass phenomenon, one which more than anything else distinguishes our times musically from earlier epochs. Electronics in music—and especially in pop music—have all of a sudden become something to be taken for granted, but for a long time it was mainly used only superficially and not properly exploited. After the contributions of **Chuck Berry** (1931–), **Bo Diddley** (1928–) and the old blues greats, the most important turning point came with **Jimi Hendrix** in the late sixties. Joachim-Ernst Berendt writes: "Hendrix used to play 'on' the electronics as if they themselves were the instrument—not as if he was just playing an electronically amplified instrument". Those who saw Hendrix play will strongly confirm this—the concentration and extreme sensitivity with which he was always charming exciting new sounds from his guitar. Hendrix played with these sounds, he exploited them more thoroughly and over a wider range than anyone before him. It was not just the electric guitar that was in the foreground of all this but also the

possibility of volume levels approaching the pain threshold, which gave even the most ordinary sounds unimagined dimensions and nuances. Since then these two things have often gone together in Electric Jazz—the whole arsenal of electrical and amplified acoustic instruments, and the monstrous sound levels. Amplification gave conventional instruments like the trumpet, saxophone or even the drums a new sound. It is also one of the technical conditions that had to be met if instruments like the violin and the flute, long shut out of jazz, were to break through and hold their own. "Sound" is the great slogan that links electronics and music. Every instrument and every element of the instrument/amplifier system derives from its design and construction a particular sound; and musicians now experiment with and around this sound just as seriously and thoroughly as sax-players used to do with the mouthpieces of their instruments.

What is true of the violin and the flute is even more true of one of the oldest jazz instruments, the double bass. To the question whether it is really only in the last ten or fifteen years that the bass has been emancipated from its original role in a jazz band, many bass men will answer that this is only partly true. The musical emancipation of the bass happened back in the forties, but only now can their instrument really make itself heard; only now has it been emancipated in terms of volume and thus become even better suited to this kind of music.

Jimi Hendrix

In contemporary jazz particular scope and importance is accorded to the various kinds of instruments grouped under the collective term "keyboards". The synthesizer was developed in the late fifties by the American Bob Moog. The trade press greeted it as "the most sensational instrument of recent times", with the result that it came to be fundamentally misused in commercial music making. As its name suggests, the synthesizer produces "synthetically", by means of various switching combinations, any sound you care to think of. Its range of possible sounds is so overwhelmingly vast, that it became necessary to record the switching sequence for a particular sound in card indexes and catalogues. This is the only way in which

167

Wolfgang Dauner with keyboards and synthesizer

a particular sound can be called up at will.

Apart from **Sun Ra**, that great outsider of Free Jazz, **Herbie Hancock** was among the first to make use of the synthesizer's capabilities in jazz, and this despite its wide variety of forerunners in experimental electronic music. His LP *Sextant,* which appeared under the CBS label, is important in this context. Another notable synthesizer player is the German **Wolfgang Dauner** who has devoted years to exploring the possibilities and problems of the instrument, years in which he has put many new sources of sound to good use in jazz. Many pianists were relatively quick to switch to the synthesizers, electronic pianos, various types of organ and other

keyboards, all of which they use in any combination you care to name, often together with the conventional acoustic piano. But these new instruments bring with them new demands on the technique of the pianist, and only a very few have risen to this challenge in a truly individual and distinguished way—people like **Herbie Hancock, Joe Zawinul, Wolfgang Dauner, George Duke** or **Jasper van't Hof**. In 1973 the Swiss pianist and arranger **George Gruntz** (1932–) assembled the whole range of different keyboard instruments together with six keyboard players. This was on the occasion of a Piano Conclave, where some 20 different keyboards combined to produce a sound spectrum that had never been heard before.

Throughout the history of jazz, rhythm has always been one of its key features. The rhythm of a piece provides the jazz musician with one of the important areas in which freedom of musical expression can be exercised—in fact the space in which he moves. The psychological make-up of the player is particularly clearly reflected in his relationship to rhythm. But seldom has rhythm come to the fore in jazz as it has in the past few years. Miles Davis goes so far as to regard rhythm as the key aspect for him and for the modern jazz heritage. In a discussion with the two French journalists Dominique Farran and François Jouffa in 1973, Miles had this to say about the music of the group he then had: "Our melodies are always getting shorter and shorter,

168

and we play fewer and fewer of them. For every melody you can think of has already been booked and exploited by the record industry. It's all *déjà vu*—you always seem to have heard it somewhere before. And because of this we are now paying much more attention to rhythm, and especially to polyrhythm. And the melody is to be found again in the rhythm of the bass and the drums . . . we are three orchestras in one—an African, an occidental and an oriental". It is not just the bass that has liberated itself from its former sole function of providing rhythm and harmonic support for the improvisations of the melody instruments. The drums too are going through a similar development. Especially since **Elvin Jones** (1927–) and **Tony Williams** appeared on the scene, the beat, as the real rhythmic and metrical foundation of the musical happening, is being played and varied in more and more complex forms. At the same time the percussion instruments play an increasingly important part in the production of melody. The drumming of **Tony Williams**, **Billy Cobham** or **Alphonze Mouzon** sometimes sounds like a complete percussion orchestra with a powerful, broad tone colour that is no longer just "horizontal" but can shift in pitch too.

To these enhanced capabilities of the conventional drum must be added on the one hand the numerous percussion instruments with which South American music in particular is so well provided, and on the other the influence of various exotic musical cultures. Among those who come from South America are **Airto Moreira** and **Dom Um Romao**. It is thanks mainly to Airto, an outstanding percussion player, and the way he made his name with Miles Davis and later with Chick Corea too, that so many "electric" bands try to make their sound more rich and varied with the many rhythm instruments of South American origin. Dom Um Romao is a member of the group *Weather Report,* where Airto too played for a short time.

The change from Free Jazz is particularly marked in the case of rhythm and is characterized by the way in which most people have again come to like their metres regularly beaten out. People are playing again these days in three/four or four/four time, and much more frequently than ever in the past in "bent" metres like 11/8, 15/8 and so on. Fantasy knows no bounds, and the effect is at once enigmatic and delightful. This beating out of the time, which is required above all in the unbalanced metres, makes heavy calls on emotional energy, concentration and discipline. Behind it, there seems to be often something like a passionate yearning or at least a strong desire to repeat the shared experience of the beat within the group every second. But in many respects the new jazz is an answer to Free Jazz. It takes Free Jazz trends further; it circumscribes and occasionally redefines Free Jazz phenomena. Further, the jazz of the seventies is turning back to material which Free Jazz rejected and which has to some extent been used in other developments of style running parallel to Free Jazz. Over and above all this there is something like a generally accepted "recognition theory" of New Jazz, a basic tenet of all who represent it—namely its eclectic character.

In 1973 the pianist **Keith Jarrett** (1945–) brought out with the Munich record company ECM a cassette embracing three LPs under the title *Solo Concerts Bremen/Lausanne.* This recording characterized—one might almost say exemplified—this key aspect of the jazz of recent years. The Free Jazz musicians wanted to play themselves free and yet found themselves cramped again by new constraints. In New Jazz "free will" means having really free and available at your fingertips everything that the jazz musician sees as important and necessary for his playing. Categories are no more—one plays over and beyond them. Keith Jarrett and other protagonists of this new "free will by eclecticism" have shown a preference for solo concerts. Pianists, guitarists and indeed even trombonists like **Albert Mangelsdorff,** bassists and violinists play unaccompanied. Many of them love the inwardly intensified atmosphere of the unaccompanied solos, to give full rein to the flow of their ideas, and to play themselves really free in a monologue which becomes a dialogue of the musician with himself. In Jarrett's long piano improvisations echos of Schumann, Chopin, Debussy and Schubert are directly and meaningfully linked with ecstatic blues

Keith Jarrett

and gospel *motifs*. And yet his music is no dilettante or potpourri-like stringing together of musical quotations. Because *he* plays this music, because he improvises on it in a single creative process, it is *his* music, unrepeatable in the conditions that gave birth to it and in its essence. Keith Jarrett writes on this topic: "The importance [of these recordings] for me is the truth in them. An artist spontaneously creates something that is defined by the atmosphere, the public, the place (in terms both of space and of geographical location) and the instrument. All these things are consciously shaped and worked on by the artist as he plays, so that here more than anywhere else success or failure belong wholly to the artist. The artist is responsible every

170

second... for a group this does not apply to the same extent, nor should it. To begin with each player is responsible to the others and therefore the circle is not quite closed on itself, not quite pure. No one knows *exactly* whose mistake or responsibility, failure or success has a critical effect in each case. This lies in the nature of a group and the associated relationships. The link with the public is less strong because one is in close communion with the rest of the group". Jazz was always eclectic, but now eclecticism has become "style". Thus jazz-rock synthesis—a term which surely covers a great deal of what is now being played—does not mean the synthesis of "two" musical trends. "Jazz" and "rock" are part of a larger continuum; strictly speaking both are simply terms for particular forms of manifestation. "Eclecticism" spreads out from "jazz" and "rock" and likewise from "jazz-rock". Admittedly of course in this context "Electric Jazz" is also a category, but no-one who writes about music or any art can dispense with categorizing, even if both the writer and his subject object to the idea of categorisation.

Not only traditional jazz but modern jazz too are now more popular than ever before. Not the least important reason for this is that the spectrum of what jazz is was never so wide before. After the musically advanced rock of the late sixties came mainly to a sticky end in the clutches of commercialism, a large part of the rock public turned to New Jazz. In the second half of the sixties Free Jazz had become for many musicians—of whom **Chick Corea** is a text book specimen—something for insiders—and this despite the powerful urge of Free Jazz for communication. Corea and the many other representatives of the "reaction to Free Jazz" have proved in recent years that it is not only the public that has to change its attitude to the music, but *vice-versa*. The same goes for the music, maybe even to a much greater extent. New Jazz did not have to sacrifice any of its jazz quality to reach a wider public; it simply had to become something different, something broader, wider in scope—in a word something more eclectic. In 1974 **Herbie Hancock** received a golden disc in the USA for his LP *Head Hunters.* In the American music business this means sales reaching the million mark. As the American magazine *Rolling Stone* remarked, this was the first time that "an album of advanced musical improvisation" made the Top Ten and "1974 became the year of jazz rock". In that year **Miles Davis**, **John McLaughlin**, **Chick Corea**, **Herbie Hancock** and Weather Report found a forum matching their music—music in which the directness, expressiveness and extrovert character of the best moments of rock were truly integrated with the best qualities of jazz.

Joachim-Ernst Berendt

Epilogue

Glosses on a Philosophy of Jazz

Jazz, as we said at the beginning of this book and have seen throughout it, is many things at once and different things for different people. Many interpretations of jazz are contradictory; indeed they even seem mutually exclusive—and yet each one of them is valid and effective for the person who himself hears it and lives it. As I see it, jazz more than any other art belongs in a world of "both-and", of "not only-but also"; it is thus opposed to the world of the "either-or".

The world of the "either-or" is the white world of the nineteenth century whose ghosts still flit round in our heads, the world of causality and linearity in which every cause had its effect and could necessarily have only one effect, the world whose rationality has drained us and itself, transforming itself into a gigantic machine which runs on and on and on. Jazz came into the world and grew up as the thinking and artistic approach of the nineteenth century was found wanting and finally became scientifically untenable. It owes its start in life to the march music of New Orleans—the musical apotheosis of causality and linearity. But these origins vanished into thin air to reappear turned inside out—literally, for the accent was now on the weak beats instead of the strong ones. It was no longer "*left* two three four" but "one *and* two *and*", the accent elevating the word "and" from a mere additive or summing meaning to its original conjunctive one. Nonetheless the bar still began on "one". Stressing the "and", the weak link, gave the beat, which in European music has a dividing function, a uniting one. And that was exactly what jazz musicians from that point on were to do over and over again—to unite, in rhythm, in metre, in melody, in harmony, in form, in style . . . Of the thoughts that follow it is often pointed out that this indication is significant in itself, yet the questions of what it means in terms of artistic and cultural history remain unasked. The birth of jazz happened at a time in which fundamental and often radical innovations prevailed in almost every field—innovations which led into what we now know as the "image of the modern world". In physics—to start

173

there—statistics took the place of causality; Planck's quantum of action no longer had just one possible effect but many different, contradictory and unpredictable ones. The Heisenberg Uncertainty Principle and Einstein's Theory of Relativity made the world relative. At a stroke the same phenomenon could have different, contradictory causes; the same cause could bring about contradictory phenomena. Polarity was weakened; opposites were drawn together by their shared cause. In biology the direct linearity of Darwin's doctrine of inheritance was broken up. In philosophy—to take things that far, as we must—Hegel with his dialectic established a "thinking in opposites". It was discovered that "the dialectical approach could sometimes explain the contradictory behaviour of philosophical systems" (Max Bense). Soon every branch of the humanities and natural sciences had to have its dialectic—dialectic materialism, dialectic theology and "dialectic idealism", as Existentialism has been defined. Finally an admission, suppressed for centuries, broke through from Asia: "But there are countless truths, that is views of reality expressed in words, and each one of them is just as true as it is false" (Hermann Hesse in *Chinesische Legende*). It is not just the "both-and" that belongs to dialectic—and to jazz. To both of them there also belongs rhythm, the real and highest meaning of which is precisely the union of opposites. Hegel's doctrine of the swing of the pendulum between thesis and antithesis, leading to synthesis, which in turn becomes another thesis and gives rise to a further antithesis in endless progression, is first and foremost a rhythmic doctrine—in fact in the last resort it adds up to rhythm. Those who see how, consciously and unconsciously, this doctrine has put its stamp on the thinking of our century can even talk of the whole cutural life of these times in terms of a "discovery, a rediscovery of rhythm". This rediscovery is the key innovation of our times, irreconcilable as it is with the strict, as it were "ruled" arhythmic linearity that formerly held sway. In German idealism, the German classical period—the *Auf-Klärung*, the Reformation—for centuries rhythm was suppressed.

Now it broke out. Spengler's philosophy of history—his concept of the rhythmic succession of cultures and the rhythmic development of each individual culture—is just as rhythmic in nature as that of his opposite number Arnold Toynbee, who took the doctrine further and for whom history progresses in the interplay of challenge and response. Rhythm becomes the motive force of history. Musicologists, notably Rudi Blesh, and specialists in the ethnology of music such as Ernest Borneman have identified the essence of jazz as "call and response"—call and response developed from forms of African and black American spiritual music-making in which the question of the priest . . . of the lead singer, of the lead dancer, of the medicine man . . . is followed by the response of the congregation . . . , of the audience, of the community. Bergson—surprisingly for up till then such thoughts belonged to Africa or Asia rather than Europe—spoke of "rhythm as an element of the living". The principle of symmetry that governs life in all its forms, the mirror-image form of the leaf or of the body—all this he saw as rhythm. In a flash they came crowding round—bio-rhythmics and psycho-rhythmics as independent branches of science, and the rest. People talked of the "rhythm of the earth" as a force governing our life and wellbeing, of "biological rhythm research", of "the full spectrum of human rhythm". In biology the "environment" brought rhythm into the linearity of the doctrine of inheritance. Rudolf Kassner wrote of "rhythm as an intellectual category" in literature. Arthur Köstler named rhythm, together with "realism" and "relevance", as an "experimental yardstick for the dominant tendencies in the novel".

Here I can only scratch the surface of all this. But it gives me all the more pleasure to do so when I am sending this book to the publishers who twenty five years ago brought out my first book—*Jazz—eine zeitkritische Studie* (Deutsche Verlags-Anstalt, Stuttgart 1950). This little volume is long since out of print; today much of it strikes one as out of date and green. But in it I treated the essence of what I have said above on dialectic and rhythm more thoroughly than I have since had the chance to do elsewhere. Those who write about jazz are writing

174

mainly for the followers of jazz. As I quickly learnt the hard way, the followers of jazz take no great interest in anything that extends beyond their own field. Only today, a quarter of a century later, when we can stand back a little from everything that we were directly concerned with at that time and that had to be worked through after the persecution of jazz by the Nazis—only today does the need more and more often arise to take a peep over the boundary wall with which the followers of jazz have literally shut off their music from all surrounding phenomena and to break down the isolation which they have imposed not only on themselves but on their music. In coming back to the publishers of the *Zeitkritische Studie*, may I also return to what I wrote in 1950: "It is a 'thinking in rhythm' that characterizes the thinking of our time and that does not leave untouched even those who basically think arhythmically ... It is thus understandable that even musicology is increasingly making rhythm a valid criterion. The fact that there is talk of 'atrophy of rhythm' in the same breath as 'the music of the white races'; that 'at the end of all abstract-orientated, multi-part music based on accord ... lies the hidden goal of the arhythmic flow of melodies and harmonies'; that finally people come to speak of the completely opposite nature of 'two concepts of music of which one emphasizes rhythm, the other melody and harmony' (H.H. Stuckenschmidt)—all that would have been unthinkable as late as the turn of

the century ... thoughts like this have ... a physical and mechanical momentum. Physics is like a holograph, projecting its images on every imaginable plane. The physicist has long since known—just to stand back and say it out loud for once—that things are "made of rhythm". In quantum mechanics matter is nothing other than vibration, and energy nothing other than a certain concentration of vibration. If there is anything left in the theory of quantum mechanics that is 'comprehensible' or 'imaginable'—if there is a single word that can be visualized, it is the word 'vibration'. And here the word 'vibration' is simply a rather more precise physical term for 'rhythm'. If modern physics has it that my pencil is 'vibration', then it is 'rhythm'.

"But it is not just physical and atomic processes that have to be understood in terms of rhythm if they are to be understood at all. The same is true of every technological process ... rhythm lies ... not only in the process, but way back in the origin, in the very metaphysics of engineering. It is inherent in the 'relativity' of engineering, as Ortega y Gasset put it in his *Betrachtungen über die Technik*, (Reflections on Technology)—perhaps the finest work ever written about technology. One aspect of these thoughts could be seen as an 'environmental theory of engineering' by analogy with the environmental theory of biology created by Jakob von Uexküll. Here technology becomes a function of the variable human life plan.

What was formerly said about biology now becomes valid for technology—and in a still more radical sense, so that 'to be an engineer, it is not enough to be an engineer' and 'mankind, technology, wellbeing ... are in the last resort synonymous'. In all these thoughts rhythm appears in the same role as the fire of Heraclitus or the water of Thales—as a basis, a point of departure, a basic material, a driving force not just of technical procedures but of the technical mind too; and not just of the technical mind but of the human mind; and not just of the mind but of the whole being.

"All this is reflected with extraordinary fidelity in jazz too ... in physics material dissolves in rhythm; in jazz music dissolves in rhythm. In jazz melody, harmony, form and style are blurred in the oscillations of 'uncertainty'; in physics radiation oscillates with corpuscle, space with time, absolutism with relativity, speed with acceleration ...

"It becomes increasingly clear—and not just in the context of these thoughts but in the broader one of musical development—that the question about the explicit meaning of jazz music is identical with the other question about the explicit meaning of rhythm. Rudolf Kassner, who pondered much on these things, once said that it was a property of rhythm 'that, so to speak, something answers you at the other end and comes to meet you ...' He contrasted this with tempo where 'nothing comes to meet you and instead you are always having to chase or catch up with something. And that makes a very big difference'. Tempo belongs in the world of the straight line, of progress, of development—the world in which things continuously move apart and contrasts become sharper. Rhythm on the other hand has the dialectic art of bridging, balancing and resolving contradictions.

". . . Thus at the heart of rhythm lies the need to relate. It is therefore natural that rhythm wherever it appears—in music, the visual arts, architecture or poetry—comes as a symbol of union, of tolerance and of the possibility for opposite opinions to coexist. Hostility towards rhythm—and here perhaps lies the real, existential nub of the hostility to jazz to be found in almost all dictatorships of right and left alike . . .—hostility towards rhythm thus nearly always runs in harness with a deep-rooted secret hatred of those who think differently. One might think of this hostility as the 'artistic sensibility of the dictator'—as the artistic sensibility of the man who is incapable of bearing with the answer of those who think differently . . ."

Enough of these quotations from 1950, all of which are plausible rather than profound. What was then said with reference to Ortega and Kassner, to Hesse and von Uexküll, to Bergson and Köstler adds up to experiences since gone through by thousands of musicians and millions of young people without any intellectual training.

Dialectic, rhythm between thesis and antithesis, swing, every kind of "both and" imply ambiguity. "Uncertainty" in music matches that of physics, always in the sense of the Heisenberg Principle. In physics as in art a point is defined by coordinates. But the Uncertainty Principle states that the more sharply I fix one coordinate in my gaze, the less sharp the other becomes. This is the real reason for the contemporary aporia in general and for the aporia of writing about jazz and its reception in particular. It is also the reason for the problems that "jazz people" have amongst themselves—jazz critics most of all, but also everyone who loves jazz and is concerned with it without himself being a practising musician. Where breadth and tolerance are not part of the approach to life—as they are with most musicians—the "uncertainty" that calls for breadth and tolerance produces only still greater fanaticism, still more relentless bigotry. An attempt should be made to carry over what we have tried to bring out about rhythm to the other characteristic elements of jazz too. The first question to be asked then is whether there is not a common element that unites the three main characteristics of jazz—and the "umbrella" element. The reader will recall that the attempted definition reproduced in the early pages of this book talks of swing, improvisation and tone colour as the key characteristics of jazz, each of them related of course to certain procedures, techniques, styles and historical developments in jazz.

To take swing first, it creates just not intensity but also a certain form of rhythmic spontaneity. This stems from the completely personal, irreproducible shifts of rhythmic accents; from the way the accents lie exactly where they would not be expected to lie in conventional music; and hence from the tension that arises between these "queue-jumping" new accents and the conventional metre. In the extreme—and I am using this example simply to highlight the situation by *reductio ad absurdum*—the solos of the great jazz drummers—of Max Roach for instance or now of Billy Cobham—cannot be copied. At any rate no-one has ever copied them—and if anyone tried the result would be rigid, dead and mechanical.

Second, tone colour, sound. This creates intensity and spontaneity from the way in which each individual player brings his personal sound into the music without reference to tonal traditions—notably the tone standards of concert music. This personalized and individualized sound can only be convincing if the player pushes himself in his music to the limit of his physical, spiritual and emotional powers—if he transforms into musical sound his most intimate and personal experiences. That is the real reason why sound is so important for jazz, and for many of its bi-products and offshoots—the player makes his instrument the voice of his innermost feelings and experiences. That way he has no ear and no feel for traditional standards of sound and the way, as we find in conventional concert music, that these put their stamp on almost everything and can only be varied at a pinch. What a jazz musician has to say fills him so completely that it breaks out from the conventions—indeed it is only beyond the conventions that the message can be musically articulated. Where this is not so it is not worth the jazz musician's while to try to articulate it—anyone else could do it just as well.

Third then improvisation, which creates intensity and spontaneity by making the path from player to hearer shorter and more direct than it is in our European music. For this path no longer leads through scoring and the work of a composer who may have lived centuries ago and about the right interpretation of whom musicologists squabble; it runs direct from the improvising musician to his audience. Classical music is unthinkable without an "interpreter"; he interprets for the ear of the listener what the composer intended. Jazz music by contrast may be made meaningless by interpreters. For there is nothing to interpret here. A jazz musician plays his own music, and this is what "jazz improvisation" (which is very rarely free, unconstrained, careless extemporizing) is really about. Even when his improvisation is based on someone else's theme, he is, to the extent that he is improvising, his own composer. Just as he does with the sound, he translates into music, directly and by the shortest route, his own experience, thoughts and feelings.

Thus intensity and spontaneity are umbrella concepts for almost everything that happens in jazz. Both are essentially modern concepts, which have only established themselves in the human consciousness since the turn of the century and have steadily gained in importance since then. Again, in the twentieth century and in complete contrast to earlier times, artists in other fields too are coming to depend more and more on intensity and spontaniety. But there is no modern art—sport and games apart, probably no aspect of modern life—in which intensity and spontaneity are as important as they are in jazz. Of the two spontaneity is the more fertile from the philosophical point of view. This has taken its place in philosophy since the time of Kant—characteristically very little up to then. Kant set spontaneity up as the opposite of "receptivity". It is interesting to realize—although we can scarcely appreciate it fully today—that in Kant's time spontaneity and receptivity (the ability of quiet reception and contemplative absorption) must really have been opposites. Through the nineteenth century the concept of spontaneity continuously broadened so that today—and here we use jazz only as an example—"receptivity" and "capacity for absorption" are also comprehended within spontaneity (in jazz in the case of John Coltrane, for instance).

"Spontaneous" comes from the dog Latin *spontaneus,* meaning "full of initiative, independent, sudden, surprising" (the Latin word "sponte" means voluntarily!). Almost all the philosophical reference works and dictionaries which I have been able to consult relate spontaneity to the problem of freewill—the 1973 edition of the Brockhaus Encyclopedia, for instance: "In philosophy the position adopted with regard to the problem of freewill is decided by the reply to the question whether and to what extent man is capable of spontaneous actions." Herder's *Neues Lexikon der Pädagogik* (1971) sees a contrast between spontaneity and authority. The spontaneous man sets himself against everything authoritarian and is for his part unauthoritarian.

The whole discussion over the problem of spontaneity only really got under way and began to bear fruit around the turn of the century—at the same time, as already mentioned, in which spontaneity began to play a part in art—and most of all in jazz. It is here that the contrasts lie—the mediaeval artist created from a "receptive" attitude, the jazz musician creates from a spontaneous one. (It goes without saying here, as I said above, that receptivity is to be found in jazz, even in the most recent jazz; and on the other side of the coin that we cannot conceive of the mediaeval artist without spontaneous reactions. But that is in the very nature of their presentation—that it cannot be achieved without relativities, without an element of statistics, without the establishment of foci, all of which have to be related. There was *more* receptivity among artists of earlier epochs, and there is *more* spontaneity among artists of today—and there is

177

most spontaneity of all in jazz).

Spontaneity implies directness, vitality, playfulness, impulsiveness—and with them irrationality, the abandonment of causality and its replacement by statistics—(just as is the case with modern physics, where statistics have replaced causality to an ever greater extent). These are all phenomena and modes of behaviour which are of the highest importance in the understanding of the modern world, scientifically, politically, socially and psychologically alike. Nowhere, in no other art are all these phenomena and modes of behaviour to be found so highly concentrated as they are in jazz.

One striking thing is the hostility to spontaneity of Marxist philosophy—or at least of the variants of it which have degenerated into the dogmatic ideology of government, art and life of the socialist states. Lenin said: "Communists have no room for spontaneity ... communists teach the masses organized, purposeful, wholehearted, timely, mature action ..." And Lenin again: "Their task is a struggle against spontaneity". The Marxist-Leninist dictionary of philosophy published in the German Democratic Republic defines spontaneity as: "Clumsy, ill-organized and purposeless behaviour, which can have harmful effects and can be exploited by reactionary and counter-revolutionary forces". Spontaneity is associated there with "the dependence on nature and limitations of social conditions in earlier periods ... the class division into exploiter and exploited ..."

It is with a certain ironic amusement that we read of this heresy-hunt against spontaneity as an elementary behaviour pattern without which freedom appears to be unthinkable. Once again we find—as in so many cultural and artistic statements coming from the USSR and its sphere of influence or indeed in their whole style of life—an astonishing conservatism and retrogressiveness. Men may have thought that way (at least about the abstract assessment of spontaneity) in the Middle Ages, but today ... ?

Perhaps we have here another reason for the unwavering hostility to jazz in the USSR and many countries that lie in its power. Jazz as a music of spontaneous, free, personal, impulsive, surprising, playful decisions—which simply doesn't fit into their kind of society, or at least not when a noteworthy number of young people are identifying with it, and this means identification with freedom and individualism. "Where spontaneity is, the subjective is; and where the subjective is there is spontaneity". This sentence, according to Francke's *Lexikon der Pädagogik* "constitutes an inseparable in recent thought". Here the subjective stands in contrast to "the world of things, objects and everything mechanical"; it is broadly defined as: "ego, soul (also spirit, reason), person, monad, individuum ..."

For centuries—basically throughout the heyday of occidental art and philosophy, and by no means least under Christian influence—spontaneity was to some extent or other suspect. Spontaneous, personal actions, spontaneous decisions could—and of course had to—be accepted, but the chance that they would lead to erroneous actions and wrong decisions—in Christian terms to "sin", to inadequate suppression of the personal and the physical—was considered to be disproportionately large. Thus in the last resort it was considered better, safer and more reliable to dispense with spontaneity completely, or at least as far as possible. The notion that, by contrast, quick, direct spontaneous reaction may stem from natural harmony and virtue is, it is true, difficult to justify in rational terms but maybe all the pithier and more convincing for that. It is a discovery that only started to come to light around the turn of the nineteenth and twentieth centuries.

The picture fills out when we see that our second umbrella concept too—intensity—has been subject to the same kind of intensification as spontaneity. In the few lines that I could find on the word "Intension" (*"Intensität"* was unheard of then) in the 1866 edition of the *Allgemeine deutsche Real-Enzyklopädie für die gebildeten Stände* (General German Practical Encyclopedia for the Educated Classes), there is the fine sentence: "We call a life intensive when it is assessed not by the passing of time but by its inward effectiveness and its content". A century later there is an almost inescapable abundance of definitions of intensity in physics, radiation theory, spectral analysis, biology, farming, psychology and so on, to the point where an appropriate work of reference recommends that further extension of the word "intensity" should be avoided, "so as not further to overload the meaning of this word". All that has remained is the meaning of the time dimension, always in the sense of a conquest of time, the attainment of independence of time and a collapse of space in time. Now however this is related to theoretical physics and no longer linked to the "inward effectiveness" of an intensive life but to precise formulae derived from the Relativity Theory.

For intensity is not just—as they thought in the last century—a "plus" in power or effectiveness. The "plus" itself creates a new quality. "Intensification of colour changes the tone; amplification of sound changes the role of the partial; indole smells of flowers when highly diluted, of faeces when concentrated . . ." (Henning, *Psychology of the present*). But increases in intensity are not just quantitative increases, whether it be in physics, psychology, music or jazz. They create a new dimension, a new and hitherto unknown quality. Thus they are in the true sense positive and creative in the context of the energy concepts of theoretical physics and artistic or psychological processes alike.

Jean Gebser, the important Swiss philosopher, whose work *Ursprung und Gegenwalt* (Origin and Present) on the understanding of the radical change of consciousness that mankind is now going through is still not receiving the attention it has long deserved, points out: "Intensities cannot be measured, unless that is we confuse them with thrust, pressure or tension. Where we measure them we disperse them . . ." Gebser sees a contradiction between the time element "intensity" and the extended quality of space. "Extensity" expands space, intensity fills time. For Gebser time, understood as intensity, must be "the main theme of the new mutation" which mankind must undergo if it is not to succumb to its problems which are no longer capable of rational solution. "The breakthrough of time into our consciousness—this event is the great and unique theme of the world in our time". (This, and other quotations from Gebser, come from *Ursprung und Gegenwalt*).

For men of this century there has opened in one sweep a whole spectrum of possible manifestations of time—no more just as conventional "clock time", but as "natural time, cosmic time or star time; as biological duration, rhythm, metre; as mutation, discontinuity, relativity; as vital dynamics, psychic energy . . . as a unit of past, present and future; as a creative force, an imaginative force, as work, even as motor activity . . ." For this abundance of possible times "the three dimensional world of our father's conceptualization had no sensorium. For them, in the hard-frozen world of space which they inhabited, the world of time was a disruptive factor which could be suppressed by ignoring it or falsely converting it into a spatial component . . . Werner Gent, a leading connoisseur of the theories and philosophies of that epoch, could say of it that it had downgraded time and degraded it to a mere mathematical quantity".

As early as the end of the last century (1889) Bergson was complaining about "the confusion of duration with extent, of succession with simultaneity, of quality with quantity". That was why he devoted to the concepts of "intensity" and "duration" the first two chapters of his book *Time and Free Will*.

I have pointed out again and again, not just in the *Zeitkritische Studie* mentioned above but in other publications too (*The Jazz Book* and *Variationen über Jazz*) that jazz more than any other art is an art in time. Swing, the distinguishing rhythmic principle of jazz, is only understandable as a primary temporal phenomenon—as the superimposition of two different levels of time—and hence of two levels of existence: one European and rational, one African and magical—time counted and time lived. This is the reason for the substantial inadequacy of all attempts to explain swing in terms of musicology—an inadequacy admitted by many music experts. Most musicologists who interest themselves in jazz are either ignorant of any form of time philosophy such as Rudolf Kassner, Bergson or, within music itself, Stravinsky developed. Indeed it seems to them needless and inappropriate—a strange and paradoxical attitude in the light of the overwhelming importance that almost all manifestations of time have for music, as the "art in time". The temporal character of things musical culminates in jazz.

And not just in swing. Improvization too is a primary temporal phenomenon to the extent that it liberates music from its dependence on spatial components such as notation, scoring or repeatability. Most of all intensity is also a time dimension—intensity which has been inherent in jazz from the start and has steadily mounted as it developed. Swing, jazz sound, jazz phrasing, jazz improvization—as we have said all of these can be summed up as facets of intensity. They form the drive that keeps the wheels of jazz history rolling, from style to style, from mode of execution to mode of execution. The whole history of jazz can be written under this heading—the struggle for ever greater intensity broken only by a few years of "coolness" and resignation now and then after which the assault on the next higher level of intensity is resumed all the more energetically.

I highlighted the temporal character of swing and improvization way back in the fifties before anyone had any idea of the tremendous breakthrough in intensity that the Free Jazz of the sixties brought with it or of the significance of intensity as a component of time. Of course it took Gebser's understanding of intensity to flesh out this picture: "An intensity cannot make itself evident by merely thinking, because the only language thinking knows is that of spatial succession ... as long as we go on thinking that we can master intensities and through them time by forcing them into a system, all we shall achieve is the breakup of these systems".

And that is just what the "intensive" assault of Free Jazz did. All the systems under which jazz had "functioned" until then came apart. And that is by and large just what will happen in every aspect of our thought and lives—outside music, jazz and art too—as long as we go on misunderstanding intensity and time and thinking of the former just as a "plus" and the latter mainly in the terms of theoretical physics as a fourth dimension of space or, to simplify still further, just as "clock time". All the systems will come apart, indeed they are already splitting at the seams. That is what is happening today.

For Gebser it is a misunderstanding—let us say a hippie-like, pardonable inexactitude—to talk of "extension of consciousness" as the new dimension of consciousness that mankind needs today. It is not extension of consciousness that we need but, according to Gebser "intensification of consciousness". But here again this intensification is not simply a stepping up of the old consciousness; this has failed and we should only make its failure still more terrible if we intensified it. What is needed is a new "quality"—something different, new, that cannot yet be put into words.

The desperation with which the Free Jazz men battled for ever greater intensity; the desperation which with men like Coltrane and Albert Ayler ended in depression in face of their most recent failure to reach the next, so far unattainable "intensity of consciousness"—and despite this the repeated, foolhardy storming of still higher levels of intensity; the bursting apart like a bubble of jazz as it had been up till then; the resigned slide into a routine intensity that in the last resort is no more than "accomplished" and has now become the standard practice of innumerable jazz musicians. From the background we have set it against, all this gains a significant and illuminating importance going far beyond "fan-like" enthusiasm for the music as such. (Nonetheless this "fan-like" enthusiasm does at least bring about an unconscious grasping of the situation, for which we must be grateful). Only after the dismantling of existing systems could there evolve a process connoisseurs of Free Jazz call "the discovery of beauty in chaos", in other words the taming and ultimate mastery by beauty of the chaos with which mankind will have to live for a time and which thus, just like former "worlds" in which man has lived, needs to be tamed and overpowered by art and the artist. Gebser again: "We shall then be able to perceive a new sound, a new shape, a new vision where we now seem to hear nothing but shrillness and dissonance". For those who have lived with Free Jazz for better or for worse this has already happened—they have been able to perceive a new sound, a new shape, a new vision.

It is a characteristic of the artistic approach and artistic experience of European man to test the soundness of his artistic experiences and developments against the philosophical and humane implications inherent in them. This is an inseparable part of the art of self-discovery and self-realization that forms an important element—for the Greeks the most important—in artistic activity and experience. This "sounding" has taken place in every field of modern art too—with the distinguishing exception of jazz. Why then this exception? If, as stands out from the pages of this book, jazz occupies a key position in the artistic and intellectual development of our century, this omission should be remedied. It should be remedied not simply in an "epilogue" at the end of a book devoted to the musical and stylistic developments of this music, but as comprehensively and thoroughly as has been done in other fields of modern art. The striking of a spark, a little prod—that and no more is the intention of these glosses.

Bibliography

It should be noted that competent treatments of many aspects of jazz do not yet exist, and this is especially true of studies of outstanding individual musicians; also, there are no fully up-to-date general discographies.

I Reference Works

a) General
John Chilton: *Who's Who of Jazz* (London, 1970)
Leonard Feather: *Encyclopaedia of Jazz in the 70s* (New York, 1976)

b) Discographies
B.A.L. Rust: *Jazz Records 1897–1931* (Hatch End, Middlesex, 1961)
B.A.L. Rust: *Jazz Records 1932–42* (Hatch End, Middlesex, 1965)
Jorgen Jepsen: *Jazz Records 1942–62* Vols. 1–8 (Holte, Denmark, 1966–7)
Walter Bruyninckx: *50 years of Recorded Jazz 1917–67* (Mechelen, Belgium, 1969)

c) Bibliographies
Robert Reisner: *Literature of Jazz* (New York, 1954; rev. 2/1959)
Carl Mecklenburg: *International Jazz Bibliography 1919–69* (Baden-Baden, 1969)
Donald Kennington: *Literature of Jazz* (London, 1970)
Steven Winick: *Rhythm—an Annotated Bibliography 1900–70* (Metuchen, N.J., 1974)

II Historical and Sociological Studies

a) General Histories
Marshall Stearns: *Story of Jazz* (London, 1956)
Nat Shapiro & Nat Hentoff, eds.: *Hear Me Talking to You* (London, 1956)
Wilfrid Mellers: *Music in a New Found Land* (London, 1964)
Eileen Southern: *Music of Black Americans* (New York, 1971)
John Storm Roberts: *Black Music of Two Worlds* (London, 1973)
Joachim-Ernst Berendt: *The Jazz Book* (London, 1976)

b) Histories of Specific Styles, Periods and Regions
Leonard Feather: *Inside Bebop* (New York, 1949)
Paul Oliver: *Blues Fell This Morning* (London, 1960)
Samuel Charters & Len Kunstadt: *Jazz—a History of the New York Scene* (Garden City, N.Y., 1962)
Ira Gitler: *Jazz Masters of the 40s* (New York, 1966)
Henry Kmen: *Music of New Orleans 1791–1841* (Baton Rouge, La., 1967)
Paul Oliver: *Story of the Blues* (London, 1969)
Tony Russell: *Blacks, Whites and Blues* (London, 1970)
Ross Russell: *Jazz Style on Kansas City and the South West* (Berkeley, Calif., 1971; rev. 2/1973)
William Shafer & Johannes Riedel: *The Art of Ragtime* (Baton Rouge, La., 1973)

c) Sociological and Related Works
Nat Hentoff: *The Jazz Life* (London, 1962)
Neil Leonard: *Jazz and the White American* (London, 1964)
Robert Gold: *A Jazz Lexicon* (New York, 1964)
Paul Oliver: *Conversation with the Blues* (London, 1965)
Charles Keil: *Urban Blues* (Chicago, 1966)
Ralph Ellison: *Shadow and Act* (London, 1967)
Paul Oliver: *Screening the Blues* (London, 1968)

III Theory, Analysis, Criticism

Winthrop Sargeant: *Jazz Hot and Hybrid* (New York, 1938)
Ralph de Toledano, ed.: *Frontiers of Jazz* (New York, 1947)
Sidney Finkelstein: *Jazz—a People's Music* (New York, 1948)
André Hodeir: *Jazz—its Evolution and Essence* (London, 1956)
Raymond Horricks, ed.: *Jazzmen of Our Time* (London, 1959)
Nat Hentoff & A.J. McCarthy, eds.: *Jazz—New Perspectives* (London, 1960)
Leroy Ostransky: *Anatomy of Jazz* (Seattle, 1960)
Michael James: *Ten Modern Jazzmen* (London, 1960)
Benny Green: *The Reluctant Art* (London, 1962)
Richard Hadlock: *Jazz Masters of the 20s* (New York, 1965)
André Hodeir: *Toward Jazz* (London, 1965)
A.J. McCarthy, ed.: *Jazz on Record 1917–67* (London, 1968)
Gunther Schuller: *Early Jazz* (New York, 1968)
André Hodeir: *The Worlds of Jazz* (New York, 1972)
Max Harrison: *Modern Jazz—the Essential Records 1945–70* (London 1975)
Max Harrison: *A Jazz Retrospect* (Newton Abbot, Devon, 1976)

IV Studies on (or by) Individual Jazzmen

Louis Armstrong: *Satchmo—My Life in New Orleans* (London, 1955)
Sidney Bechet: *Treat It Gentle* (London, 1960)
Richard Sudhalter: *Bix Beiderbecke* (London, 1974)
Michael James: *Miles Davis* (London, 1961)
Larry Gara: *The Baby Dodds Story* (Los Angeles, 1959)
Vladimir Simosko: *Eric Dolphy* (Washington, 1974)
Michael James: *Dizzy Gillespie* (London, 1959)
Walter Allen: *Hendersoniana* [Fletcher Henderson] (Highland Park, N.J., 1973)
Billie Holiday: *Lady Sings the Blues* (London, 1958)
Mezz Mezzrow: *Really the Blues* (London, 1947)
Alan Lomax: *Mister Jelly Roll* [Morton] (London, 1952)
Walter Allen: *King Oliver* (London, 1957)
H.O. Brun: *The Story of the Original Dixieland Jazz Band* (London, 1961)
Max Harrison: *Charlie Parker* (London, 1960)

Ross Russell: *Bird Lives!* [Charlie Parker] (London, 1973)
Max Abrams: *The Book of Django* [Reinhardt] (Los Angeles, 1973)
Artie Shaw: *The Trouble with Cinderella* (London, 1955)
Paul Oliver: *Bessie Smith* (London, 1959)
H.J. Walters: *Jack Teagarden* (Stanhope, N.J., 1960)
Charles Fox: *Fats Waller* (London, 1960)

V Periodicals

At the time of publication, the only current periodical in English which can be recommended is *The Journal of Jazz Studies* (c/o Transaction Inc., Rutgers University, New Brunswick, N.J. 08903, U.S.A.). However, the annual *Popular Music Periodicals Index* and *Index to Popular Music Record Reviews* (both published by the Scarecrow Press, P.O. Box No. 656, Metuchen, New Jersey 08840, U.S.A.) will be found useful for tracing the items of interest which occasionally appear in the many fan magazines.

Appendices

Discography and Photos

This is not a true discography, for such would give the recording dates and locations and full personnels of every track of all the LPs listed below. That in itself would occupy a book larger than the present volume, and most of the information is already obtainable elsewhere (see section Ib of the Bibliography). What follows is, instead, a minimal listing of recommended recordings, carefully selected to illustrate all phases of jazz up to the present.

By no means all of these items are currently available, for jazz LPs pass in and out of the catalogue with the speed of pop discs. They have all been obtainable at one time or another though, and apart from occasionally being (briefly) reissued, they appear on the shelves and in the mailing lists of specialist dealers in jazz records. They are worth searching, and waiting, for.

Although every effort has been made to ensure that all information is correct, neither the publishers nor the authors can accept responsibility for any errors in record numbers which may affect purchases.

I Blues and related forms

Anthologies

   Afro-American Songs Library of Congress L52
   Alabama Country 1927–32 Origin OJL14

All-Star Blues Polydor 423243
American Folk Music: Religious Folkways FA2952
American Folk Music: Social Folkways FP253
American Skiffle Bands Folkways FA2610
Angola Prison Spirituals 77 LA12/13
Atlanta Blues RBF RBF15
Backgrounds of Jazz Victor X-Vault LX3009
Back to the Country Bounty BY2205
Bad Luck and Trouble Arhoolie F1018
Barrelhouse Style Piano Swaggie JCS33747
Been Here and Gone Folkways FA2659
Blues and All That Jazz Decca DL9230
Blues and Trouble Arhoolie FS1011/2 (2 LPs)
Blues Fell This Morning Philips BBL7369
Blues from Maxwell Street Heritage 1004
Blues in the Mississippi Night Nixa NJL8
Blues People Highway H102
Blues We Taught Your Mother Prestige-Bluesville BLP1052
Boogie Woogie Riverside RLP12–114
California Blues Polydor 423242
Can't Keep From Crying Bounty BY6035
Carolina Blues Arhoolie R2005
Chicago Blues: the Early '50s Blues Classics BC8
Chicago Rhythm and Blues Sounds Storyville SLP176
Conversation with the Blues Decca LK4664

Country Blues RBF RBF1
Country Girls 1927–35 Origin OJL6
Country Spirituals Storyville SLP135
Decades of the Blues: 1950s Vols. 1 and 2 Highway H100/1 (2 LPs)
Deep South: Sacred and Sinful Prestige INT25005
Detroit Blues: the Early '50s Blues Classics BC12
Dixieland Jug Blowers Swaggie JCS33711
Eastern and Gulf Coast States Postwar Blues PWB3
Eastern Shores Prestige INT25008
Georgia Blues 1926–31 Roots RL309
Georgia Sea Islands Vols. 1 and 2 Prestige INT25001/2 (2 LPs)
Going to California Heritage HLP1003
Going Up the Country Decca LK4931
Gospel Song: an Introduction RBF RBF5
Great Blues Singers Riverside RLP12–121
Hammer and Nails Riverside RLP3501
Harlem Congregation Ducretet-Thompson TKL93119
Harmonicas, Washboards and Fiddles Roots RL311
Honky-Tonk Train Riverside RLP8806
I Have to Paint My Face Arhoolie F1005
In the Spirit Vols 1 and 2 Origin OJL12/13 (2 LPs)
Jackson Blues 1928–38 Yazoo L1007
Jug Bands RBF RBF6
Jump Kansas City Folkways FJ2810

Kings of the 12-String Guitar Piedmont 13159
Let Me Tell You About the Blues Blue Horizon LP2
Living with the Blues Realm RM209
Louisiana Country Yazoo L1004
Memphis Area 1927–32 Roots RL307
Memphis Jug Bands Collectors' Classics CC2
Mississippi Blues 1927–40 Origin OJL5
Mississippi Blues Roots RBF RBF14
Missouri/Tennessee Roots RL310
Modern Chicago Blues Bounty BY6025
Murderers' Home Nixa NJL11
Music from the South: Elder Songsters Vols. 1 and 2
Folkways FP655/6 (2 LPs)
Music of Alabama Vol. 2 Religious Folkways FP418
Negro Church Music London LTZ–K15214
Negro Folklore from Texas State Prisons Bounty
BY6012
Negro Prison Camp Worksongs Folkways FP475
Negro Religious Songs Library of Congress L10
Negro Spirituals Vogue LAE12033
Nothing But the Blues Fontana TFL5023
Old Time Religion Fontana 688520ZL
Out Came the Blues Ace of Hearts AH72
Party Blues Melodeon MLP7324
Piano Blues Rarities London AL3565
Pioneers of Boogie London AL3506
Postwar Blues: Detroit Postwar Blues PWB5
Primitive Piano Jazz Collector JGN1001
Prison Worksongs Louisiana Folklore LFS–A5
Rambling on My Mind Milestone MLP3002
Rare Blues of the 1920s Historical ASC5829–1/4 (4
LPs)
Rent Party Style Piano Swaggie JCS33746
Rhythm and Blues Pye GGL0280
Roots of the Blues London LTZ–K15211
Rural Blues Xtra 202
Screening the Blues CBS 63288
Sound of the Delta Testament T2209
Southside Chicago Blues Decca LK4748
Spiritual and Gospel Festival Fontana TL5243
St Louis Town 1927–32 Yazoo L1003
Story of the Blues 1928–68 Vol. 1 Columbia
G30008 (2 LPs)
Story of the Blues 1928–68 Vol. 2 CBS 66232 (2
LPs)
Ten Years in Memphis 1927–37 Yazoo L1002
Texas Country Music Roots RL312
They Sang the Blues Historical ASC5829–17
Treasury of Field Recordings Candid 8026/7 (2
LPs)
Tub, Jug and Washboard Bands Riverside
RLP8802

Uncloudy Day Fontana 688515ZL
Vintage Country Blues Vols. 1–3 Down D200/2 (3
LPs)
Washboards, Jugs and Kazoos RCA RD7893
White Spirituals London LTZ–K15212
Witness for the Lord Ace of Hearts AH142
Women of the Blues RCA RD7840
Texas Alexander: Texas Alexander Jazz Society
LP14
Kokomo Arnold: Bad Luck Blues Brunswick 87504
Barbeque Bob (Robert Hicks): Atlanta Blues RBF
RBF15
Scrapper Blackwell: Mr Scrapper's Blues Xtra 5011
Blind Blake (Arthur Phelps): Blues in Chicago
Riverside RLP8804
Bob Brookmeyer: The Blues Hot and Cool HMV
CLP1438
Bill Broonzy: Trouble in Mind Fontana 688206ZL
Rev Pearly Brown: Georgia Street Singer Folk-Lyric
FL108
Bumble Bee Slim (Amos Easton): Bumble Bee Slim
Fontana 467–182TE
Leroy Carr: Blues Before Sunrise CBS BPG62206
Peter Clayton: Doctor Clayton RCA RCX7177
Ida Cox: Sings the Blues London AL3517
Big Boy Crudup: Bluebird Blues RCA RD778B
Georgia Tom (Dorsey): Georgia Tom and His
Friends Riverside RLP8803
Sleepy John Estes: The Legend Delmark DL603
Blind Boy Fuller: Blind Boy Fuller Blues Classics
BC11
Jazz Gillum: You Got to Reap What You Sow RCA
INT1177
Smokey Hogg: Smokey Hogg Crown 5226
John Lee Hooker: John Lee Hooker Advent LP2801
Lightning Hopkins: Sings the Blues Realm RM128
Son House: The Legendary Son House CBS
BPG62604
Howling Wolf (Chester Burnett): Big City Blues
Ember EMB3370
Mississippi John Hurt: Folk Songs and Blues
Piedmont PLP13157
Mahalia Jackson: In the Upper Room Columbia
33SX1753
Blind Lemon Jefferson: Blind Lemon Jefferson Vol.
1 Roots RL301
Blind Willie Johnson: His Story Folkways F63585
Robert Johnson: King of the Delta Blues Singers
CBS BPG62456
Bishop Kelsey: Congregation of the Temple of God in
Christ Polydor 623201
B.B. King: Blues in My Heart Crown 5309

Leadbelly (Huddie Leadbetter): The Library of
Congress Recordings Elektra EKL301.3 (3 LPs)
Big Maceo (Merriweather): Big Maceo RCA 130246
Tommy McClennan: Tommy McClennan RCA
130274
Blind Willie McTell: The Early Years Yazoo L1005
Memphis Minnie (McCoy): Memphis Minnie Blues
Classics BC13
Memphis Slim (Peter Chatman): Willie's Blues
Prestige-Bluesville BVLP1003
Muddy Waters (McKinley Morganfield): Down on
Stovalls' Plantation Bounty BY6031
Rev Louis Overstreet: An Evening Arhoolie F1014
Charley Patton: The Country Blues Origin OJL1
Ma Rainey: Ma Rainey Vol. 1 London AL3502
    Ma Rainey Vol. 2 London AL3538
    Ma Rainey Vol. 3 London AL3558
    Gertrude Ma Rainey Riverside RLP8807
    Ma Rainey Riverside RLP12–108
    Ma Rainey Ristic LP19
    The Immortal Ma Rainey Milestone MLP2001
Jimmy Rushing: Listen to the Blues Fontana
FJL405
Bessie Smith: The World's Greatest Blues Singer
Columbia GP33 (2 LPs)
    Any Woman's Blues Columbia G30126 (2 LPs)
    The Empress Columbia G30818 (2 LPs)
    Empty Bed Blues Columbia G30450 (2 LPs)
    Nobody's Blues But Mine Columbia G31093 (2
LPs)
Clara Smith: Clara Smith Vol. 1 VJM VLP15
    Clara Smith Vol. 2 VJM VLP16
    Clara Smith Vol. 3 VJM VLP17
Otis Spann: Otis Spann is the Blues Candid
CJM8001
Victoria Spivey: Victoria Spivey Fontana 17264
Roosevelt Sykes: Mr Sykes's Blues Riverside
RLP8819
Tampa Red (Hudson Whittaker): Don't Tampa with
the Blues Prestige-Bluesville BLP1030
Sonny Terry: Washboard Band Folkways FP6
Rosetta Tharpe: Sister Rosetta Tharpe Mercury
MPL6529
Joe Turner: Boss of the Blues Atlantic 590006
Clara Ward: Gospel Concert Roulette R25233
Peetie Wheatstraw (William Bunch): Peetie Wheat-
straw Blues Classics BC4
Bukka White: Sky Songs Fontana 688804ZL
Big Joe Williams: Blues on Highway 49 Esquire
32–191
Sonny Boy Williamson: Sonny Boy Williamson Blues
Classics BC3

Sonny Boy Williamson No. 2 (Rice Miller): *Down and Out Blues* Pye NPL28036
Jimmy Yancey: *Chicago Piano* Atlantic SD7229

II Ragtime

Anthologies
Black and White Ragtime Biograph BLP12047
Creative Ragtime Euphonic CSR1206
Cylinder Jazz Saydisc SDL112
Golden Age of Ragtime Riverside RLP12–110
Pianola Jazz Saydisc SDL117
Ragtime Piano Roll Vol. 1 London AL3515
Ragtime Piano Roll Vol. 2 London AL3523
Ragtime Piano Roll Vol. 3 London AL3542
Ragtime Piano Roll Vol. 4 London AL3563
Eubie Blake: *Wizard of Ragtime Piano* 20th-Century Fox 3003
Marches I Played on the Old Ragtime Piano 20th-Century Fox 3039
William Bolcom: *Heliotrope Bouquet* Nonesuch H71257
Brun Campbell/Dink Johnson: *The Professors Vols. 1 and 2* Euphonic ESR1201/2 (2 LPs)
Ann Charters: *A Joplin Bouquet* Sonet SNTF631
Scott Joplin: *Ragtime Pioneer* Riverside RLP8815
Scott Joplin/James Scott: *Ragtime Piano Rolls* Riverside RLP12–126
Joseph Lamb: *Rags* Folkways 3562
New Orleans Ragtime Orchestra: *A Ragtime Nightmare* Sonet SNTF632
Tony Parenti: *Ragtime* London LTZ–U15072
Ragtime Jubilee Jazzology J21
Joshua Rifkin: *Scott Joplin Rags Vol. 1* Nonesuch H71248
Scott Joplin Rags Vol. 2 Nonesuch H71264

III New Orleans Jazz

Anthology *The Sound of New Orleans 1917–47* Columbia C3L30 (3 LPs)
Emile Barnes: *Emile Barnes* American Music AM641
Louis Nelson Delisle: *Big Eye Louis Nelson Delisle* American Music AM646
Billie and Dédé Pierce: *Billie and Dédé Pierce* Storyville 670178
Lee Collins: *Jones-Collins Astoria Hot Eight* HMV 7EG8084
Louis Dumaine: *The Jazzola Eight* HMV 7EG8119
Irving Fazola: *New Orleans Express* EmArcy EJL1264

Halfway House Orchestra: *The Halfway House Orchestra* VJM VLP19
Kid Howard: *Kid Howard's Band* Icon LP8
Papa Laine: *Papa Laine's Children* Oriole MG20002
George Lewis: *George Lewis with Kid Shots Madison* American Music AM645
Sam Morgan: *Sam Morgan's Jazz Band* VJM VLP32
Jim Robinson: *New Orleans Band* Riverside RLP369
Thomas Valentine: *Sonnets from Algiers* Icon LP3
Wooden Joe (Nicholas): *New Orleans Band* American Music AM640
Young Tuxedo Brass Band: *New Orleans Today* London LTZ-K15234

IV Post-New Orleans Developments

Henry Allen: *Henry Red Allen* RCA LPV–556
Sidney Bechet: *Bechet Memorial* Fontana TFL5087
Blues in the Air RCA 430216
Bechet-Mezzrow Quintet Concert Hall KJ1257/8 (2 LPs)
Charlie Creath: *Jazz from St Louis* Parlophone PMC7157
Johnny Dodds: *New Orleans Bootblacks and Wanderers* Philips BBL7136
Johnny Dodds Vol. 1 London AL3505
Washboard Band HMV DLP1073
The Georgians: *Complete Recordings Vol. 1* VJM VLP12
Bunk Johnson: *Bunk Johnson's Band 1944* Storyville SLP128
Bunk Johnson Storyville SLP152
Bunk's Brass Band Dixie LP107
Bunk Johnson's Band 1945 Storyville SEP401
Freddie Keppard: *17 Rare Selections* Herwin 101
George Lewis: *New Orleans Stompers Vol. 1* Blue Note BST81205
The Climax Session Vogue LAE12005
Jelly Roll Morton: *The 1923–24 Piano Solos* Fountain FJ104
Rareties Rhapsody RHA6021
King of New Orleans Jazz Vol. 1 RCA RD27113
Hot Jazz RCA RD–7807
Stomps and Joys RCA LPV–508
King of New Orleans Jazz Vol. 2 RCA RD–27184
Mr Jelly Lord RCA RD–7914
Library of Congress Sessions Riverside RLP9001/12 (12 LPs)
New Orleans Memories Fontana TL–5261
New Orleans Rhythm Kings: *New Orleans Rhythm Kings* Milestone M47020 (2 LPs)

Albert Nicholas: *Albert's Blues* 77 LEU12/20
King Oliver: *Creole Jazz Band 1923* Riverside RLP8805
King Oliver's Jazz Band Parlophone PMC7032
Dixie Syncopators Vol. 1 Ace of Hearts AH34
Dixie Syncopators Vol. 2 Ace of Hearts AH91
King Oliver and His Orchestra RCA 430592
King Oliver's Orchestra 1929–30 RCA 10017
King Oliver in New York RCA LPV529
Original Dixieland Jazz Band: *Original Dixieland Jazz Band* RCA 730703/4 (2 LPs)
Kid Ory: *Tailgate* Vogue LAG12104

V Chicago Jazz

Anthologies *Chicago Jazz 1927–28* Odeon MOEQ27010
The Sound of Chicago 1923–40 Columbia C3L32 (3 LPs)
Lovie Austin: *Blues Serenaders* Fountain FJ105
Bix Beiderbecke: *Bix Beiderbecke and the Chicago Cornet Kings* Milestone M47019 (2 LPs)
Bix and His Gang Parlophone PMC1221
Bix and Tram 1927 Parlophone PMC7064
Bix and Tram 1928 Parlophone PMC7100
Bix and Tram 1929 Parlophone PMC7113
Jimmy Blythe: *South Side Chicago Jazz* London AL3529
Tommy Ladnier: *Blues and Stomps* London AL3524
Clarence Lofton: *A Lost Recording Date* London AL3531
Jimmy Noone: *Jazz at the Apex Club* Ace of Hearts AH84
Muggsy Spanier: *The Great Sixteen* RCA RD27132
Jack Teagarden: *Jack Teagarden* RCA RD7826
Clarence Williams: *Clarence Williams 1926–30* Fontana 682088TL

VI New York

Anthologies *Early Harlem Piano* London AL3540
Thesaurus of Classic Jazz Columbia C4L–18 (4 LPs)
Charleston Chasers: *Charleston Chasers 1925–28* VJM VLP26
Bunk Johnson: *Last Testament* Philips BBL7231
Charlie Johnson: *Charlie Johnson 1927–29* RCA 741065/6 (2 LPs)
James P Johnson/Luckey Roberts: *Harlem Party Piano* London HB-U1057
James P Johnson Blue Note BLP7011
James P Johnson Xtra 1024

James P Johnson/Luckey Roberts: *Harlem Party Piano* London HB-U1057
Ladd's Black Aces: *Ladd's Black Aces Vol. 1 1921-22* Fountain FJ102
Eddie Lang/Lonnie Johnson: *Blue Guitars* Parlophone PMC7019
Eddie Lang/Joe Venuti: *Stringing the Blues* CBS BPG62143/4 (2 LPs)
Miff Mole: *Mole's Molers Vol. 1* Parlophone PMC7120
   Mole's Molers Vol. 2 Parlophone PMC7126
Red Nichols: *The Five Pennies* Ace of Hearts AH63
   Syncopated Chamber Music Audiophile XL326
   Rare Vertical Jazz Historical HLP8
Luckey Roberts/James P Johnson: *Harlem Piano Solos* Good Time Jazz LAG12256
Jabbo Smith: *Jabbo Smith* Melodeon MLP7326/7 (2 LPs)
Joe Venuti/Adrian Rollini: *The Sound that Swung the 1930s* Music for Pleasure MfP1161
Fats Waller: *Young Fats Waller* HMV DLP1111
   Young Fats at the Organ RCA 741052

VII Swing

Anthologies *From Spirituals to Swing* Vanguard 8523/4 (2 LPs)
   In the Groove RCA RDS6651/6 (6 LPs)
   The Sounds of Harlem Columbia C3L33 (3 LPs)
Mildred Bailey: *All of Me* Ember CJS830
Count Basie: *Jumping at the Woodside* Ace of Hearts AH111
   One o/clock jump Fontana TFL5077
   Super Chief CBS M67205 (2 LPs)
Bunny Berigan: *Bunny Berigan and His Orchestra* RCA LSA3108
Chew Berry: *Stompy Stevedores* Columbia FPX299S
Pete Brown: *High in a Basement* 77 LA12/8
Cab Calloway: *Calloway Classics* CBS 62950
Benny Carter: *With the Ramblers* Decca 154062
   Benny Carter 1940-41 RCA 430686
Casa Loma Band: *Casa Loma Classics* Brunswick 87534
Charlie Christian: *Charlie Christian Vol. 1* Realm RM-52538
   Charlie Christian Vol. 2 CBS BPG62581
Bill Coleman: *In Paris* HMV HXT40328
Tommy Dorsey: *The Best of Tommy Dorsey 1937-41* RCA 731129
Harry Edison: *Sweets at the Haig* Vogue LDE118
Roy Eldridge: *Arcadia Shuffle* Jazz Archives JA-14
   Roy Eldridge Vogue LD507-30

Ella FitzGerald: *Ella Sings Gershwin* Ace of Hearts AH45
Benny Goodman: *B.G. 1927-34* Vogue-Coral LVA9011
   The Vintage Goodman Columbia CL-821
   The Golden Age of Goodman HMV DLP1116
   Trio, Quartet and Quintet RCA 430230
   B.G.: the Small Groups RCA LPV-521
   1938 Carnegie Hall Concert CBS BPG66202 (2 LPs)
Bobby Hackett: *Hackett Horn* Epic EE22003
Edmond Hall: *Celestial Express* Blue Note B6505
Lionel Hampton: *Open House* Camden CDN129
Coleman Hawkins: *Coleman Hawkins* RCA LPV501
   Vintage Hawk Music for Pleasure MfP1128
   Hawk in Holland Ace of Clubs ACL1247
   Classic Tenors Stateside SL1017
   Hollywood Stampede Capitol T20435
   The Moods of Coleman Hawkins Verve VLP9113
   Disorder at the Border Spotlite 121
Coleman Hawkins/Chew Berry: *The Big Sounds* London HMC5006
Fletcher Henderson: *A Study in Frustration* CBS BPG62001/4 (4 LPs)
Earl Hines: *57 Varieties* CBS BPG63364
   Quintessential Recording Session Chiaroscuro CR101
   Grand Terrace Band RCA RD7720
   Spontaneous Explorations Stateside SL10116
Billie Holiday: *The Golden Years Vol. 1* Columbia C3L-21 (3 LPs)
   The Golden Years Vol. 2 Columbia C3L-40 (3 LPs)
Claud Hopkins: *Claud Hopkins* Jazz Panorama LP13
Spike Hughes: *All-American Orchestra* Ace of Clubs ACL1153
Andy Kirk: *Clouds of Joy* Ace of Hearts AH105
Harlan Leonard: *Harlan Leonard and His Rockets* RCA LPV531
Jimmy Lunceford: *Rhythm is Our Business* Ace of Hearts AH155
   Lunceford Special Philips BBL7037
McKinney's Cotton Pickers: *McKinney's Cotton Pickers* RCA 430637
Mills' Blue Rhythm Band: *Mills' Blue Rhythm Band* Jazz Panorama SD3
The Missourians: *The Missourians* RCA 430385
Bennie Moten: *Kansas City Jazz* RCA 130282
   Kansas City Jazz 1929-30 RCA 10023
Don Redman: *Little Giant of Jazz* RCA 741061
   Don Redman Realm RM52539

Django Reinhardt: *Djangologie Vols. 1–18* Pathé C054-16001/18 (18 LPs)
Luis Russell: *The Luis Russell Story* Parlophone PMC7025
Artie Shaw: *Concerto for Clarinet* RCA DPM2028 (2 LPs)
   The Gramercy Five RCA LSA3087
Willie Smith: *Willie Smith Six* Vogue EPV1090
Eddie South/Stephane Grappelly: *South with Grappelly* HMV 7EG8324
Jess Stacy: *Jess Stacy* Brunswick BL54017
Art Tatum: *Here's Art Tatum* Ace of Hearts AH109
   The Art of Tatum Ace of Hearts AH133
   God is in the House Onyx OR1205
Fats Waller: *Memorial Album* Encore ENC181
Chick Webb: *Stomping at the Savoy* Realm RM52537
Dickie Wells: *Dickie Wells in Paris* HMV CLP1054
Lee Wiley: *I've Got the World on a String* Ember CJS829
Teddy Wilson: *The Teddy Wilson Piano Solos* CBS 62876
Lester Young: *Memorial Album Vol. 1* Fontana TFL5064
   Kansas City Five and Six Stateside SL1002
Lester Young/Nat Cole: *Trio* Score LP4019
Lester Young/Coleman Hawkins: *Jubilee All-Stars* Spotlite 119
Lester Young: *Lester Leaps Again* Fontana FJL128
   Lester Young Memorial Vol. 1 Realm RM132
   The Great Lester Young Vol. 1 Liberty LBY3048
   Just You, Just Me Summit AJS-8
   Pres is Blue Summit AJS-12
   Pres Verve MGV8162
   The President Columbia 33CX10031
   It Don't Mean a Thing Verve MGV8187
   Lester Young in Paris Blue Star 84069

VIII Swing Continuations

Charlie Barnet: *Classics in Jazz* Capitol LCT6018
Bob Brookmeyer: *Kansas City Revisited* United Artists UAL4008
Don Ellis: *Electric Bath* CBS BPG63230
Erroll Garner: *The Dial Masters* Spotlite 129
Bill Harris: *The Herdsmen* Mercury SMWL21038
Stan Hasselgard: *Stan Hasselgard* Capitol EAP1-466
Coleman Hawkins: *The Hawk Flies High* London LTZ-K15117
Woody Herman: *The Thundering Herds* Columbia C3L25 (3 LPs)
Jo Jones: *Jo Jones Special* Vanguard PP111002

Red Norvo: *Move!* Realm RM158
Anita O'Day: *Anita O'Day Sings the Winners* Verve MGV8283
Oscar Peterson: *My Favourite Instrument* BASF BMP20671-8
Mel Powell: *Thingamajig* Vanguard VRS8502
　Out on a Limb Vanguard VRS8528
Ike Quebec: *It Might as well be Swing* Blue Note BLP4105
Boyd Raeburn: *Boyd Raeburn* Savoy MG12025
Earle Spencer: *Concert in Jazz* Tops LP1532
Art Tatum: *Solo Piano* Capitol 5C052.80800
　Solo Masterpieces Pablo 2625703 (13 LPs)
　The Tatum Group Masterpieces Pablo 2625 706 (8 LPs)
Jack Teagarden: *The Legendary Jack Teagarden* Roulette 2682034 (2 LPs)
Lucky Thompson: *Lucky Thompson* Ducretet-Thompson D93038
Fats Waller: *Fats on the Air* RCA RD7552/3 (2 LPs)
Mary Lou Williams: *Mary Lou Williams Plays in London* Vogue LDE022
Lester Young: *Lester Swings* Verve 2683066 (2 LPs)
Lester Young/Teddy Wilson: *Pres and Teddy* Verve 2683025 (2 LPs)

IX Louis Armstrong

Louis Armstrong in New York 1924–25 Riverside RLP8811
Louis Armstrong V.S.O.P. Vols. 1/7 CBS 62470/6 (7 LPs)
Louis Armstrong V.S.O.P. Vol. 8 CBS 62750
A Rare Batch of Satch RCA RD27230
Satchmo Collectors' Items Decca DL8327
Armstrong Jazz Classics Ace of Hearts AH7
Louis Armstrong's New Orleans Jazz Brunswick OE9287
Town Hall Concert Plus RCA RD7659
New Orleans Nights Ace of Hearts AH18
Satchmo on Stage Decca DL8330
Louis Armstrong Plays W.C. Handy Realm Jazz RM52067
Satchmo: a Musical Autobiography Brunswick LAT8211/4 (4 LPs)

X Duke Ellington

The Duke—1926 London AL3551
Early Duke Jazz Panorama LP-12
The Ellington Era 1927–40 Vol. 1 Columbia C3L-27

(3 LPs)
The Ellington Era 1927–40 Vol. 2 Columbia C3L-39
(3 LPs)
At His Very Best RCA RD27133
Piano in the Foreground CBS BPG62204
Back to Back HMV CLP1316
Side by Side HMV CLP1374
Masterpieces by Ellington Columbia 33CX1022
It's Duke Ellington Ember EMB3327
In a Mellotone RCA RD27134
Such Sweet Thunder Realm Jazz RM52521
Daybreak Express RCA LPV-506
Duke Ellington Odeon OS1075
Jumping Punkins RCA LPV517
Duke Ellington's Greatest HMV DLP1007
Johnny Come Lately RCA RD7888
Ellington's Harlem Hot Chocolates VJM VEP27
Duke Ellington Tax LP9
The Indispensable Duke Ellington RCA RD27258/9
(2 LPs)
Band Call World Record Club TP-86
Historically Speaking Ember CJS809
Concert in the Virgin Isles Reprise R6185
Ellington at the Cotton Club Camden CDN119
Ellington Uptown Philips BBL7443
Seattle Concert RCA 430206
Anatomy of a Murder Philips BBL7338
The Big Sound Columbia 33CX10136
Treasury of Jazz No. 10: Duke Ellington RCA 130280
Solitude Philips BBL7229
Rare Duke Ellington Masterpieces VJM VLP9
Jungle Jamboree Parlophone PMC1154
Cotton Club Days Vol. 1 Ace of Hearts AH23
Cotton Club Days Vol. 2 Ace of Hearts AH89
Cotton Club Days Vol. 3 Ace of Hearts AH166
Duke Ellington HMV DLP1094
Treasury of Jazz No. 31: Duke Ellington RCA 430616
Ellington '65 Reprise R6122
Ellington '66 Reprise R6154
The Duke Steps Out RCA RD7731
Liberian Suite Philips BBL7287
Great Ellingtonians World Record Club T479/80 (2 LPs)
Stepping into Swing Society Coral CRL57255
Rocking in Rhythm Parlophone PMC1184
The Duke in Harlem Ace of Hearts AH47
The Ellingtonians Vogue VJD525 (2 LPs)
This One's for Blanton Pablo 2335728
Far-Eastern Suite RCA LSA3063
The Ellington Suites Pablo 2335743
New Orleans Suite Atlantic SD1580
Alan Cohen: *Black, Brown and Beige*

XI Bop

Joe Albany: *Proto-Bopper* Revelation REV16
Serge Chaloff: *Lestorian Mode* Realm RM113
Charlie Christian: *Harlem Jazz Scene* Society SOC996
Buddy de Franco: *King of the Clarinet* MGM MGM112
Gil Fuller: *Tropicana* Vogue EPV1052
Dizzy Gillespie: *The Small Groups 1945–46* Phoenix LP2
Dizzy Gillespie/Sonny Berman: *The Dial Masters* Spotlite 132
Dizzy Gillespie: *Dizzy Gillespie* RCA RD7827
　The Greatest RCA RD27242
　Big Band in Concert Vocalion LAE540
　Paris Concert Columbia 33CX1574
　The Dizzy Gillespie Story Realm RM114
Wardell Gray: *Memorial Album* Prestige 7343-2 (2 LPs)
Al Haig: *Jazz Will o' the Wisp* Xtra 1125
Coleman Hawkins: *Bean and the Boys* Prestige PR7824
J.J. Johnson: *Boneology* Realm RM195
　The Eminent J.J. Johnson Blue Note BLP1505/6 (2 LPs)
Dodo Marmarosa: *The Dial Masters* Spotlite 128
Howard McGhee: *The Dial Masters* Spotlite 131
James Moody: *Moody's Workshop* Xtra 5017
Fats Navarro: *Memorial Vol. 1* Realm M52192
　Memorial Vol. 2 Realm M52208
　The Fabulous Fats Navarro Blue Notes BLP1531/2 (2 LPs)
Red Norvo: *Red Norvo's Fabulous Jam Session* Spotlite 127
Charlie Parker: *Charlier Parker on Dial* Spotlite 101/6 (6 LPs)
　The Savoy Sessions Realm RM120/3 + RM131 (5 LPs)
　Historical Masterpieces Vols. 1–3 MGM MGMC986/8 (3 LPs)
Charlie Parker/Dizzy Gillespie/Bud Powell: *The Greatest Jazz Concert Ever* Prestige 24024 (2 LPs)
Bud Powell: *The Bud Powell Trio* Columbia 33SX1575
　Vintage Years Verve VLP9075
　The Amazing Bud Powell Vols. 1 and 2 Blue Note BLP1503/4 (2 LPs)
　Jazz Original Columbia 33CX10069
　The Lonely One HMV CLP1294
　Blues for Bud Columbia 33CX10123
　Strictly Powell RCA 430212

Sarah Vaughan: *Sarah Vaughan Sings* Masterseal MS-55
George Wallington: *Trios* Prestige S7587

XII Bop Continuations

Sonny Berman: *Jam Session* Esoteric LP322
Clifford Brown: *The Complete Paris Collection* Vogue VJT3001 (3 LPs)
Serge Chaloff: *Blue Serge* Capitol T742
Teddy Charles: *New Directions* Atlantic ATLP3
Sonny Criss: *Up, Up and Away* Prestige PRLP7530
Tadd Dameron: *Study in Dameronia* Prestige PRLP7055
   Fontainebleau Esquire 32–034
Miles Davis: *Double Album* Blue Note BST81501/2 (2 LPs)
   Miles Davis and the Modern Jazz Giants Esquire 32–100
   Round about Midnight CBS BPG62323
Kinny Dorham: *Whistle Stop* Blue Note BST84063
Jon Eardley: *Hey There!* Esquire 20–074
Dexter Gordon: *The Chase* Spotlite 130
Al Haig: *Special Brew* Spotlite LP8
Tubby Hayes: *100% Proof* Fontana TFL5410
Elmo Hope: *Hopeful* Riverside RLP408
Milt Jackson: *Milt Jackson* Blue Note BST81509
J.J. Johnson: *First Place* Fontana TFL5005
   Blue Trombone Fontana TFL5137
Duke Jordan: *Jordu* Prestige 7849
Yusef Lateef: *Eastern Sounds* Fontana 688202ZL
Alonzo Levister: *Alonzo Levister* Debut DEB125
Charlie Mariano: *Portrait* Regina 286
Howard McGhee: *Together Again!* Contemporary LAC12291
Charles Mingus: *Jazz Experiments* London LTZ-N15087
   Jazz Composers' Workshop London LTZ-C15058
Modern Jazz Quartet: *Looking Back at the M.J.Q.* Esquire 32–124
   Concorde Prestige PR7005
Thelonius Monk: *Genius of Modern Music Vols. 1 and 2* Blue Note BLP1510/1 (2 LPs)
   Monk's Moods Esquire 32–119
   Work! Esquire 32–115
   Golden Monk Stateside SL10152
Phineas Newborn: *A World of Piano* Contemporary LAC535
Charlie Parker: *The Definitive Charlie Parker Vol. 1* Metro 2356059, *Vol. 2* 2356082, *Vol. 3* 2356083, *Vol. 4* 2356087, *Vol. 5* 2356088, *Vol. 6* 2356091, *Vol. 7* 2356095, *Vol. 8* 2356096

Bernard Peiffer: *Lullaby of Birdland* Polydor 623210
Boyd Raeburn: *Boyd Raeburn* Savoy MG12040
Henri Renaud: *Henri Renaud All-Stars* Vogue LAE12046
Sonny Rollins: *Worktime* Xtra 5026
   Saxophone Colossus Stateside SL10164
   Sonny Boy Xtra 5022
   Way Out West Contemporary LAC12118
   At the Village Vanguard Blue Note BLP1581
Zoot Sims: *Trotting* Xtra 5001
Lennie Tristano/Red Rodney: *Bebop 'n' After* Mercury SMWL21028
René Urtreger: *Modern Piano from Paris* Felsted EDL87020
Sarah Vaughan: *Swinging Easy* EmArcy EJL1273

XIII Cool Jazz

Chet Baker/Russ Freeman: *Quartet* Vogue LAE12119
Teddy Charles: *Ezzthetic* Xtra 5004
Al Cohn: *Cohn's Tones* Realm RM155
Miles Davis: *Pre-Birth of the Cool* Cicala BLJ8003
   Birth of the Cool Capitol T1974
   Collectors' Items Prestige 24022 (2 LPs)
Miles Davis/Gil Evans: *Miles Ahead* CBS BPG62496
   Porgy and Bess CBS BPG62108
Kinny Dorham: *Quiet Kenny* New Jazz NJLP8226
Gil Evans: *Big Stuff* Xtra 5034
   Roots Fontana 688003ZL
   Great Jazz Standards Fontana 688000ZL
   Out of the Cool HMV CLP1456
   Into the Hot World Record Club T748
   Individualism Verve V6-8555
   Gil Evans Ampex A10102
   Svengali Atlantic ATL40528
Tal Farlow: *Interpretations* Columbia 33CX10029
Buddy de Franco: *Free Sail* Choice CRS1008
Tony Fruscella: *Tony Fruscella* London LTZ-K15044
Stan Getz: *Greatest Hits* Stateside SL10161
   The Steamer World Record Club T341
   At Storyville Vogue LAE12158
Lars Gullin: *Fine Together* Sonet SLPD2542 (2 LPs)
Lee Konitz: *Lee Konitz Collates* Esquire 32–027
   Lee Konitz with the Gerry Mulligan Quartet Vogue LAE12181
   Lee Konitz Plays Vogue LDE060
   Lee Konitz with Warne Marsh London LTZ-K15025
   Inside Hi-Fi London LTZ-K15092

   Very Cool Columbia 33CX10119
   The Real Lee Konitz London LTZ-K15147
   Motion Verve MGV8399
John LaPorta: *John LaPorta* Debut DLP10
John Lewis: *The John Lewis Piano* Atlantic 1272
Warne Marsh: *The Art of Improvising* Revelation REV22
Modern Jazz Quartet: *Odds Against Tomorrow* London LTZ-T15181
   No Sun in Venice Atlantic 1284
   Fontessa Atlantic 1231
Brew Moore: *Quartet and Quintet* Vocalion LAE564
Gerry Mulligan: *Historically Speaking* Xtra 5009
   Gerry Mulligan Quartet Vogue LAE12050
   Concert Jazz Band Verve VLP9037
Gerry Mulligan/Paul Desmond: *Two of a Mind* RCA RD7525
Jimmy Raney: *In Three Attitudes* HMV CLP1264
Claude Thornhill: *The Early Cool* Ember CJS828
   The Thornhill Sound Harmony HL7088
Lennie Tristano/Buddy de Franco: *Cross Currents* Capitol 5C05280853
Lennie Tristano: *Lines* Atlantic 590031
Richard Twardzik: *The Last Set* Vogue LAE12117

XIV West Coast Jazz

Buddy Collette: *Nice Day* Contemporary LAC12092
Bob Cooper: *Bob Cooper* Capitol KPL102
Teddy Edwards: *Together Again!* Contemporary LAC12291
Clare Fischer: *The Reclamation Act* Revelation REV15
Herb Geller: *Stax of Sax* Jubilee JLP1094
Jimmy Giuffre: *The Jimmy Giuffre Clarinet* London LTZ-K15059
Chico Hamilton: *Quintet* Vogue LAE12039
Bill Holman: *Fabulous Bill Holman* Coral LVA9088
Stan Kenton: *Solo—Stan Kenton without his Orchestra* Creative World ST1071
Lou Levy: *Solo Scene* RCA LPM1267
Shelly Manne: *Manne and his Men* Vogue LDC072
   Manne and his Men Contemporary LAC12062
   Shelly Manne and his Friends Contemporary LAC12100
   The Two and The Three Contemporary LAC12276
Frank Morgan: *Frank Morgan* Vogue LAE12012
Gerry Mulligan/Shorty Rogers: *Modern Sounds* Capitol T2025
Lennie Niehaus: *The Quintet* Contemporary

LAC12167

Art Pepper: *Art Pepper Meets the Rhythm Section*
Contemporary LAC12066
  Getting Together Contemporary LAC12262
  Smack Up Contemporary LAC12316
  Intensity Contemporary LAC553
Carl Perkins: *Carl Perkins Trio* Dootone DLP211
Shorty Rogers: *The Swinging Mr Rogers* London
LTZ-K15023
  Cool and Crazy HMV DLP1030
  Martians, Come Back! London LTZ-K15056
  Big Band Express RCA LPM1350
Howard Rumsey: *Lighthouse All-Stars Vol. 1* Vogue
LDC146
  Lighthouse All-Stars Vol. 3 Contemporary
LAC12182
  In the Solo Spotlight Vogue LDC151
  Music for Lighthouse-Keeping Contemporary
LAC12086
  Bud Shank: *Quartet* Vogue LAE12041
Cy Touff: *Having a Ball* Vogue LAE12040
Claude Williamson: *Claude Williamson* Capitol
KPL103

XV Hard Bop

Art Blakey: *Hard Bop* Philips BBL72120
  A Night at Birdland Vol. 1 Blue Note BLP1521
  Buhaina's Delight Blue Note BST84104
Tina Brooks: *True Blue* Blue Note BST84041
Donald Byrd: *The Cat Walk* Blue Note BST84075
Sonny Clark: *Leaping and Loping* Blue Note
BST84091
John Coltrane: *Blue Train* Blue Note BST81577
Dexter Gordon: *Doing Alright* Blue Note
BST84077
Johnny Griffin: *The Congregation* Blue Note
BLP1580
Ernie Henry: *Seven Standards and a Blues* Riverside
RLP12-248
Jackie McLean: *Bluesnik* Blue Note BST84067
Charles Mingus: *Pithecanthropus Erectus* London
LTZ-K15052
Hank Mobley: *Roll Call* Blue Note BLP4058
Thelonious Monk: *Five by Monk by Five* Riverside
RLP12-305
J.R. Monterose: *The Message* Jaro JAM5004
Lee Morgan: *The Sidewinder* Blue Note BLP4157
Sonny Rollins: *Sonny Rollins Vol. 2* Blue Note
BST81558
  Newk's Time Blue Note BST84001
Wayne Shorter: *Speak No Evil* Blue Note

BST84194
Horace Silver: *Horace Silver and the Jazz Messengers*
Blue Note BST81518
  Finger Popping Blue Note BST84008
  The Jody Grind Blue Note BST84250

XVI Further Developments

Benny Bailey: *Big Brass* Candid 8011
Dollar Brand: *Anatomy of a South African Village*
Fontana 688314ZL
Jaki Byard: *Here's Jaki* New Jazz NJLP8256
Teddy Charles: *Tentet* London LTZ-K15034
John Coltrane/Thelonious Monk: *At the Five Spot*
Jazzland JLP46
John Coltrane: *Giant Steps* London LTZ-K15197
  My Favourite Things Atlantic ATL5022
  Africa Brass HMV CLP1548
Chris Cross: *Remember that Broadcast from Mars?*
Melos MLP4973
Tadd Dameron: *Mating Call* Prestige PRLP7070
Miles Davis: *Kind of Blue* CBS BPG62066
  My Funny Valentine CBS BPG62510
  E.S.P. CBS BPG62577
  Sorcerer CBS BPG63097
  Nefertiti CBS BPG63248
  Jack Johnson CBS 70089
Duke Ellington: *Money Jungle* United Artists
ULP1039
Bill Evans: *Explorations* Riverside RLP12-351
  Empathy Verve VLP9070
  Conversations with Myself Verve VLP9054
  A Simple Matter of Conviction Verve VLP9161
Art Farmer: *Portrait* Contemporary LAC12197
Jimmy Giuffre: *The Jimmy Giuffre Three* London
LTZ-K15130
Barry Harris: *Luminessence* Prestige S7498
Hampton Hawes: *The Green Leaves of Summer*
Vocalion LAC579
Andrew Hill: *Point of Departure* Blue Note
BST84167
Bobby Hutcherson: *Dialogue* Blue Note BST84198
Duke Jordan: *Trio and Quintet* Savoy MG12149
Steve Lacy: *The Straight Horn* Candid 8007
Harold Land: *The Fox* Vogue LAE12269
Teo Macero/Teddy Charles: *Something New,
Something Blue* Columbia CL1388
Dodo Marmarosa: *Dodo's Back!* Argo LP4012
Hal McKusick: *Jazz Workshop* RCA LPM1366
  Cross-Section Saxes Decca DL9209
Charles Mingus: *The Clown* London LTZ-K15164
  East Coasting Parlophone PMC1092

Tia Juana Moods RCA RD7514
Blues and Roots London LTZ-K15194
Mingus Ah Um Philips BBL7352
Black Saint and Sinner Lady HMV CLP1694
Let My Children Hear the Music CBS 64715
Modern Jazz Quartet: *At Music Inn Vol. 1* London
LTZ-K15085
  The Comedy London HA-K8046
Thelonious Monk: *The Unique Thelonious Monk*
London LTZ-U15071
  Brilliant Corners London LTZ-U15097
  Thelonious Himself London LTZ-U15120
  Nica's Tempo Savoy RM52223
  The Man I Love Black Lion 2460197
Wes Montgomery: *Go!* Fontana FJL109
Gerry Mulligan: *Sextet* EmArcy EJL101
Herbie Nicholls: *Trio* Blue Note BLP1519
Max Roach: *Percussion Bitter Suite* HMV CLP1522
  Drums Unlimited Atlantic 1467
Sonny Rollins: *Sonny Rollins and the Big Brass* MGM
MGMC776
  Freedom Suite Riverside RLP12-258
  The Bridge RCA RD7504
  On Impulse HMV CLP1915
George Russell: *Jazz Workshop* RCA RD7511
  Stratusphunk Riverside RLP341
  Ezz-thetics Riverside RLP375
  The Stratus Seekers Riverside RLP412
  In Kansas City Decca DL4183
  At the Five Spot Decca DL9220
  The Outer View Fontana 688705ZL
  Jazz in the Space Age Decca DL9219
Cecil Taylor: *Jazz Advance* Transition TRLP19
  At Newport Columbia 33CX10102
  Looking Ahead! Contemporary LAC12216
  Love for Sale United Artists UAL4046
Lucky Thompson: *Lucky Strikes* Prestige PR7365
Lennie Tristano: *The New Tristano* Polydor 590017
Tommy Vig: *In Budapest* Mortney MR71425
Mal Waldron: *The Quest* Xtra 5006

XVII Third Stream

Anthologies *Modern Jazz Concert* Columbia WL127
  Music for Brass Columbia CL941
Neil Ardley: *Symphony of Amaranths* Regal-
Zonophone SLPZ1028
Ars Nova Chamber Jazz Ensemble: *Unpleasant for
the Peasants* Melos MSLP8379
John Benson Brooks: *Alabama Concerto* Riverside
RLP12-276

Pavel Blatny: *Third Stream Compositions* Supraphon 1150528
Don Ellis: *How Time Passes* Candid 8004
Tears of Joy Columbia G30927 (2 LPs)
Jimmy Giuffre: *Tangents in Jazz* Capitol T634
J.J. Johnson: *Perceptions* HMV CLP1536
Teo Macero/Bob Prince: *What's New?* Columbia CL842
David Mack: *New Directions* Columbia 33SX1670
Modern Jazz Quartet: *Third Stream Music* Atlantic 1345
Gunther Schuller: *Jazz Abstractions* Atlantic 587043
Matyas Seiber/John Dankworth: *Improvisations for Jazz Band and Symphony Orchestra* Saga XIP7006

XVIII Free Jazz

Art Ensemble of Chicago: *Les Stances à Sophie* Nessa N4
Albert Ayler: *Spirits* Transatlantic TRA130
Spiritual Unity ESP 1002
Ghosts Fontana 688606ZL
Bells ESP 1010
Spirits Rejoice ESP 1020
Gato Barbieri: *Under Fire* Flying Dutchman FD10156
Carla Bley: *A Genuine Tong Funeral* RCA SF8015
The Escalator Over the Hill (Box of 3 LPs, unnumbered, on the Jazz Composers' label)
Paul Bley: *Footloose* Savoy MG12182
Peter Brötzmann: *The End* FMP ST0030/40/50 (3 LPs)
Marion Brown: *Afternoon of a Georgia Faun* ECM 1004
Don Cherry: *Complete Communion* Blue Note BLP4226
Symphony for Improvisors Blue Note BLP4247
Ornette Coleman: *Something Else* Contemporary LAC12170
Tomorrow is the Question Contemporary LAC12228
The Shape of Jazz to Come Atlantic 587022
Change of the Century London LTZ-K15199
This is Our Music London LTZ-K15228
Free Jazz Atlantic 1364
Ornette London LTZ-K15241
Ornette on Tenor Atlantic 1394
At the Town Hall ESP 1006
At the Golden Circle Vols. 1 and 2 Blue Note

BLP4224/5 (2 LPs)
The Empty Foxhole Blue Note BLP4246
In Europe Vols. 1 and 2 Freedom 2383090/1 (2 LPs)
Science Fiction CBD 64774
John Coltrane: *Coltrane* HMV CLP1629
Love Supreme HMV CLP1869
Ascension HMV CLP3543
Meditations HMV CLP3575
Live at the Village Vanguard Again HMV CLP9124
Eric Dolphy: *Out to Lunch* Blue Note BLP4163
Don Ellis: *New Ideas* Esquire 32–183
Essence Pacific Jazz PJ55
Jan Garbarek: *Triptykon* ECM ST1029
Jimmy Giuffre: *Fusion* Verve V8397
Thesis Verve V8402
Free Fall Columbia CL1964
River Chant Choice CRS1008
Milford Graves/Sonny Morgan: *Percussion Duets* ESP 1013
Gunther Hampel: *Out of New York* BASF MPS20900
Joe Harriot: *Abstract* Columbia 33SX1477
Steve Lacy: *Evidence* New Jazz NJLP8271
Albert Mangelsdorff: *The Wide Point* BASF MPS2022569–0
George Russell/Bill Evans: *Living Time* CBS S65010
Terje Rypdal: *Terje Rypdal* ECM 1016
Pharoah Sanders: *Karma* Impulse AS9181
Alexander von Schlippenbach: *Globe Unity* BASF MPS20630
Woody Shaw: *Blackstone Legacy* Contemporary 7627 (2 LPs)
Alan Shorter: *Parabolic* Verve 2304060
Wayne Shorter: *The Oddyssey of Iska* Blue Note BST84363
Alan Silva: *Seasons* Byg 529342/3/4 (3 LPs)
Spontaneous Music Ensemble: *Karyobin* Island ILPS9079
Sun Ra: *Fate in a Pleasant Mood* Saturn 202
Sun Song Delmark DL411
Outer Planes of There Saturn 206
Secrets of the Sun Saturn 9954
Magic City Saturn 403
When Angels Speak of Love Saturn 405
Angels and Demons Saturn 407
The Sun Ra Solar Arkestra Savoy MG12169
The Heliocentric Worlds of Sun Ra Vol. 1 ESP 1014
The Heliocentric Worlds of Sun Ra Vol. 2 ESP 1017
Nothing Is ESP 1045

Cecil Taylor: *World of Cecil Taylor* Candid 8006
At the Café Montmartre Fontana 688602ZL
Unit Structures Blue Note BLP4237
Nefertiti Fontana SFJL926
McCoy Tyner: *Sahara* Milestone MSP9036

XIX Rock Jazz

The Allman Brothers: *At Fillmore East* Atlantic SD2802 (2 LPs)
Association P.C.: *Rock Around the Clock* BASF MPS21763
Gary Bartz: *Harlem Bush Music* Milestone MSP9032
Paul Bley: *Scorpio* Milestone MSP9046
Blood, Sweat and Tears: *New Blood* Columbia KC31780
Gary Burton: *Duster* RCA LSP3835
Ray Charles: *All-Time Great Performances* ABC SD-731 (2 LPs)
Chicago: *Chicago Transit Authority* Columbia GP8 (2 LPs)
Billy Cobham: *Spectrum* Atlantic SD7268
Chick Corea: *Return to Forever* ECM ST1022
Larry Coryell: *Offering* Vanguard VSD79319
The Cream: *Wheels of Fire* Atlantic 2700 (2 LPs)
Wolfgang Dauner: *Et Cetera* BASF MPS2121432
Miles Davis: *Bitches' Brew* CBS 66236 (2 LPs)
The Dreams: *Dreams* Columbia 30225
Roberta Flack: *Quiet Fire* Atlantic SD1594
The Flock: *Dinosaur Swamp* CBS S67278 (2 LPs)
Aretha Franklin: *Amazing Grace* Atlantic 2–906 (2 LPs)
Dave Goliath: *Ghengis Cohn Rides Again!* Melos MSLP9645
George Gruntz: *Noon in Tunisia* BASF MPS20640
Herbie Hancock: *Sextant* Columbia STKC32212
Jimi Hendrix: *Electric Ladyland* Polydor 2612002 (2 LPs)
Keith Jarrett: *The Mourning of a Star* Atlantic SD1596
Janis Joplin: *Cheap Thrills* Columbia KC32168
Roland Kirk: *Blacknuss* Atlantic K40358
Dave Liebman: *Drum Ode* ECM 1046
Bennie Maupin: *The Jewel in the Lotus* ECM 1043
John McLaughlin: *Birds of Fire* Columbia KC31996
Pink Floyd: *Ummagumma* Electrola 1C188–04222/3 (2 LPs)
Jean-Luc Ponty: *Plays the Music of Frank Zappa* Pacific Jazz 20172

Carlos Santana: *Caravanserai* Columbia KC31610L
Soft Machine: *Third* Columbia G30339 (2 LPs)
Jeremy Steig: *Legwork* Solid State SS18068
Weather Report: *Sweetnighter* Columbia KC32210
Tony Williams: *Turn It Over* Polydor 244021
Larry Young (Khalid Yasin): *Unity* Blue Note
BST84221
Frank Zappa: *The Grand Wazoo* Reprise
STMS2093
Joe Zawinul: *Zawinul* Atlantic SD1579
Attila Zoller: *A Path Through the Maze* BASF
MPS21282